Korean Families
Continuity and Change

Edited by Korean Family Studies Association

SNUPRESS
Seoul National University Press

Korean Families

Continuity and Change

Copyright © Korean Family Studies Association, 2011
Printed in Seoul, Republic of Korea

Seoul National University Press
1 Gwanak-ro, Gwanak-gu, Seoul 151-742, Republic of Korea
E-mail: snubook@snu.ac.kr
Home Page: http://www.snupress.com
Tel: 82-2-889-4424
Fax: 82-2-888-4148

First Printing: December 30, 2011

ISBN 978-89-521-1257-6 93330

Preface

Korean Families: Continuity and Change is designed by The Korean Family Studies Association and written by member scholars of the Association.

The Association was established in 1977 to perform joint research with scholars of family studies in various fields so that they could share their individual research outcomes. With the spread of globalization in academic societies, we, the members of the Association, agreed that we would need a book on Korean families written in English for Korean students taking English lectures, for English-speaking foreign students in Korea, and for readers all over the globe who have an interest in Korean families. Therefore, we decided to publish a book, and created a task force in 2009 to prepare the book on Korean families. During the map-out stage, the members of the task force chose topics and recommended authors. Later, some members served as writers while others contributed as reviewers.

The main aim of the book is to provide an English-language textbook that may help many foreign readers and students who study English lectures make knowledgeable of the current trends in Korean family life. Historically, family studies have received scholarly attention in numerous academic fields. However, the contributors of this book came from the fields of sociology, anthropology, feminism, and human ecology, in which our Association members are majorly involved at present. Two historical articles are included to expand and deepen the readers' insight into the historical background of the contemporary meaning of the Korean family.

The book is organized into an introduction and five subsequent parts with 13 chapters overall. The introduction provides a brief overview of the continuity and changes in the patrilineal culture of the current Korean family. Part I, Traditional Korean Families, presents a historical analysis of the family/kinship system and women's life during the Goryeo and Joseon Dynasties. Part II, Family and Society, includes two chapters on changes in the family population and families with the concept of 'compressed modernity', and examines family issues at the macro level. Part III, Family, Change, and Space, includes three chapters on family life among the rural, urban, and lower classes based on intensive qualitative research. Part IV, Family and Gender, includes three chapters on the image of the Korean family, love and marriage, and work-family reconciliation as discussed from feminist perspectives. Part V, the Family in Life Stages, includes three chapters on the early, middle, and late years of the family, focusing on family relations.

I hope this book, edited from an interdisciplinary perspective, will be a useful guide and reference for those who expect a deeper understanding of the Korean family. I acknowledge and appreciate the great efforts of all of the members who have contributed to this book.

I am thankful for the suggestions I received from my dear insightful reviewers, including Chung Grace of Seoul National University, Park Hye Jun of Seoul National University, Kim Myung-hye of Chonnam National University, Lee Mi-sook of the Catholic University of Korea, Sohn Seong Young of Dongduk Women's University, Chin Meejung of Seoul National University, and Kwon Hee-Kyung of Changwon University. I also thank the anonymous reviewers for their English proofreading. Thanks also to goes out to Janette Douglas, who helped with the English editing. Finally, I am grateful to the editors and editorial staff of the Seoul National University Press.

2009-2010 President of the Korean Family Studies Association

Ok Sun Wha

Contents

III
Family, Change, and Space

IV
Family and Gender

V
Family in Life Stages

Continuity and Change in Patrilineal Culture of Korean Families[1]

Ok, Sun Wha (Seoul National University)

1. Introduction

Family culture is composed of inherent principles that determine how family members are organized and form relationships, as well as family's systems, rules and values. These inherent principles are based on the patrilineal family system that has been maintained for a long time in Korean history. However, recently, rapid socio-cultural change has altered the old family-related system, and, within this turmoil of change, Korean family culture appears to be struggling to find its identity.

By understanding changes in social systems and values, which

---

1 Part of this paper presented at The 2nd International Symposium of Multicultural Human Ecology Center in Seoul National University, Korea in December 2008.

are important factors to potentially change family culture, we can grasp the changes in family culture. Therefore, in this chapter, the following will be discussed. First, change in the patrilineal family system will be examined through changes in Korean laws related to family. Secondly, to understand changes in the value of children, the meaning of children in the Korean family and the birth-sex ratio will be discussed. Finally, after examining the bi-lateralization phenomenon in Korean families, the streams of continuity and change in patrilineal family culture will be discussed.

2. Change in Family System: From Patriarchal Family to Gender-Equal Family

1) Patriarchal Family System

Since "Gyeong-guk Daejeon(經國大典)" — National Code promulgated in 1471 to define the administrative structure of the Joseon Dynasty — was codified in the Joseon Dynasty, the history of the establish- ment of laws related to the family system can be explained as follows (source: http://www.moleg.go.kr/main/main.do). Under Japanese colonization, "The Joseon Civil Affairs Ordinance" was enacted in March 1912. After the restoration of independence, the Civil Law of the Republic of Korea was proclaimed in February 1958 and came into effect in January 1960. The Family Register Law was established in 1960 to prescribe regulations on one's legal domicile and the head of family and family members. The Family Register Law established in 1960 was essentially a patriarchal family law. Under this law, a patriarchal head of family was recorded first, and, following this, lineal ascendants of the head of family, a spouse of the head of family, lineal descendants of the head of family and their spouses were recorded in order. We can learn that a family is defined as a patriarchal family by looking at the definitions of a head of family and family members in Chapter 2 of the Civil Code on Relatives before abolition of "head of family system." According to Article 778, entitled "Definition of Head of Family," "a person who has succeeded to the family lineage or has set up a branch family, or who has established a new family or has restored a family for any other reason, shall become the head of a family," and, according to Article 779, entitled "Scope of Family Members," "The spouse and blood relative of the head of a family, and the spouses of the blood relative, and any other person who has his or her name entered in the family register in accordance with the provisions of this Act shall become members of the family." Although several amendments have been made to family-related sections in the civil law since its establishment, gender inequality still remains as well as remnants of the patriarchal family system. However, "head of family system" was abolished in March 2005, and, as a result, "The Family Register Law" was also abolished in May 2007. Therefore, articles related to the patriarchal family system, for the most part, have been deleted.

2) Gender-Equal Family System

After the abolition of 'The Family Register Law' in May 2007, which followed the abolition of the "head of family system" in March 2005, new laws about family relation registration were enacted in January 2008. As a result, a new system replaced the "head of family system," and the constitutional ideology of the dignity of the individual and gender equality came to be realized. New laws about family relation registration are procedural laws of the family system that changed remarkably starting on January 1st, 2008. Under the new laws, new systems such as 1) amendment of the principle of succeeding father's surname, 2) change of surname, and a 3) full adoption system were executed. Therefore, an individual forms a family relation register based on a registered address, replacing the way in which a family register is formed per family based on a head of family. In other words, the idea of permanent domicile — in which a family register was based on a family address — was eliminated, and the idea of a "reference place of registration" was adopted as a basis to process various reports for civil affairs. Every member of a family need not have the same "reference place of registration"; thus, an individual can change it freely (Supreme Court of Korea 2008).

Compared to the old laws which contained the idea of permanent domicile based on the patrilineal head of family and the rule of succeeding father's surname,[2] these new laws have brought remarkable changes to the basic framework of the Korean family

---

2 Refer to Civil Act (amended 2002.1.14 by Act No. 6591), Article 781 (Entry into Family Register and Surname and Origin of Surname of Child) (1) A child shall succeed his or her father's surname and origin of surname and shall have the name entered into his or her father's family register.

system.

3. The Value of Children

1) Meaning of Children

Familism has been emphasized as a family value of the traditional family, which was a patrilineal family form firmly established since the mid Joseon Dynasty. Familism is composed of the ideas of putting family first, respecting parents, continuing patrilineal family relationships, and socio-economic ties among siblings and relatives. Under familism, the family unit takes precedence over individuals and society (Ok 1989).

A basic form of the patrilineal descendant family is an extended patrilineal descendant family set up by parents and the married eldest son's family living together. This form of family has contributed to make patrilineal relative groups functional in the process of exchanging mutual help between more extended patrilineal relative groups. Due to the family structure centered on the relation of the father and the eldest son, a strong preference for boys was developed, and a hierarchy between generations and within a generation was emphasized.

To maintain and develop this form of family, children have special meaning within the family to the extent that the primary purpose of marriage is to give birth to a child. In particular, from Joseon Dynasty until recently, a preference for boys has been pervasive in society in order to maintain the family lineage. In other words, since it was considered that the permanence of the family is dependent on the existence of children, boys have therefore been preferred. In addition, there was a natural preference for having many children in an agrarian society.

However, the implicit value which modern parents put on their children has changed. Modern parents have conflicting thoughts about children; on the one hand, they consider them to be a reward for life and marriage, but, on the other hand, they see them as burdensome in reality, interfering with the rhythm of life. Although there are variations of this phenomenon according to age, gender, and region, we can say that in general parents have ambivalent attitudes toward their children (Ok, et al. 2000).

Recently, there has been a change in the physical and emotional benefit provided by children; compared to the past, the financial contribution from children has decreased, while the cost of investment in children has dramatically increased. In addition, Confucian norms have changed, so it has become difficult for parents to expect that children will accept the duty to care for their elderly parents or provide them with material support. Therefore, today the meaning of children has changed, from the idea of an investment good for the succession of the household production function, to the idea of a consumption good needing affection. Due to pressure from the increase in female employment, women prefer to have a smaller number of children, and parents want to have only one child in order to provide a higher quality of life, leading to a low birth rate (Shin, et al. 2008).

2) Preference for Boys and Birth Sex Ratio

In modern society, both urban and rural, it is reported that there is low support for a preference for boys (Ok, et al. 2000). However, there are still cases of people who want to give birth to a boy, as the patrilineal tradition has not entirely disappeared since the Joseon Dynasty, when the relation between the father and the eldest son was the center of the family. In particular, in the 1990s this phenomenon appeared as an artificial control in the birth sex ratio. For example, the sex rate of newborns in 1990 was 116.5 (Korea Statistical Information Service 2011), meaning 116.5 boys were born for every 100 girls born.

Shin (2008) and her associates explained the changing pheno-menon on boy preference as follows. This imbalance in the birth sex ratio has been shown to improve over the years. In 2007, the number of boys born was 106.1 per 100 girls born, recovering to the normal sex ratio (103-107) for the first time in 25 years since 1982. Looking at the birth order, the birth sex ratio for the first child was 104.4 and for the second child was 105.9; thus, this indicates the birth sex ratios for the first and second child were at a normal level without abortion or artificial manipulation. However, it is difficult to conclude that the preference for boys has completely disappeared, because, in the case of third and fourth children, the third child has a birth sex ratio of 115.2, and the fourth child, 119.4. In other words, boys were born at rates of 15.2 % and 19.4 % higher than girls. On the other hand, in the case of regional birth sex ratio, there were significant regional differences in the 1990s, and remarkable differences continued until 2006, but relatively even birth sex ratios were shown over regions in 2007. However, according to one recent survey, people who intended to have children more often said "yes" to the question "do you think you need to have at least one son?" This seems to show that there still remains a preference for boys in our society to a certain extent.

3) Birth Rate

(1) Family Planning

Changes in the population structure can be considered to also reflect changes in family culture in a society. In particular, Korea has continuously pursued a birth control policy since its independence from Japanese colonization in 1945 in order to reduce pressure from overpopulation. Until 1950, the family planning program was simply to encourage people to have an appropriate number of children at their own discretion. However, in 1961, the family planning program was strengthened as the Family Planning Association was formed, suggesting a specific number of children.

The family planning slogan was, "Let's participate in the 3, 3, 35 plan." This suggested having 3 children, spacing 3 years apart, before the age of 35. The government took the initiative and advertised that the appropriate number of children was 3. This number of "3", which represented the family planning program in the 1960s, was changed to the number "2" in the 1970s, at which time the well-known slogan, "Whether girls or boys, have two children and raise them well" was adopted. In the 1980s, it was even suggested that people have only one child. The "population control policy" announced in 1981 was the final edition of the family planning program. Families participating in the family planning program received benefits-income support was given to the families undergoing birth control medical operations and children's medical fees were reduced. On the other hand, maternity leave was not provided for a third or more children. The government even formed teams to provide "visiting birth control medical operations."(Wizhankook, November 17, 2008) This family planning project as birth control policy continued until 1996.

(2) Total Fertility Rate

Korea's total fertility rate hit its record of 6.0 in 1960s, but, by 1983, had dropped to a replacement fertility level of below 2.1, to a very low fertility level of 1.47 in 1998, and then to 1.08 by 2005, among the world's lowest fertility levels (Korea National Statistical Office 2007).

Since total fertility rate set the lowest record of 1.08 in 2005, it appears to have increased slightly, as it was 1.12 in 2006 and 1.23 in 2010. However, this increase seems to be affected by demographic factors, such as a rise of the female population in their late 20s (due to the 3rd baby boom effect) and socio-cultural factors. In particular, the birth distribution ratio of first children has been gradually increasing from 47.2 % in 2000 to 53.5 % at present, while that of second children has been continuously decreasing from 42.4 % in 2000 to 37.1 % now. Therefore, it can be inferred that this recent birth rate increase is due to the effect of temporary socio-cultural factors (Statistics Korea 2011).

(3) Policy to Overcome Low Birth Rate

Generally, when a society's total fertility rate is under 2.1 — a population replacement level needed to maintain the same population level — that society is called a low birth rate society. This means that one fertile woman (age between 15 and 49) should give birth to more than 2 children to maintain a stable level of population. Even though the birth rate had dropped to 2.08 in 1983, below the population replacement rate (2.1), the South Korean government continued a birth control policy until 1996. However, as the birth rate dropped to 1.08, a very low birth rate level, the government began to review this issue and commenced a policy on low fertility and aging society on September 1st, 2005.

We can expect the birth rate to increase when the basic environments to give birth and raise children are improved by policies on low fertility. Every country with a low fertility problem is looking for a fundamental cause in the socio-cultural aspects of society. However, unlike European countries, it is believed that the low fertility problem in South Korea is caused by high educational expenses due to excessive competition to get into universities. However, according to the results from analyzing the factors affecting the birth rate decrease based on the data collected in various cities from 1983 to 2006, financial variables — such as educational expenses, economic growth rate, and pay increases for women — were not significant, while socio-demographic variables — such as age of women at first marriage, divorce rate, and employment rate of women — were significant. On the other hand, based on the survey results, it seems that private educational expenses have a significant effect on mid- to lower-class people. Further, more women already raising one child answered that they intend to have another child than did other women, if the cost of raising a child and educational expenses were reduced by 50 %. It is believed that, if these costs are reduced, women who do not intend to have a child at present would be influenced more effectively. Therefore, the policy on low fertility should be applied differently depending on whether people already have a child or not. In addition, the effect of a reduction in the cost of raising a child is greater for mid- to higher-class people who do not receive government child benefits. Therefore, to solve the low fertility problem, the range of classes who receive government child benefits needs to be expanded (Shin, et al. 2008).

To improve the efficiency of the policy on low fertility, the lowest total fertility rate of each major OECD country, year reached, and the level of improved fertility achieved need to be reviewed, and the Korean government needs to model their policies on successful examples.

4. Bi-lateralization of Family Relations

Analysis on the results of the preceding research on the bi-lateralization of family relations can be divided into two perspectives (Sung 2006). The first point of view, more pervasive in the media than in the academic field, considers this to be a positive change that moves away from the exclusively patriarchal culture of the Korean family. In this viewpoint, it is assumed that kinship interaction is not limited to the paternal side and is expanded to the maternal side as well, affecting the perception of people. The second point of view, focusing on the blind spots of the present observed phenomenon of bi-lateralization, considers the bi-lateralization of relations in the Korean family to be asymmetrical and no different from neo-familism that emphasizes solidarity among blood relations. They believe that it consolidates the lack of differentiation between generations, causing negative functional effects on the intergenerational relations.

One report from a daily newspaper said, "It is no longer surprising to see people living with the wife's brothers and sisters, or even in the wife's parents' home." Some call this phenomenon, in which the boundary between "maternal family" and "paternal family" is blurred, a "neo-matrilineal society," while others argue that it is premature to conclude that this is the case. Some criticize that "the use of terms such as 'neo-matrilineal society' makes it sound like women's rights are improved, when in fact the wife's mother's labor is exploited." Some also argue, "Although it is true that patriarchal family culture is changing, the family culture principle in which ancestral rites or taking care of parents is based on the patriarchal blood line remains strong." (Kukinews 2007, December 9) In addition, another report argues that the claim of "neo-matrilineal society" that women become the center of the family in fact embellishes the transfer of women's "responsibility and burden." (SBS News 2007, May 3)

On the other hand, according to the results of analysis of in-depth interviews with middle-aged married men and women, Sung (2006) found that equal meaning was given to both sides of the family. In the case where both sides of the family were democratic, both spouses were emotionally and financially independent from the paternal side of the family and relatives, and the couple maintained a companionate relationship, bi-lateralization of interactions between both sides of the family were accepted. Therefore, for the desired bi-lateralization of family relations, it can be concluded that couples need to maintain their relationship as companions, while financial and emotional independence is established between generations. Superficial bi-lateralization without independence between generations causes dependency between generations, unrealistic expectations, and despair when such expectations are frustrated, worsening intergenerational relations as a result.

On the other hand, according to the preceding studies about bi-lateralization of kinship relations, which seemed to appear notably in the 1990s, it is argued that bi-lateralization in Korean families is different from that of families in Western countries, since, in reality, Korean family relations have become bilateral or maternal-centered, while their family rules still emphasize paternal-centered relations. This demonstrates that, while Korean society appears to have departed from the patriarchal family structure, this has not completely occurred in reality.

Bi-lateralization in Korean families can be seen as increasing the use of the wife's family network according to practical needs such as social support. In other words, since bi-lateralization in Korea is selective due to women's needs, it does not appear to be true bi-lateralization in which there is interaction with both sides of the family equally. This indicates that asymmetric kinship relations still exist 30 years after the beginning of study on the changes in kinship relations in the 1970s.

5. Conclusion

Korea's patrilineal family culture, considered traditional morals and customs, has been gradually changing since society has accepted western culture. In particular, over the past 10 years, in which time gender equality has been adopted as a basic idea of every government policy, gender discrimination has been criticized and revised in full measure in most public areas. However, the fundamental structure of patrilineal family culture — the paternal line descent rule — continues to exist in the social order and standards of everyday life as well as public areas.

However, the system, centered on the patrilineal family, has been dramatically altered, as the "head of the family system," which was recently abolished, and new laws, regarding family relation registration, have been enacted and implemented in 2010. Of course, the patrilineal family culture will not be changed instantly nor fundamentally in everyday life. However, the fact that the principle of succeeding the father's surname has been amended after enduring for hundreds of years, allowing for surname changes, has a special meaning regardless of how many people actually choose to do so. This can be a beginning of change in the previous meaning of family where family lineage was only through the paternal line descent.

As well, the amendment of the unilateral paternal line descent rule and the abolition of the "head of family system" will allow for the unraveling of conscious and unconscious issues on the continuation or extinction of family. The recent research on people's values regarding children showed almost no preference for boys, but, in reality, this preference continues to exist due to the socio-cultural system and environments. Nonetheless, the birth sex ratio in 2007 has regained a normal level, and the change in the family system is expected to dramatically reduce the unethical artificial adjustment of the birth sex ratio.

It is clear that the birth rate was successfully reduced after the 1970s by the implementation of a birth control policy as a government family planning project — unimaginable in the past when the purpose of marriage was to give birth to a boy — caused a serious low birth phenomenon entering into 2000, as did increases in the employment of married women, the cost of raising children, and educational expenses. However, even though the number of births dropped dramatically, this does not mean the value of children also diminished. Rather, the expectations placed on a small number of children became greater, and the value of children remained high.

As the number of births was reduced and the size of the family shrunk considerably to a nuclear-family-centered unit, the relationship between a small number of children and their parents has been reinforced, and it is expected that a nuclear-family-centered familism, different from the one in the old patrilineal family system, will be strengthened. The enthusiasm families in Korea show for private education to a degree not seen elsewhere and their unlimited protection of and involvement with their children are also examples of a highly cohesive Korean family culture. These phenomena are comparable to those of the traditional family culture, which emphasized the functional consolidation of the family/kin structure for the perpetuation of a patrilineal family.

To conclude, it is expected that Korean patrilineal-family-centered culture will be transformed into a family culture centered on the nuclear family and that this family-centered culture will be maintained. On the other hand, this gradually spreading bi-lateralization of family relations is currently in transition and appears to be selective. In the future, however, the family culture reinforcing the relationship within the nuclear family will stabilize in the context of the greater understanding of gender equality and the spread of the family with a small number of children. It is anticipated that such a change will form a new family culture where all three nuclear families — a nuclear family consisting of children and parents, and each parent's nuclear family of origin — together engage in multi-functional interaction.

References

Korea National Statistical Office (2007). Birth Statistics. Retrieved from http://www.nso.go.kr.

Korea Statistical Information Service (2011). Birth Sex Ratio. Retrieved from http://kosis.kr/wnsearch/totalSearch.jsp

Ministry of Government Legislation (2008). Gajokgwangyeui deungnok deung-e gwanhan bumnyul (Act on Family Relations Registration). Retrieved from http://www.moleg.go.kr/main/main.do.

Ok, S. W. (1989). Han-gukinui gajokjuuigachie daehan yeon-gu (A Study on Familism in Contemporary Korean Families; in Korean). Ph. D. Dissertation. Seoul National University. Seoul.

Ok, S. W., Sung, M., & Shin, K. Y. (2000). Dosi mit nongchon geojujaui gajok mit chinjokgwallyeon gachigwan bigyo (A Study on the Family and Kinship Value in Urban and Rural Families of Korea; in Korean). *Dae-han-gajoenghakhoeji (Journal of the Korean Home Economics Association)* 38(9): 1-17.

Shin, Y. J., Sung, T. E., & Choi, E. Y. (2008). *Chulsane yeonghyangeul michineun boyuk, Gyoyukbi budame gwanhan yeon-gu (A Study on the Burden of Cost of Raising Children and Educational Expenses which Influences Childbirth*; in Korean). Korea Institute for Health and Social Policy. Policy Report 2008-17.

Statistics Korea (2011). Total Fertility Rate Retrieved from http://kostat.go.kr/wnsearch/search.jsp.

Sung, M. (2006). Jiljeok yeon-gureul tonghan han-guk gajogui yang-gyehwa hyeonsang-e daehan jindanjeok jeopgeun (Bilaterization Phenomenoa in Korean Families: A Qualitative Research; in Korean). *Han-gukgajeong-gwallihakhoeji (Journal of Korean Home Management Association)* 24(3): 59-72.

Supreme Court of Korea (2008). Retrieved from http://help.scourt.go.kr/minwon/min_17/min_17_1/index.html.

Kukinews (2007, December 9). My children and husband say that they feel comfortable in my family's home. Retrieved from http://www.kukinews.com/news/article/print.asp?arcid=0920740378.

SBS News. (2007, May 3). Neo-matrilineal society? Only women's burden has increased. Retrieved from http://news.sbs.co.kr/section_news/news_read.

jsp?news_id=N1000251726.

Wizhankook (2008, November 17). Family Planning. Retrieved from http://
    pdf.hankooki.com/wz/view_wz.htm?exec=viewpage&height=2886&G
    CC=AG01299&PaperDate=2008-11-17&PageNo=1850317&PageName
    =28&CNo=51832438&COI=&NCT=&scope=&keyword=&period=&sta
    rtdate=&enddate=&page=&page_size=&idx=

I
Traditional
Korean Families

Chapter 1
Family/Kinship System under the Goryeo and Joseon Dynasties

Chapter 2
From a Daughter to Daughter-in-law

Chapter one

Family/Kinship System under the Goryeo and Joseon Dynasties

Yi, Jong Seo (Ulsan University)

1. Differences between the Korean Kinship System before and after the seventeenth century

Korea's kinship system changed dramatically in the seventeenth century, as the second half of the Joseon Dynasty period was beginning. The essence of that change was a new emphasis on the "paternal" relationships among all people. Since the seventeenth century, Koreans have used the terms "ancestors" and "descendants" in a "paternity-centric" way. Unlike the Western world's concept of the family tree, Korean families feature a single line from the father to father's grandfather to grandfather's father and so on until it reaches the ultimate founder of the line. The female's line is not considered nor featured. The same rule applies to one's descendants as well, traveling from son to grandson to great-grandson and so on until it reaches the most recent descendant. Again, female lines are not considered as legitimate lines of descendants. The range of descendants forms a pyramid, and the entire group is collectively labeled with their last name. For example, the "Gimhae Kim house" or the "Jeonju Yi house" indicates a group of paternal descendants who originated from a single founder bearing the name of either Kim or Yi. More than 4 million people who share the last name "Gimhae Kim" are now considered descendants of Kim-Suro-wang, who is known to have founded a small country in the Gimhae region in A.D. 42. Only recently has a person been allowed to change their last name. Previously, people had no choice but to follow the father's last name, except under extreme, often humiliating circumstances, called "changing one's last name," essentially an act of expulsion from the family.

In such a paternalistic society, the status of females had little or no meaning. Although daughters were considered as offspring of the family, once they had married they became members of their husband's family; however, the offspring of a married daughter were considered members of their fathers' houses. Furthermore, this hierarchic family pattern of paternity was also reflected in the practice of property inheritance and distribution. Since the seventeenth century, property inheritance by daughters continued to decline, and, eventually, their right to inherit properties was denied. If parents did not have a son, they would adopt a male from a paternal relative, who would inherit their properties, leaving nothing to their daughters.

Such practices reflect the emergence of a new paternal view

that perceived sons and daughters very differently, not in terms of their gender or their social roles but in terms of values they came to embrace. They essentially considered a paternal grandson as "ours" (mine), and a maternal grandson as "theirs" (yours). Different terms were employed to refer to them as well. In English countries, the father of parents is generally referred to as "grandfather," and the male offspring of one's sons as "grandson." Yet in Korea, "grandfather" refers only to a "paternal" grandfather, while the "grandfather" of a female is referred to as "the other grandfather," just as there is a "grandson" and "the other grandson." "The other(外)" refers to relationships that involve females, and it literally means 'outside.' Meanwhile, the "sisters" of the parents are also identified differently. In Western countries they are referred to as "aunt," regardless of whether they are the sisters of the father or the mother. In Korea, however, the sister of the father is called "Gomo," while the sister of the mother is called "Imo." Although they share the same distance from the offspring of either their brothers or their sisters, they are referred to by different names, emphasizing the paternal relationship.

Because paternal relationships were considered more important than maternal relationships, a person's residence was determined by familial relationships as well. Marriage was no longer considered an equal merging of a male and a female but came to mean the act of a female being assimilated into the male's household. When a paternal father died, it was primarily the son and the daughter-in-law who had the right and obligation to mourn. So, when daughters married, mothers would utter, "you are now a member of your husband's house, even after you die." Thus, the population of a village was composed of males sharing the same last name and the women who married them, and they would be buried there as well, even the daughters-in-law.

However, before the seventeenth century, during the Goryeo Dynasty (918-1392) and the early half of the Joseon Dynasty (1392-1592), Korean society was based on an entirely different familial and kinship system. There was no distinction between paternal and maternal relationships. Ancestors and their descendants included ancestors and descendants from both the male and female families. "Ancestors" referred to all of one's elder, blood-related relatives, and descendants could choose specific figures that were either honorable or at least useful when emphasizing their heritage. This is exemplified by the lineage of the Goryeo royal family (see Figure 1).

As we can see, females are included in the official lineage of Taejo Wang Geon, which was neither exclusively based upon a paternal order nor a maternal order. We can see as well that the graph indicates ancestors were selectively chosen, perhaps, to emphasize more what must have been considered the politically more desirable heritage and identity of Wang Geon. This approach to lineage, where both the paternal and maternal lines were considered ancestors and descendants, changed in the post-

Figure 1 The Lineage of Taejo Wang Geon, Founder of the Goryeo Dynasty

seventeenth century Joseon society. In that society, only paternal figures were considered as ancestors and descendants.

Thus, after the seventeenth century, a person's last name was an indicator of a group of people who had paternally-connected blood-relationships, unlike the Goryeo Dynasty period, where it was merely an indicator that one was a father or a son. It did not indicate an ancestor-descendant relationship. Furthermore, sometimes a last name would have to be changed. In Goryeo, for example, people were required change their last name, if it was the same name as the king, according to orders issued in 1198 and 1344. Usually, the name was replaced with either the mother's last name, or, in cases where the father and mother shared the same last name, the last name of either the father's mother or the mother's mother would be used. Thus, people were allowed to use various last names.

Beginning in the latter half period of the Joseon dynasty, altering a last name in this fashion was impossible, and it is still almost impossible today. Additionally, if a last name required a change, then all members of that house would have to change their names to the new name. However, before the restrictions of the Joseon Dynasty, the Goryeo people allowed discretionary decisions when choosing either the last name of a mother or a paternal grandmother or a maternal grandmother, because the last name merely confirmed the relationship between a father and a son, not a relationship between an ancestor and a descendant.

There was no distinction between paternal and non-paternal relationships, which was mirrored in the kinship terms. Similar to Western countries, as well as Japan, people were distinguished only by their gender, and kinships, according to their distance from a particular person, were considered as equally close relatives of that person. In other words, there was no paternal or maternal distinction. The Goryeo people did not have "grandfathers" nor "other grandfathers." There had only "grandfathers." There were only "aunts," who were sisters of either the father or the mother alike, and there were only "uncles," who were either brothers of the father or the mother alike. If they were blood-related, then they would be considered as relatives in an ancestor-descendant relationship. No particular recognition or status was given to relatives who were linked paternally.

This was reflected in the property distribution patterns as well. Goryeo people distributed their properties to their sons and daughters equally, and, when parents refused to distribute their properties equally, the action was often reversed. Social positions or governmental posts that could not be divided equally among a person's offspring were either passed on to a son or, if there were no sons, then to an offspring on the mother's side. Property distribution documents well into the first half of the Joseon Dynasty provide further support of equality in the distribution patterns during this period.

During the Goryeo Dynasty and the early half of the Joseon Dynasty, the concept of marriage was also different. Unlike the post-seventeenth century period, when marriage meant the incorporation of females into the male household, in the Goryeo and early Joseon periods, both males and females retained their original web of blood-relationships, which were merged, equally, in their union. Both the male and the female could retain ownership of the properties they inherited from their respective parents, and they were not allowed to take ownership of the other's property or inherit them without due process. Once they had children, the couple could divide the properties among them equally. If the couple did not have children, their properties would be inherited by other blood-related relatives.

Furthermore, contrary to the post-seventeenth century period, in the Goryeo and early Joseon periods, upon marriage, males moved into the home of their wife. Thus, in a village, there would be females who had grown up in that village, and males who had married into the family, all living together, and both the wives and the husbands would be buried there as well. So, males sharing the same paternal lineage did not reside in the same place. Instead they were scattered throughout the country, residing in their wives; hometown. Although similar to the residence patterns of a matriarchal society, this pattern was somewhat different as well. It was a social practice based upon the equality between males and females, but it was also convenient. Furthermore, males were not incorporated into the females' homes. Rather, they freely moved out of the females' homes to other locations for various reasons.

2. The Familial/Kinship System in the Latter Half of the Joseon Dynasty and Its Relationship to the Chinese System

As mentioned before, the Korean familial/kinship system changed considerably in the seventeenth century, due, primarily, to the conscious efforts of the *yangban*, an elite class of civil or military leaders who considered the Chinese system honorable. The *yangban* was expected to hold public office, follow the Confucian doctrine through study and self-cultivation, and help cultivate the moral standards of Joseon society (Lee 2004). This Chinese system refers to the Chinese "Clan Code (宗法)."

Clan codes were established in ancient China and were the method used to organize families under a paternal (patriarchal) system that reinforced and consolidated familial relationships. The Obok practice (五服制), which dictated the level of mourning a person should display toward various types of his or her relatives, called mourning periods, is a good example of how clan codes worked. Neither intimacy nor a person's value system or preference toward specific relatives could override the Obok practice (五服制). Familial and kinship members were classified into five groups. The relative's class, according to the Obok practice (五服制), determined what mourning attire to wear, the amount of sorrow to exhibit, and how to display such sorrow. People who fit inside these five classes were referred to as a collective of Obok relatives (五服制).

As we can see from Table 1, even when blood relationships are separated by the same distance from a person, the paternal relationship is given a much higher class than the maternal relationship. For the brother of a father, 12 months of mourning was required but only five months for the brother of a mother. Furthermore, males were instructed to mourn the death of their paternal relatives, while females were instructed to mourn the death

Table 1 The Five Classes of Relatives in the Mourning System (Obok-chin)

Class	Period of mourning	Object of Mourning	
		Paternal figures	Non-paternal figures (non-related figures)
1	25 months	parents	parents of the husband
2	12 months	grandparents, sons, (unmarried) daughters, brothers of the father, (unmarried) sisters of the father	brothers of the husband's father
3	9 months	(married) sisters of the father, cousins of the father, sons of the father's cousins	(married) daughters
4	5 months	second cousins of the father, sons of the father's second cousins	parents of one's mother, brothers and sisters of one's mother
5	3 months	sons of the father's third cousins	parents of the wife, sons of mother's sisters and brothers and sons of father's sisters

of the paternal relatives of their husbands. Males mourned the death of their parents for 25 months, but they only had to mourn three months for the death of their wives' parents. Females had to mourn the death of their husband's parents for 25 months as well. Clearly, paternal relationships took precedence over other relationships, and wives became a part of their husbands' network of blood relationships. Once the clan codes were implemented, males gained a network of paternal relationships with women bound to that network.

Figure 2 indicates the relationship among relatives within the range of five classes. The point person (Ego) is a member of a large paternal blood-related community with a single great-great-grandfather at the top as the ultimate ancestor. Some of the relatives connected through a non-paternal relationship were also

Figure 2 Structure of the "Five-Class Mourning System"

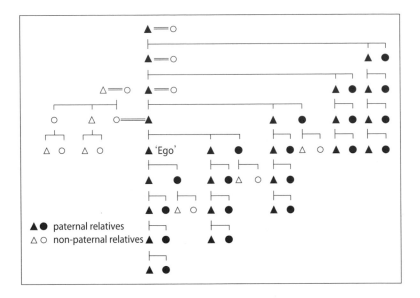

acknowledged as relatives. Yet there were very few of them, and they were assigned only to the lower classes without the hope of a significant role.

As the Figure implies, families and kinship relationships in ancient China were organized paternally. Additionally, many customs and rituals were established to maintain and reinforce the practice, for example, coming-of-age ceremonies, wedding ceremonies, funerals and memorial services. Among these, funerals and memorial services reflected the nature of the clan codes the most, establishing and reinforcing ritual rules and codes of conduct. For example, all five classes of relatives gathered for a funeral. Relatives connected paternally generally cooperated eagerly, as they were descendants of the same ancestor, but people who were not connected paternally remained marginalized. Even when the same degree of relationship distance existed between a person and two relatives, the one with the paternal relationship was granted more power and obligations than the non-paternal relationship. For funerals, people with non-paternal relationships had extremely limited roles, while the task of cleansing the dead body and putting it inside the coffin was the duty of paternal relatives who were allowed to see the body. For example, a paternal grandson would be allowed to see his grandfather's body, yet a maternal grandson would not.

A similar order was reflected in the memorial services held for ancestors as well. Memorial services were held on the day a person died, or sometimes on other important anniversaries, and usually only paternal descendants were invited. Other relatives were not allowed to participate in the service, even when they were within the five-class range. The memorial services for fathers, grandfathers, great-grandfathers, and great-great-grandfathers strengthened the relationship among clansmen.

All these institutions, designed to display and reinforce the clan codes, were renovated by the Southern Sung dynasty's Ju Hi (朱熹, 1130–1200). Ju Hi developed a new form of Confucianism, Seongnihak (Neo-Confucianism), and, while resurrecting the old clan codes, he also eradicated things that did not serve the present. The result was a protocol manual self-authored and entitled "Ga-rye (家禮)," which means "rules to be observed inside the house." Ga-rye continued to influence Korean society after the latter half period of the Goryeo Dynasty. The regulations and institutions of Ga-rye were regarded as standard principles to live by, and people who observed the rules were commended by the authorities. The Joseon people were extremely determined to live by the rules of this book. Thus, the leadership of Joseon and the intellectual Yangban acknowledged the righteousness and legitimacy of the teachings inside *Ga-rye* and praised a person's life that abided by the rules.

Yet the number of Yangban figures who actually understood the spirit of this *Ga-rye* and maintained them at all costs was actually not that high. In appearance, they built familial shrines and held services for the spirits of their dead ancestors, according to the rules established inside *Ga-rye*. Yet they only abided by the instructions of *Ga-rye* in terms of the structure of the shrine, food to prepare for the service, and the procedural order to be adhered during the service. The actual objects of those services were selected by the people themselves, contrary to *Ga-rye*. *Ga-rye* dictated that the shrine and services be for the paternal ancestors and descendants only. Yet the Yangban figures, who lived in the early half of the Joseon Dynasty period, enshrined many ancestors, both paternal and maternal, with different last names. A grandson would enshrine the tablet of the father of his mother, or the brother of his mother, and then hold memorial services for them. Services in the early half of the Joseon Dynasty's were never held exclusively for paternal ancestors and descendants. Brothers, sisters, and grandchildren from the father's side and the mother's side would stand together and hold services. Although such actions were in direct violation of the clan codes' philosophy, the Joseon Yangban figures maintained these variations of the customs for over two hundred years.

3. Embracing and Understanding the Theory of Shared Energy

Although early Joseon's Yangban figures believed and considered *Ga-rye* as the ultimate standard of conduct for households, they could not act upon the clan codes, because they could not understand nor tolerate the suggestion of the superiority of paternal relationships in *Ga-rye*. With only the clan codes and a scarcity of explanations, the people found it difficult to accept the mandate that non-paternal relationships should be excluded from the range of ancestors and descendants. However, once they studied and understood the theory of "shared energy," they ultimately began to believe in it.

In ancient China, people believed that when a person died that person would be split into a consciousness (魂) and a spirit (魄). The classic Confucian text, *Si-gyeong* (詩經), has a line that says, "father gave birth to me, and mother raised me." This is an expression of a belief that the father was the source of life, and the mother was merely a caretaker. Ju Hi (朱熹) explained this belief in terms of metaphysics, arguing that a person would inherit "energy (氣)" from the father. When the energy was drained the person would die, and the dissipated energy would become Consciousness and a Spirit. The former would ascend to the sky and the latter would percolate into the ground. Hi also argued that through the memorial services the dissipated and separated consciousness and spirit would be merged with each other once again, and the dissipated energy of the ancestors would feel the energy of the descendants, sharing the same energy, which could be felt by the descendants during the memorial service.

This placed a lot of importance upon the relationship between ancestors and descendants. Hi said, "If a person has a descendant, then we cannot say that there is no energy (氣)." He also said, "Where the body of the descendant is, there is the energy of the ancestor present as well." This "energy" was referred to an energy that would be inherited only from father to son and from ancestor to paternal descendant. In other words, only paternal relationships were considered the true ancestors and descendants, sharing the same energy.

Hi's disciple, Jin Sun (陳淳, 1159–1223), explained Hi's theory of shared energy in a way that would be more easily understandable. He argued that, if one did not have a son, then they would have to adopt the son of a person who shared the same energy as his own in order to have a son. Sun told a story, a folklore tale actually, of a person who adopted a male child from a non-paternal relative, and later, when the male child held a memorial service for his step-parents, the child's biological parents were summoned and appeared at the memorial service not the spirits of his step parents.

The theory of shared energy, reinterpreted by Ju Hi and explained in more simply by Jin Sun, served to reinforce and strengthen the system of paternal lineages in the Chinese society. Like China, the theory of shared energy played a similar role in Korea as well. Once it was introduced to the Korean population, it reinforced a paternal consciousness of relationships and realigned the familial and kinship order throughout the society.

Beginning in the fourteenth century, the last century of the Goryeo Dynasty, Korean intellectuals began to explain ancestor-descendant relationships based on the concept of "energy," due in part to the significant role of the relationship between China and Korea at the time. For example, Goryeo became part of the Mongol Yuan imperial order, and although it retained its sovereignty to a certain degree, there were vibrant interactions between Goryeo and China. Additionally, the official academic mainstream of the Yuan society followed Neo-Confucianism beliefs, which included Ju Hi's theory of shared energy.

Thus, Ju Hi's theories came to carry a lot of weight and authority not only in China but also in Korea. People even began to determine the difference between right and wrong based upon the concept of energy. Several quotes from this period highlight its importance such as "When the energy gathers, a figure will be formed, a character will be built, but when the energy dissipates, the spirit would fall to the ground and the consciousness would go up in the sky," or "When the parents die, their consciousness, the energy, relies upon the offspring." They also believed that life and death, a living person and a ghost, were essentially one, sharing the same energy. For example, when grandparents were laid peacefully under the ground, the descendants could feel peace. Thus, they protested the Buddhists' practice of cremation (火葬).

Through the early half of the Joseon Dynasty people relied more and more on the concept of energy to explain life and death, consciousness and spirit, as if the relationship between ancestor and descendant was solidified through the memorial service. Nam

Hyo On (1454–1492) argued that a person would separate into a consciousness and a spirit at death and became ghosts. Although ghosts, he believed, did not have a form, nor a heart or the ability to make a sound, when descendants faithfully and sincerely prepared a memorial service, the "energy" would come and make itself felt. Furthermore, he argued that because the ancestor and descendants shared the same energy, there was no difference between life and death.

These examples explain the relationship between ancestors and descendants and the concept of "energy" and why the memorial service served as an occasion where the consciousness and spirit of the ancestors would come and feel their descendant's sincerity and faith. It is possible Koreans came to acknowledge, or at least became aware of, the purported superiority of paternal relationships at this time.

Yet people's everyday lives exhibited a different aspect of familial relationships as well. The kinship customs of the early half of the Joseon Dynasty, as well as those of the preceding Goryeo Dynasty, continued to include all kinds of blood relationships, not only the paternal ones. Toward the end of the Goryeo Dynasty and the beginning of the Joseon Dynasty people began to denounce the paternally-focused customs and conventions of the time as barbaric. Even the Confucian scholars in Korea blamed themselves for not relinquishing such practices. Their world was still hanging on to practices of the past, but Neo-Confucianism was also beginning to take hold.

There was a significant impact on the Goryeo society by the

theory of shared energy as well. Wills and property distribution documents of this period contain countless remarks and orders regarding the distribution of property for a person without blood relationships. Additionally, a new document required that all ancestors and descendants "in either directions." Granting only blood-related relatives status as legitimate heirs, and accounting for all blood-related relatives is indicative of the attitude at the time whereby people were perceived as belonging to two groups— blood-related or not blood-related. This is believed to be a result of the theory of shared energy.

The general theory of metaphysics that explained the concepts of life and death was Buddhism in the Goryeo Dynasty period. In a secularized belief of Buddhism, humans were considered as independent individuals that were born with a borrowed body from their parents. It was believed that there were many lives, the prior ones, the current ones, and the next ones, and it was thought they actually rotated. It was also believed that all the relationships in the present were made possible because of the relationships forged in people's prior lives. So in this kind of belief system, it was not the "ancestors" whom one never had the chance of actually meeting or knowing, but the parents one had during "prior" lifetimes that were valued more. The Goryeo people prayed for the resting peace of their parents in their current life, as well as their parents in prior lifetimes. They prayed for their parents not because they were blood-related figures but because they gave birth to them and raised them. So, in this sense, the mother was valued more than the father. And since people believed relationships of the present were the result of relationships of the past, people did not hesitate to adopt infants with no blood-relationship to them.

However, intellectuals who embraced the theory of shared energy considered blood-relationships as far more important than people who followed the Buddhist version of spirits. Toward the end of the Goryeo period, the relationship between ancestors and descendants was explained as the continuation of energy and the custom of cremating an ancestor's body was considered an act of incinerating one's very root. Certainly, the theory of shared energy was exerting its influence on people's perception of the concept of ancestors and descendants.

Shared energy theory, introduced to the Goryeo people alongside Neo-Confucianism during the early half of the Joseon Dynasty, was unable to realign the entire network of human familial and kinship relationships in terms of patriarchy, it did establish a distinction between blood-relationships and non-blood-relationships. It also established the attitude and custom of excluding non-blood related figures from the family and the rite of kinship. By the latter half of the Goryeo Dynasty and the early half of the Joseon Dynasty, shared energy theory strengthened further people's awareness of the significance of blood-relationships and the general negation of non-blood-relationships.

4. Understanding Shared Energy Theory in the Latter Half of the Joseon Dynasty and the Strengthening of Paternal Order

In the early half of the Joseon Dynasty, Yangban figures did not distinguish and emphasize paternal lineage. Nonetheless, the Joseon government recognized the Chinese clan code as a standard that should be observed and implemented policies accordingly. In 1437, the Succession Law (立後法) was introduced, dictating that, if a couple did not have a son, then a male from a paternal relative [同宗支子] in the same generation should be named as the successor. In the legislation of this law, the theory of shared energy, theorized by Jin Sun, was cited as the basis for legitimizing such legislation. The government essentially supported and enforced the theory that only males from the paternal line could be named as successor-sons.

In spite of the law, forcing people to observe a patriarchal social order, individuals continued to observe their own customs and practices. However, in the mid-sixteenth century, they began to voluntarily embrace patriarchal order and to change their lives accordingly. Additionally, some Neo-Confucian scholars voluntarily supported the clan code and the protocols and determinations emphasized in *Ga-rye*, and academic opinion helped to establish the new meaning of memorial services. Yi Hwang (1501–1570), a renowned academician of the history of Neo-Confucianism in Joseon, publicly denounced the memorial services observed by descendants on the mother's side and acknowledged the legitimacy of only those memorial services observed by descendants of paternal lineage, drawing on the description of "Bon (本, Origin)." He argued there could be only one origin for an individual, so enshrining the tablet or spirit of a person who carried a different last name in the house's shrine was wrong. He reasoned that it was wrong to acknowledge two origins for a single person. For example, a person could not hold a memorial service for the father of his mother, because it was the duty of the grandfather's paternal descendant. In other words, in Joseon, the theory of shared energy was understood just as it had been in China since the sixteenth century.

In subsequent periods, discrimination against non-paternal lineages and denouncing the legitimacy of non-paternal relationships, based upon the concept of shared energy, increased. For example, in his diary, Yi Weon Ik (1547–1634) described the relationships among father, son, and grandson as a relationship through which a same energy was relayed and shared [一氣相傳]. Ju Hi provided a similar description when he emphasized the meaning and importance the memorial services served for paternal descendants. Eventually, the Joseon people came to regard the memorial services held by non-paternal descendants as "an obscure service [淫祀]," because they do not share the same energy. They also believed that "abandoning the son of a brother and naming the son of a daughter is a crime." Also, as noted earlier, adopting a non-paternal descendant caused the spirit of the descendant's biological father to appear at the service, which made people nervous.

As I heard, in the past, there was a minister who annually held a memorial service for his father. Every year, a young, handsome male would come to the service and shove the minister's father aside and take some of the food that was on the table. It was so odd, he told the story to his mother. His mother said, "Your father had once served as a magistrate in the Yeongnam region, and, when he reported for duty to that region, I tagged along. I met a servant while I was there, who was about 14 years old and very attractive and lovable. I invited him to my side and had him serve me. One night, I invited him into my room, and we spent the night together and you were conceived. He is your real father, so he is the one that deserves a meal at the memorial service. There is this energy, and we can see that it is in operation, so be aware. After hearing this, the minister secretly visited Yeongnam. He found the grave of that servant and held a memorial service for him, claiming he had some good will to pay. There may be more cases like this in the world, in houses with lax order. The sages have taught us that the father is more important than the mother. This story is a good example of this.

The story of a biological father "appearing" at a memorial service and "taking away" the prepared meals is a common story in many households at the time. Obviously, the Joseon society had embraced the theory of shared energy and accepted the new patriarchal order of the society. This kind of tale, taught by the Neo-Confucian scholars, helped to reinforce the importance of paternal lineages and relationships, as well as the memorial services they would receive once they died, to the general population. At this point, the Chinese theory of shared energy stopped being an ideology for social change and became an established social norm. Even in Korea today, the elders joke that the male provides seeds, while the female serves as cropping fields. And yet another saying is "one should love an insect more than loving a son born from the daughter." These phrases reinforce the belief that males are the source of life and that sons from daughters cannot be recognized as a true descendant.

5. The Residences' Location Pattern in the Latter Half of the Joseon Dynasty and Changes in the Familial Relationships

1) Changes in Graves' Location

(1) Location of Males' Graves in the Early Half of the Joseon Dynasty
In the seventeenth century, the familial/kinship system changed considerably. People of this time period came to harbor a different mentality and sentiment. Such changes in the people's thinking and mentality can also be traced to in the new location of graves that belonged to the Yangban males. In the Gyeongsang-do and Jeolla-do provinces, where many Yangban houses were located, the location of graves of the Kim Jong Jik (金宗直, 1431–1492) house and the Yu Hi Chun (柳希春, 1513–1577) house changed.

Kim Jong Jik was a Neo-Confucian scholar of the fifteenth century, and he considered paternal lineages and relationships very important. Based on age old documents, he traced his direct ancestors from the paternal line in order to identify ancestors who fell in the five classes of the Chinese clan code. This was a very different pattern of scholarship from other Neo-Confucian scholars in this time period. Yet, in terms of familial customs and kinship relationships, he still abided by the old customs.

Kim Jong Jik considered his great-great-grandfather very important, however he did not know where he was actually buried. The oldest ancestor whose burial place he was able to identify was his great-grandfather. Yet because his great-grandfather and great-grandmother were from the same hometown, it was not certain why his great-grandfather was buried there. So we can only identify why a figure was buried in a specific place not his great-grandfather but his grandfather. Kim's grandfather's grave was located in the same place as the grave of his mother-in-law. Thus, we can see that Kim's grandfather lived his entire life in his wife's house and then was buried in the same place as his in-laws. Kim's father led a similar life as well. Upon marriage, he lived in his wife's house, except periods when he served with the government or attended the funeral and mourning period for his own father. In his final days, he lived with his daughter, as his sons were married and left. Before he died, he asked that he be buried at beside his mother-in-law's grave.

After he married, Kim Jong Jik moved into his wife's house as well, and he continued to live there, except when he was in the capital. His wife died young, and his offspring were buried there as well. However, because he remarried after his first wife died, he was not buried there. After retiring from government service, he moved into his own house and was eventually buried in the region where his father had been buried. Had his first wife not died early,

Map 1 Location of Graves of Yu Hi Chun and His Mother Choi's Paternal Relatives

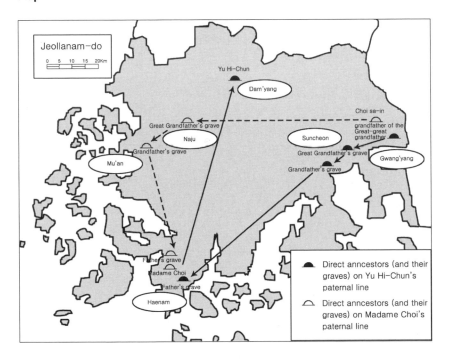

Jeollanam-do

0 5 10 15 20Km

Yu Hi-Chun

Dam'yang

Choi sa-in

Great Grandfather's grave

grandfather of the
Great-great
grandfather

Naju

Suncheon

Grandfather's grave

Great Grandfather's grave

Gwang'yang

Mu'an

Grandfather's grave

Father's grave

Madame Choi

Father's grave

Haenam

⬛ Direct anncestors (and their
graves) on Yu Hi-Chun's
paternal line

△ Direct anncestors (and their
graves) on Madame Choi's
paternal line

he would have been buried where his offspring and in-laws were buried. The same pattern is also confirmed by the grave locations of other figures that belonged to the Yu Hi Chun lineage as well.

The above map indicates the locations of graves that belonged to Yu Hi Chun, his mother Choi, and their paternal ancestors. The first direct paternal ancestor of Yu Hi Chun, whose tomb location is verified by his sixth ancestor, is located in Gwang-yang. The location was unknown until Yu Hi Chun found it and repaired it. Gwangyang was where the house of the mother and wife of this 6th ancestor was located. A true Neo-Confucian scholar, Yu Hi Chun, was thrilled to find his sixth ancestor's grave, although he was unable to find the grave of his fifth ancestor or that of his great-great-grandfather.

The location of the graves of his great-grandfather, grandfather, and father are now confirmed. Yu Hi Chun's great-grandfather and grandfather were buried in Suncheon, although they are buried in different locations inside Suncheon suggesting Yu Hi Chun's grandfather was not buried there because his own father was buried there as well. Yu Hi Chun's father was buried in Haenam, where the house of his wife was located. Yu Hi Chun was buried in Damyang, where his wife had lived since childhood. As the map shows, the locations of graves continued to change with each passing generation. The pattern of males moving to the regions of their wives' homes can also be seen from the grave patterns of the paternal ancestors of Yu Hi Chun's mother as well.

Yu Hi Chun's mother was born in Haenam, the region of her mother's home, before she married Yu Hi Chun's father.

The location of graves for the Yu Hi Chun house in the Jeolla-do province shows a similar pattern to that of the Kim Jong Jik house in the Gyeongsang-do province. Also, from the Yu Hi Chun house, it is possible to determine the familial relationships among graves located in the same graveyard. Relationships among graves in the Haenam region where Yu Hi Chun was born, can be explained as in Figure 3 below.

Evidently, males with various last names were buried in the same graveyard, when they shared the same hometown as their wife. Yet, the tomb of a brother of Yu Hi Chun indicates otherwise as well. So, obviously, neither paternal nor maternal relationships were

Figure 3 Relationships among Graves Located in the Haenam Graveyard

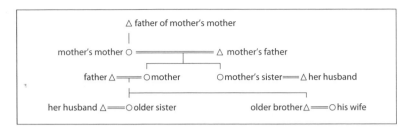

considered exclusive or definitive when deciding a burial grave. Furthermore, at the time, daughters usually cared for their parents. For example, Yu Hi Chun's sister moved to another location to care for her grandparents who were living there at the time.

(2) Location of Graves of Males during the Latter Half Period of the Joseon Dynasty

In the houses of Kim Jong Jik and Yu Hi Chun in the early half of the Joseon Dynasty, most males moved to their wives' houses where they lived out their lives there and were buried, while the females usually lived their entire lives in the town where they were originally born.

However, in the latter half of the Joseon Dynasty, the paternal relatives of both the Kim Jong Jik house and Yu Hi Chun house established burial sites for their relatives in the same place. For example, the grave of Kim Jong Jik's great-grandson Kim Mong Ryeong (1551–1580) show this new pattern. Kim Jong Jik's son and grandson lived in the house of their wives and were buried there. Yet his great-grandson, Kim Mong Ryeong, was buried in the region where his father had been buried, and his descendants were buried there as well, establishing a paternal burial site for Kim Mong Ryeong and his descendants.

Yu Hi Chun's lineage also shows a paternal burial site was established around the seventeenth century beginning with the tomb of Yu Ik Won (1579–1645), the great-grandson of Yu Hi Chun located near his father's tomb. After the death of Yu Ik Won, all his paternal descendants were buried there as well, although a few did stray and were buried in other locations. However, they were still buried close to the grave of Yu Hi Chun.

Around the seventeenth century, other houses also began to establish paternal graveyards as well. Many records and articles from this period describe people's conviction to the legitimacy of this new trend. Most articles quoted Neo-Confucianism's metaphysical theories in order to justify the relocation of a grave rather than practical necessity. Thus, people relocated the graves of their brothers and mothers to the side of their fathers and described the act as being 'just [義],' and 'in the will of gods [神理].' Notably an article written by Yi Weon Ik (1547–1634) described the philosophy that led the Yangban figures of the seventeenth century to secure and establish paternal graveyards owned only by paternal descendants. They argued a father, a son, and a grandson would like to live together, always, and, after their deaths, stay together. Further, they noted, they were "entities that shared and transmitted the same Gi (energy)[一氣相傳]," so naturally a son should be buried in a place next to his father's grave. Yi Won Ik's warning to his descendants reflects the theory of Shared Energy well.

As we can see, the Joseon Yangban figures of the seventeenth century embraced the theory of Shared Energy, held onto the paternal principles of familial relationships, and changed their own patterns of life. Their efforts were also based upon pure determination, so they were also destined to find themselves at odds with the existing sentiments of the time. They were born in their mothers' childhood homes and spent most of their lives in wives' hometowns. Yet they were convinced that this way of life was not right and were determined to change it. So, even in the seventeenth century when the familial order was being realigned to a paternal system, they were still deeply attached to their daughters, non-paternal relatives, and familial members. The following letter illustrates the inner conflicts between an attachment to the old order and a desire to support the new order.

> Letter to my baby [daughter]
> We released you from our care, and we imagine that you would be missing us. Daughters always leave their parents. That's the way it is. Your mother is well, so don't worry. I am losing weight, but don't worry. As I heard, Jeong-Il seemed sad for parting with his grandmother. He should be cared for. Tell him to stay put, and study hard. Until next time. May 3rd.

This letter was sent by a high-ranking government official, who died in 1633, to his youngest daughter. From the letter, it is clear the parents' youngest daughter and her husband had been staying with them and had recently left. The mother seems to have made a visit to the daughter's house and told her husband their grandson missed them. So the father wrote a letter, saying he missed his daughter and grandson. The letter shows the clash between a natural sentiment for their children but a conviction to the new ways and order.

Thus, before the sixteenth century, it was customary to live in the home village of a wife, but, by the seventeenth century, the Yangban found such a practice to violate the Neo-Confucian order. Men came to believe that it would be prudent to move into their own houses. Parents released their daughters, believing "females should be living with the parents of their husbands," and invited their daughters-in-law into their homes instead. Fathers and sons began to live together in life, as well as death. The Yangban established their own graveyard in the seventeenth century based upon a new conviction that "daughters are to leave their parents once they're married."

2) Changes in the Perspective Viewing the 'Parents,' and the Stepmothers' Obtaining the Status of 'Mothers'

(1) Changes in the Meaning of a "Father" and a "Mother"

Men, who lived during the Goryeo Dynasty and the early Joseon Dynasty, lived their whole lives in their wives' home towns and villages, and they were buried there as well. Yet, after the theory of Shared Energy exerted its influence, people began to consider the father figure as the source of life, and men began staying in their childhood homes with their wives as well. This led to an enormous change in the meaning and status of the words "father" and "mother." Now the father figure was considered the source of life, and the mother figure was considered an attachment to the father figure. This new perspective is prevalent in Korea today, where the terms of "father" and "mother" are used, synonymously, when referring to the brothers of the father and also the wives of those brothers.

> father = mother
> senior father = senior mother
> junior father = junior mother

As we can see, the older brother of the father is called "senior + father," and the younger brother of the father is called "junior + father." Their wives are called both "senior + mother," and "junior + mother." In this kind of reference system, the title "father" is used as the basis for naming a person who carries a paternal tie with the father, and the title "mother" is used to refer only to the spouses of the "fathers." If the title "mother" is used upon the same basis, then it is used upon the basis of naming a person who carries a maternal tie to the mother. So the term "senior mother" does not refer to the "spouse of the senior father" but rather to the "older sister of the mother."

The current system in Korea of referring to parents as "father" and "mother" was established after the seventeenth century; however, until the sixteenth century, the terms "father" and "mother" followed different rules of usage.

father = mother	mother = father
uncle = uncle' spouse	uncle = uncle' spouse
aunt = aunt's husband	aunt = aunt's husband

Evidently, before the sixteenth century the brothers and sisters of both the father and the mother were called "uncles" and "aunts," respectively, and recognized with the same status.

The status of familial members and relatives were granted only to figures that had a blood-relationship. The title of "mother" was granted not because she was the wife of the father but because she was the one who gave birth to the child and raised it. Yet, after the seventeenth century, the concept of mother was defined as the spouse of the father. So, before the sixteenth century, if something happened to the mother and she was eventually replaced, the sister of the mother or sister of the father would step in to assist, while, in the latter half of the Joseon period, the wives of the father's older or younger brothers stepped in, as they were the "mothers" due to their relationships with the other "senior" and "junior" fathers. Thus, after the seventeenth century, the naming system was modified, to reflect the importance of paternal relationships as the primary basis of referring to family members.

This indicates the Neo-Confucian view of the father and the mother established after the seventeenth century. Father is the source of life, while mother is defined by the relationship to the father. Accordingly, a female that is not recognized as a spouse cannot be recognized as a person's mother, even when the female gave birth to that person. Yet if the father approved a female as his spouse, then the offspring of that father had to recognize that female as his or her mother. In the sixteenth century, the Joseon Neo-Confucian scholars accepted this rule and tried to adapt to the new philosophy. The most renowned scholar of the history of Joseon Neo-Confucianism argued that the people should not observe a mourning period and wear mourning attire for the mother if she had been rejected by her spouse. While a father's second wife was still alive, the father's son or daughter was not allowed to say that they had "lost their mother." A rejected mother was not considered a mother. The "newer spouse of the father" was deemed the mother, clearly demonstrating the Neo-Confucianism principle of defining the status of a mother based upon her relationship to the father.

(2) "Stepmothers" Obtaining the Legitimate Status of "Mothers"

According to Neo-Confucian rules of order, stepmothers, who were considered the "next wife of the father," were entitled to the status of a mother, which did not exist in either the Goryeo Dynasty period or the early half of the Joseon Dynasty. A stepmothers was not considered a mother but were only the wife of the father.

Thus, women greeted their husbands into their homes, and when the husband died, the female mourned at her home. However, when the wife died, the husband mourned at the deceased wife's home. Furthermore, when a husband died and the woman remarried, she would invite him to live in her house with the children from her first marriage, because women considered it inappropriate to raise the children from their first marriage in their new husband's home, which was supported by society. Yet, if a man wanted to remarry after his wife died, he had to leave his dead wife's home, and, usually, children of a deceased mother never considered the new wife of their father as their mother.

Thus, children who lost their father usually lived with their mother, their stepfather, and any other kids who were born between the mother and the stepfather. On the other hand, it was extremely unusual for kids who lost their mother to live with their father, the stepmother, and any children who came with the stepmother. Therefore before the sixteenth century, it was the mother's death that threatened the existence of a family unit, because, when a mother died, the children were separated from the father as well.

There are many examples of this practice from the Goryeo period and the early half of the Joseon period. For example, Kim Jong Jik's mother lost her mother early, and her father remarried, she did not go with her father but was raised by her mother's mother. Kim Jong Jik's wife was raised by her mother's mother as well, when her mother died early. There are many similar examples in which a person was raised by the mother's sisters or the father's sisters. Thus, usually, children who lost their mother did not live with a stepmother, and they regarded a stepmother as only the wife of the father while the stepmother recognized the children as only the children of their husband's former wife.

With the advent of the Joseon Dynasty, a new emphasis was placed upon familial and kinship relationships based upon Neo-Confucianism. Scholars argued that children from a prior wife should treat a stepmother as their mother, and consequently, a stepmother had to do the same. To stabilize and firmly establish the stepmothers' status, the government of the Joseon Dynasty passed legislation to enforce the new code, allowing the wife of a deceased husband to retain her husband's property as long as she did not remarry. Furthermore, the children of a prior wife had to observe a funeral and memorial service for their stepmother just as they would for their biological mother. The oldest son of a prior wife had to hold a memorial service for a stepmother who left no children and was entitled to inherit a large portion of the stepmother's property.

However, since these new regulations went against the general customs in the early Joseon period, it was a long time before people adopted them. Additionally, the new legislation caused social conflicts, especially when it came to the distribution of property. In the sixteenth century, the children of prior wives disputed the law that dictated the inheritance of a father's property by a stepmother. In fact, often the life of a stepmother was threatened. Escalating the situation further, the relatives of a stepmother might become involved to support the stepmother's rights. In spite of the laws, the tie between the children and the stepmother based upon their link to the same male figure could not override previous biological relationships.

Before the sixteenth century, the children from prior marriages never lived with a stepmothers, staying in their biological mother's home, so they did not become acquainted with each other. Thus, the children considered a stepmother as a stranger, and, usually, they did develop an attachment to each other. Furthermore, a stepmother who was not able to have a child usually found themselves in a rather precarious situation, so it became common to arrange a marriage between the prior wife's son or grandson and the niece of the stepmother in order to bond the families together. In this way, the family was able to prevent or resolve any conflicts between them. Under this arrangement, stepmothers were generally treated well by their nieces and earned the status of mother-in-law to the sons of the husband's prior wives.

Yet it was not a smooth transition. The legislation protecting stepmothers caused fierce conflicts, and the people were not ready to consider the stepmothers as mothers, eventually causing some serious problems. There were many reports of stepmothers abusing or even killing the step children. For example, a tragic incident that occurred in 1654 was made into a novel named "Jang-hwa and Hongnyeon," which became an instant favorite of the Korean readers. Finally, in 1710 a new law was enacted that applied the penalty of strangulation to any person involved in a situation in which a stepmother coerced or lured her husband into intentionally taking the life of an offspring. This clearly indicates how badly the situation had deteriorated.

By the seventeenth century, however, the legislation regarding stepmothers as mothers was reinforced. Yangban figures continued to emphasize the importance of paternal relationships, supporting the newly defined roles and status of males and females. The stepmother would become "mother" to her husband's children from a previous wife. Changes in residence and a new sense of legitimacy worked in favor of the stepmothers' new status. In the early half of the Joseon Dynasty period, males lived in their wives' houses, but, according to the theory of Shared Energy theory, this acted against heaven's will. So, beginning in the latter half of the Joseon Dynasty, men, even after marriage ceremonies in their wives' home, returned to their own houses until their death. The practice of living in the wife's house continued to decline until it was finally abandoned. Females became completely incorporated into the house of a male, subordinating the status of women to that of men.

As time passed, the conflicts were assuaged. Past customs faded, and the new order was established. The new legitimacy of the family structure, based on paternal rights, was accepted. Hostility ended, and tragic incidents were averted. Although, novels published in subsequent periods were modeled after "Jang-hwa and Hongnyeon," none included scenes in which a child was killed by a stepmother or a child wanted the stepmother dead. The Neo-Confucian perspective toward the role of the father and mother had changed. People accepted the new relationships. The theory of Shared Energy prevailed.

References

Choi, J. S. (1983). *Han-gukgajokjedoyeon-gu* (*Study of Korea's Family System*; in Korean). Seoul: Iljisa, 1983.

Lee, S. Y.(2004). "Yangban: The Cultural Life of the Joseon Literati." In *Heilbrunn Timeline of Art History*. New York: The Metropolitan Museum of Art, 2000. Retrieved from http://www.metmuseum.org/toah/hd/yang/hd_yang.htm (October 2004)

Mun, S. J. (2004). *Joseonsidae jaesansangsokgwa gajok* (*Property Inheritance and*

Families of the Joseon Dynasty; in Korean). Seoul: Gyeong-in Munhwasa.

No, M. H. (1981). Goryeoui Obok-chin-gwa chinjokgwan-gye beopje (Goryeo Society's Obok Relatives and the Kinship Laws; in Korean). *Han-guk-sa Yeon-gu 33*, The Association for Korean Historical Studies.

Shin, I. C. (1992). *Hangugui sahoegujo: mibunhwa sahoeeseo bugye sahoero (Korea's Social Structure: From a Rather Undiversified Society to a Patriarchal Society*; in Korean), Seoul: Mundeoksa.

Yi, G. G. (1990). *Han-gugui gajokgwa jongjok (Korea's Families and Races*; in Korean). Seoul: Minumsa.

Yi, J. S. (2009). *Goryeo, Joseonui chinjokyong-eo-wa hyeol-yeon-uisik: Chinjokgwan-gyeui jeong-hyeong-gwa byeondong (Kinship Terms and Recognition of Blood Relationships in the Goryeo and Joseon Periods: Forms and Changes in the Kinship Relationships*; in Korean). Seongnam: Shin-gu Munhwasa.

Chapter two

From a Daughter to Daughter-in-law

Lee, SoonGu (National Institute of Korean History)

1. When a female was not considered "a member of the family"

In 1613 (5th year of King Gwang'hae-gun's reign), during the "Gye'chuk-year criminal case," Queen Dowager Inmok had to negotiate with the King Gwang'hae-gun over certain matters.

> My son (Prince Yeong'chang) has caused so much trouble and hurt my parents and my brother. I cannot afford to do nothing. I offer my hair as a token of sincerity. You can take the life of my son. Instead, please spare the lives of my father and my brother.

In this negotiation, Queen Dowager Daebi gave up the life of her own son in order to save the lives of her father and brother, and, by doing so, her the last bother as well. Considering the general nature of motherhood, the Queen's request seems unfathomable at best and outright irrational at worst. What in the world would have made her do a thing like this?

Certainly, there were some complicated political considerations behind this negotiation. Gwang'hae-gun felt threatened by the presence of Prince Yeong'chang. The Queen Dowager must have realized the fate of her son was already sealed. Therefore, she chose to save her family, even though she could not possibly save her son. At the same time, this request shows that the Queen Dowager considered saving her family as equally more crucial objective than saving her son. In that regard, by requesting the release of her father and brother, she was not acting as the Queen Dowager of a royal family or the mother of a prince, the presumptive heir to the throne. She was acting as the daughter of civilian lineage, the Yeon'an Kim house. In the aforementioned negotiation, she was negotiating as the daughter of the Kim house not as the daughter-in-law of the Joseon royal family. Why would she choose her civilian identity over her public identity?

During the early half of the Joseon Dynasty, women identified more strongly as a daughter. For example, upon marriage, men moved into the wife's home (男歸女家), so a woman stayed in her childhood home even after she married. Under such living patterns, women considered themselves more as "daughters of their parents" than as "daughters-in-law of their husbands' houses." By the seventeenth century, during Queen Dowager Inmok's lifetime, the practice began to weaken, and the number of married couples moving into the husband's house instead of the wife's house was increasing. However, psychologically, women still retained a strong sense of identity as a daughter, and their connections to their parents and their own homes were still very strong. In addition, high-ranking women inside the royal family would have found it even more difficult to give up their identity, as the actions of Queen Dowager Inmok reveal, defending and protecting her family and home.

As anyone else, during the Joseon period, women tried to secure the best possible living conditions for themselves. Whether in their childhood homes or the houses of their husbands, their place of residence would have determined their roles and relationships with others. Women who continued to live in their own homes would have retained the same relationship with their family members, while women who moved to the house of their husbands would have been forced to forge new relationships in a new residence and establish a new role for themselves. However, by the seventeenth century, the place of residence for a married couple shifted from the wife's house to the husband's house. This signified a major shift in terms of identity for Joseon women from being a daughter to being a daughter-in-law.

2. Changing marriages

In the pre-modern period of Korea, most women never pursued public occupations. Marriage absorbed a considerable portion of their lives. However, the marriage institution itself was changing and, thus, the identities of women gradually shifted from that of primarily "daughter" to that of "daughters-in-law."

Kim Jong Jik, who was considered and revered as the head of the Sarim-pa faction in the early days of the Joseon Dynasty, was born in Mil'yang, which was the hometown of his mother. His father's hometown was Seonsan, yet, after his father's marriage, he lived in Mil'yang, where Kim Jong Jik was born. Like his father, after Kim Jong Jik married a woman whose last name was "Jo" at the age of 21, he also moved to his wife's hometown, which was Gimsan (金山: known as Gimcheon today) and established a permanent presence there. The only time he left the town was when he had to report for government service in the capital. When his son, Mog'a (木兒) died, he was buried next to the grave of his mother's mother in Gimsan as well. When Kim Jong Jik was relieved from his government post and after he completed the mourning period at his own mother's grave, he returned to his house in Gimsan. Clearly, since the beginning of his marriage, Kim Jong Jik's home was in Gimsan and not Mil'yang. Yet, after he retired from the government, he spent his remaining days in Mil'yang and not Gimsan, but only because his wife Jo had died early and he remarried.

Kim Jong Jik lost his first wife, Jo, at the age of 52. He remarried three years later to the daughter of Mun Geuk Jeong (文克貞), who was only 18 years old at the time and brought his new bride to his house in the tradition of "U'gwi (于歸)," the act of "having the bride come (return) to the bridegroom's house." Kim Jong Jik's biography describes this event as one of particular significance and not a commonplace practice at the time. Ordinarily, an invitation of the bride to live in the husband's home would take a couple of years, and, in many cases, the brides did not even move into bridegroom's house at all. Kim Jong Jik must have rushed the invitation, because he was very old, living in the capital, and it was his second marriage.

The term "U'gwi" is from the Chinese *Si-gyeong (The Book of Odes)* in the Ju'nam (周南) chapter, meaning "the female is 'returning' to the house of the bridegroom [husband]." The nuance of "returning" reflects an attitude that the husband's house was the rightful place for the woman, so a woman's moving to the husband's house was considered as an act of "returning." Women who moved to their husband's house stayed there for the rest of their lives, and, more than likely, they would never return to their homes again.

> Water flows in that stream
> It flows into the Gi'su (淇水) River
> Missing the Wi (衛) country
> Every day, every night
> So I take consultation
> From all those lovely girls.[1]

This poem from "Si-gyeong" is about a woman who married a man living in a country called Je (齊). She missed her home country, everyday, yet Wi, was unable to return to it. She shared her grief with the other women who came to Je with her. And there is a following line that says, "a female, once married, is destined to

---

1 "毖彼泉水 亦流于淇 有懷于衛 靡日不思 變彼諸姬 聊與之謀"

move far away from her family (女子有行 遠父母兄弟)."

The poem shows the marriage pattern during the Chinese ancient period, and the emotional distress of married women at the time. Women moved into (or "returned to") the house of her husband ("于歸") and were homesick, because they were unable to go back to their childhood homes. Furthermore, in China, when a man "wedded" a wife or the man's family greeted the new daughter-in-law, it was described as an act of "taking (取)," while the woman's family was usually said to be "giving away" a daughter. Like in "Shi'gyeong," when a woman marries, she "returned" to the man's house.

During the Sung Dynasty (宋) in China, Jeong Ih (程頤) was frustrated that parents were more concerned with finding a suitable husband for their daughters than finding a good wife for their sons. He believed selecting the right daughter-in-law was crucial for maintaining the integrity of a house. However, parents were more careful when selecting a proper husband for their daughters, because it was the daughters that would have to leave their homes, move to other regions, and adapt to a new life. Men were grounded; they would stay in the house where they were raised. Women, on the other hand, would have to move, so, naturally, parents were very concerned for their daughter's well being. In China, women had moved into the man's house upon marriage since the ancient days. As a result, marriages and familial relationships have always displayed a paternal, male (媤家)-centric pattern.

However, in Korea, until the middle period of the Joseon Dynasty, the concept of a woman moving into her husband's house, or "returning" to it, was different. Women stayed in their childhood homes, and the husband moved to the wife's house.

> In the morning, Osu Chalbang Jeong Ji (丁至) dropped in. I asked him to serve as Wi'yo (圍繞)[2], when Gwangseon marries the daughter of the Nam'weon area's Kim Sa'gwa (金司果) in January. He said, 'Very well. I'll have the bridegroom spend a night at Osu, have him wear a new dress, and send him on into his father-in-law's house on a horse.'

On November 16th, 1575, Yu Hi Chun (1513-1577) wrote in his *Mi'am Ilgi (Diary)* that he asked Chalbang Jeong, who was the son of a friend, to serve as a Wi'yo[2], for the upcoming marriage of his grandson, Gwangseon. The phrase, "having Gwangseon ride on a horse on his way into his father-in-law's house" is described with the word 'Ibjang (入丈),' which meant, primarily, the act of going into one's father-in-law's house. This word also refers to the marriage itself. This example shows that, in Joseon society, the man would visit the woman's house, marry, and remain at the woman's house to live. Thus, during Yu Hi Chun's lifetime of the Joseon Dynasty, marriage was not an act of "taking a wife" but rather more like "going into the woman's home," according to the marriage customs of Korea at the time. So, initially, the marriage customs of Korea were clearly different from those of China.

---

2 This Wi'yo referred to a person who was selected among family members and relatives to escort either the bride or the bridegroom to the wedding. They were also called Sang'gaek/ 上客, Hu'bae/後陪, Hu'haeng/後行, or Wi'wu/位右.

The Yejo office devised a uniform code that said, "According to the old practices of the previous dynasty (Goryeo), the man would go to the women's house, give birth to sons and grandsons and have them grow up there. As a result, their relationship with the woman's mother's family became very important, and when the mother's parents or the wife's parents died, the man would be granted a 30-day leave of absence from their duties. The practice is still maintained today. It has been suggested that, in the future, officials should be relieved of duty for 20 days [and not 30] due to the death of one's mother's parents (figures who deserve the "Dae'gong/大功-level" mourning) and 15 days due to the death of one's wife's parents (figures who deserve the "So'gong/小功-level" mourning)." (*Sejong Shillok*, January, the Eulmi day, 15th year)

Ultimately, the Yejo office was questioning the wisdom of granting a government official the same amount of days off for the death of a father's parents as that of a mother's parents. The office argued that less time should be given off to officials for the death of a mother's parents. Furthermore, they believed the Korean custom should conform more to the customs of China. Thus, they began to change the marriage customs, which would lead, inevitably, to many more changes throughout society.

King Sejong exerted considerable effort in establishing the Chin'yeong-rye practice, in which the man would greet the woman and live in his house together. In 1435 (the 17th year of his reign), he arranged the marriage of Pa'weon-gun [prince] Yun Pyeong (尹坪) and Pricess Sukshin (淑愼翁主) after the Chin'yeong-rye fashion.

He believed if the royal family set the new standard for marriage practices, then the Sa-Daebu (scholar-officials) figures would follow. However, the people did not change their marriage customs. King Jungjong lamented, "Great king Sejong, in honoring the old [Chinese] traditions, arranged the marriages of princes and princesses in the fashion of 'Chin'yeong,' and had the scholar-officials follow his example. Yet the customs are still not changed, even today. In marriages, the males still move into their wives' homes. This is a shame that goes against the will of heaven (天道)."

During the reign of King Myeongjong, the government's efforts to expand the practice of 'Chin'yeong' were still unsuccessful. So, the government resorted to a compromised policy, promoting a "half-Chin'yeong" practice. The marriage customs were modified slightly, and the marriage ceremony reflected only small elements of Chin'yeong. Throughout the Joseon period, the Chin'yeong practice was never established as intended, except within the royal family. People continued to hold marriage ceremonies at the woman's house. However, although the Chin'yeong practice failed to take root initially, over time, fewer and fewer women continued to live in their childhood homes after marriage.

It is interesting to see how Gweon Sang Il (權相一, 1679–1759), a renowned government official from the Yeongnam region in the eighteenth century, described his greeting to a new daughter-in-law in his book *Cheongdae Ilgi* (淸臺日記). He wrote that on February 7th, 1725, his son left for his wife's home and wedded her there the day after his arrival. While the people who accompanied him returned home, Gweon's son stayed. Five days later, Gweon's son returned home, but his wife did not accompany him, staying at her home. Although Gweon Sang Il had not met his new daughter-in-law in person, he was happy to hear from other people that his son's wife looked smart and wise. He rejoiced that it was a very good and happy omen for the house. And a few days later, his son brought him the first letter from his daughter-in-law.

Over the next two years, his son continued to visit his wife's house on a regular basis, once every one or two months. It is not known exactly how many days he spent there, but, in one instance, he stayed there for a whole week. In the meantime, Gweon Sang Il continued to exchange letters with his daughter-in-law. Finally, after two years and five months, into their marriage, on July 22nd, 1727, Gweon Sang Il's daughter-in-law moved into her husband's family house. She had already given birth to a son, whom she carried with her when she "returned" to Gweon's house. The baby was already 7 to 8 months old.

The marriage of Gweon Sang Il's son was typical of marriage in the eighteenth century, which was arranged by family members. The wedding ceremony was held at the woman's house, and, after one or two years, the woman "returned" to her husband's house. This practice was called "Hae'mug'ih," a (reversed) remnant of the "male-returning-to-female's-house" of the past.

What kind of influences would all these changes have had upon the people's lives in general? Let's examine Kim Jong Jik's example once again. When he died at the age of 62, his brother-in-law, the brother of his first wife, and his nephew, actually the son of his sister, were put in charge of the funeral. His son, whom he had from Madame Mun, his second wife, was only seven years old then. So, while the widow was in charge of the situation in a titular sense, others were appointed to oversee the actual process. Jo Wi (曺偉), who was the brother of Kim Jong Jik's first wife, and Gang Baek Jin (康伯珍) and Gang Jung Jin (康仲珍), who were the sons of his sister, were the people in charge of the funeral. At the time, Kim Jong Jik did have some nephews from his brothers, but no one suggested that the sons of Kim's brothers instead of the sons of Kim's sisters should oversee the funeral. No one was concerned that the people put in charge of the funeral were from Kim's first wife's house and his nephews from his sisters. Jo Wi and Kim Jong Jik had been very close to each other through an academic relationship, and Jo Wi was well-versed in ritual protocols, making him the most qualified person to oversee the funeral. In addition, the sons of his sisters were grown and were well versed in the relevant protocols as well. So, at the time, it was only natural for them to take charge of the occasion. Although this may seem a little bit odd from today's perspective, where Kim Jong Jik's second wife, who was living, would take charge, there was a very different set of principles in operation then.

However, during the latter half of the Joseon Dynasty, marriage customs changed dramatically. Men no longer live in the wife's house after they married, and a paternal (patriarchal) family/kinship system was established. In the late eighteenth and early nineteenth centuries, in his final years, No Sang Chu wrote in his diary (盧尙樞日記: 1763-1829) of a clash with the main successor of his house, who was much younger. This young successor, according to Chu's account, sold the lands of the house at his own discretion and did not care for his mother. His diary was filled with contempt, blame, and criticism against this person. Why such a bitter conflict with this person? Chu was a successful government official who reached the Jong-3 pum seat, and his son passed the military examination and was serving as Hyeon'gam prefect in the Heungdeok area. Yet he was unable to control this main successor. Although Chu criticized him constantly, he was unable to criticize him in person, and he evaded him when possible. Thus, in the paternal marriage and familial system, the main successor was indeed a powerful figure, a far departure from the era of Kim Jong Jik.

The atmosphere changed for women as well. Kim Jong Jik's mother, Park, and the daughter-in-law of Gweon Sang Il lived in different conditions. While Kim Jong Jik's mother, Park would visit her husband's village, Seonsan, from time to time, she never moved into her husband's house permanently. On the other hand, although Gweon Sang Il's daughter-in-law stayed at her childhood home for two years after her marriage, eventually, she moved into Gweon's house and began her new life there as a daughter-in-law. Obviously, the lives of the two women were distinctively different. One was able to retain her life as a daughter in her family's house, while the other had to adjust to a new life as a daughter-in-law in her husband's house. The paths of women changed, inevitably forcing new, less powerful identities to emerge.

3. Shin Sa'im-dang lived more as a "daughter"

Shin Sa'im-dang is a well-known symbol of the typical faithful wife, benevolent mother, whoever she lived her life more as a daughter than as a mother or a wife. She writes,

> Leaving my old mother at home
> On my way to Seoul alone
> Raising my head and watching the Bukchon town
> White clouds are floating, and a mountain in the night is the only thing green.

Shin Sa'im-dang (1504-1551) wrote this poem, presumably on her way to Seoul, after leaving her childhood home. Why is the poem so sad and moody? The poem was written in 1541, after Shin Sa'im-dang decided to leave her childhood home, where she had lived for more than 20 years after she was married. She was moving permanently to her husband's house, so she was deeply saddened to part with her mother.

According to her biography, written by her son, Yulgok Yi Ih, she did not stay long either in her husband's house in Paju or in Seoul. After following her husband to the Bongpyeong region, she returned to Gangneung to give birth to her son, Yulgok, where they stayed until he was five years old, Shin died 10 years after she came to Seoul, but most of her life was spent in Gangneung and its adjacent areas. It is believed that Shin Sa'im-dang lived at home for so long, because either her father, Shin Myeong Hwa (申明和) was particularly fond of her and would not let her go or she stayed to observe the mourning period after her father's death. In any event, regardless of the reasons, she was able to stay in her childhood home for so long, because it was the dominant practice at the time. Although her father had lived in the capital occasionally, he finally settled in Gangneung as well. His youngest son-in-law, Gweon Hwa (權和), also lived there and cared for his mother-in-law, the wife of Shin Myeong Hwa, Madame Yi. All these examples demonstrate the marriage customs of the period, where husband's lived in the house of their wife.

Not only were marriage customs different but also property inheritance and ancestral memorial services as well. For example, in the 45th (1566) year of the Gajeong (嘉靖) era, records from the Yulgok family state:

> In year, on May 20th, brothers and sisters gathered together in order to discuss the dividing of the properties of their parents. The discussion proceeded to decide that all the lands and Nobi servants, which had been owned by both their father and their mother, would be distributed evenly and equally to all of their offspring, and, in case of servants, who had earlier been lost yet newly found again in the future, the individual who located them and secured them would be granted with the ownership of one servant among them, and then the ownership rights over the others would be determined by the order of age among offspring, according to the law dictated in *Gyeong-guk Daejeon*. Memorial services should be discussed together as well, and necessary things should be prepared. (Treasure, No.477, Yulgok Seonsaeng

Nam'mae Bunjae-gi/栗谷先生男妹分財記, Records of dividing properties, among Yulgok's brothers and sisters).

Another example is found in the foreword section of the property distribution records created by the Yulgok family, his brothers and sisters.

> Duties regarding regular memorial services (忌祭祀) would not be rotated (輪行), and shall be put in charge of the oldest son (宗子). Yet all the offspring should assist the process, by providing a certain amount of rice. Direct offspring should provide 10 Du of rice, and offspring of those direct offspring should provide 5 Du of rice. Their offspring, and children of the daughters, should provide 2 Du units of rice (Treasure, No.477, Yulgok Seonsaeng Nam'mae Bunjae-gi/栗谷先生男妹分財記, Records of dividing properties, among Yulgok's brothers and sisters).

From the beginning of the record, it is clear the properties of both the father and the mother were distributed, equally, to all the sons and daughters, primarily by age and without discrimination, according to the orders dictated inside *Gyeong-guk Daejeon*. The properties of both the father, Yi Weon Su, and the mother, Shin Sa'im-dang, were distributed in an equal fashion to all the male and female offspring. Furthermore, reflecting a level of reality, lands were distributed in a slightly unequal fashion, as some of them received a minimum of 20 Bok units of land, while others received a maximum of 40 Bok units of land. The discrepancy in land distribution was probably due to the different status of the individual land units, such as the level of fertility, or the economic status of a particular offspring. It does not appear to be the result of a discriminative practice committed against either a son or a daughter. The second daughter was given more compared to the third daughter, and the son, Yulgok, received more than his youngest brother Wi (瑋). On the other hand, the Nobi servants were equally distributed, giving 15 or 16 servants to each of the offspring. This kind of property distribution was not limited to the Yulgok family. Most property distribution records created in the sixteenth century show a similar pattern.

It is also evident that all the brothers and sisters shared the responsibility of maintaining and preparing memorial services for their ancestors. Notably, it was decided not to rotate the role of preparing the memorial services, implying that these duties had once been rotated or that it was not an unusual practice to rotate the role. According to a quote from a diary written in the early half of the seventeenth century by a Yangban woman, "For the main mourning day (大忌) observed by the Sajik-gol residence, we prepared some things and sent them over for the service. We made preparations in stead of Dat'jeot'gol Daek (a wife of husband's brother). Evidently, rotating the role had been the usual practice until the middle period of the Joseon Dynasty.

Memorial services were regarded as an obligation and duty, but it was also an important form of right when discussions of property distribution occurred. At the time, the practice of "rotating" memorial services was the norm, meaning all parties involved in the rotation cycle shared equal rights. In other words, in terms of preparing and observing memorial services, no distinctions were made between men and women. Women were considered as equally legitimate members of the family, even after they were married to other males of other houses.

Meanwhile, Shin Sa'im-dang was unable to shake the feeling of homesickness. She was 38 years old when she came to the capital, yet she missed her mother deeply.

> My mother always missed Gangneung. At nights, she would break down in tears, and she couldn't fall asleep until dawn. One day, the concubine of Shim-gong (沈公), a relative of the house, came and played the Geo'mun-go. Mother cried at the sound of the instrument and said, 'Those sounds sadden me. It makes me miss people even more.' Everyone in the room felt a profound sorrow, but they did not exactly know why.

This is the image of Shin that her son Yulgok remembered. She always missed her hometown and even cried at the mere sound of music playing. Although it may be natural for women to miss their family homes, Shin grieved deeply. It might be said that while her body was in Seoul, her mind was still in Gangneung.

> Mother was very good at pictures and calligraphy. At the age of seven she imitated the picture of An Gyeon and drew pictures of mountains and rivers. It was magnificent. She also drew grapes. I am quite sure that no one else in the world would be able to describe the figure of grapes as she did. Folding screens and

hanging pictures that imitate her paintings are now to be found everywhere.

Yulgok was convinced that no one could paint a picture as elegantly as his mother, and he was proud that people adored her style so much that many replications were created.

Unlike another figure, Madame Jang, whom we will discuss later, Shin did not believe that women should not or could not paint, and she never had any intention of quitting. Furthermore, she dared to exhibit her work. Few could challenge her sensitivity and skill for producing exceptional paintings with artistic values. Had she not been able to live for a prolonged period of time in her own childhood home, she might not have been able to exert the tremendous effort and time involved in her works. In other words, had she lived in her husband's house, she might have had the necessary time and freedom to develop her artistic skills.

Her style of educating her children also reflects aspects of her life. Her biography is admittedly not too long, but oddly enough only one line addresses the issue, saying, "When her children did something wrong, she taught not to." Apparently, Yulgok had very little to say or remember about his or his siblings education and instruction by his mother. Usually, the education of children was considered one of the most important duties of a daughter-in-law of a family, as the welfare of children ensured the future for the house. The lack of more information about his and his sibling's education might suggest Shin did not invest an extensive amount of time or effort as did other women in her day. She existed more as a daughter of her own home than as a daughter-in-law of her husband's house. It remained her identity throughout her life. Yet this does not seem to have been her choice but, rather, the result of the marriage customs at the time.

4. Madame Jang lived more as a "daughter-in-law"

Madame Jang from Andong (1598-1680) married Yi Shi Myeong, who was a disciple of her father, at the age of 19. She was born in Andong, and upon her marriage she moved into her husband's house, which was located in Yeonghae's In'yang-ri village, more than 200 ri units away from her hometown. She did not postpone over the move. Yi Shi Myeong already had two children from his late wife. Over her lifetime, Jang raised a total of 10 children, including two from her predecessor. The second son, Yi Hyeon Il, became well-known for his political and academic career.

She was the only daughter and child of Jang Heung Hyo, a notable scholar in the history of Confucian studies during the latter half period of the Joseon Dynasty. Probably because she had no brothers or sisters, she became deeply interested in the teachings of Neo-Confucianism. In Joseon society, the education of children took place at home for a certain period of time. Since Jang was an only child, it seems likely her scholarly father concentrated all his efforts in the teaching of his only daughter.

"Master Gyeongdang (敬堂) only had a daughter, so he loved her dearly. He taught her *Sohak* and *Shib'pal Sa'ryak* (十八史略),

and she learned it quite well." We can see that her father was very involved in the education of his only daughter. Thus, it is not surprising that Jang became well-versed in the Confucius and also adept at writing poems and painting pictures. Her skills might have been similar to those of Shin Sa'im-dang.

However, she eventually stopped those things, deciding writing and painting were not things women should do. What changed her mind? What things did she believe women should do? Her biography and the cooking manual *Eumshik Dimi-bang* she authored suggest Jang considered "managing the house," which would have included making preparations for memorial services and greeting guests and 'admirably educating the children' as the real tasks meant for women.

In *Eumshik Dimi-bang* she listed more than 150 types of cuisine and one third of the book dedicated to alcoholic beverages and how to produce them. In making preparations for memorial services and for greeting guests, liquor was apparently a crucial ingredient. Inside *Byeongja Ilgi*, Madame Jo recorded "Seungji Yi Hyeon and Pansa Im came, had three drinks individually, and at night, Jib'eui Gweon came and had six drinks;" "Jeong In Dong and Cheomji Yi came and had a drink;" or "After meal, he went to Panseo Yi's house in Sajik-gol and returned late, drunken." It appears visits and social exchanges among men often included liquor.

Song Shi Yeol wrote in *Gye'nyeo-seo*, which he authored for his own daughter, that all guests must be sincerely greeted. He warned that a house that did not greet its guest properly would eventually come to "repel" all visitors and would collapse under its own rudeness. Maintaining the integrity of the house and supervising the greeting of the guests was the job of the daughter-in-law of the house. Jang was well aware of that, so she studied more than 50 ways to produce liquor, which she saw as necessary for the performance of her role.

It is also interesting that when Madame Jang completed *Eumshik Dimi-bang*, she strictly instructed her daughters to copy the material but not to carry it with them. She said this book should be inherited by her own daughters-in-law and not her own daughters. She considered her own daughters, who were daughters-in-law of other houses, as members of the other houses. These examples illustrate Madame Jang's view upon the status and role of a daughter-in-law.

Madame Jang was also very eager to perform her role as a mother. According to the biography [Haengjang] written by her second son, Yi Hyeon Il, she always encouraged her children to be good (善) and hoped they would become saint-like people in the future. Her comments are presented in detail. She said, "You may have the reputation as fine writers, but I do not value that. Once in a while I hear you do some good things, and I do enjoy that and cherish that."[3] Yi Hyeon Il also noted, "Because I was slow and not that bright, and also had nothing to look for, I wasn't able to do what my mother wanted me to do. Yet I behaved myself, did not say anything mean to others, and managed to not do some bad things

---

3 『貞夫人安東張氏實記』附錄 行實記

to others. I think I was able to do so, thanks to my mother's constant warning and teaching." It appears Madame Jang was very involved in the education of her children.

She was the typical female figure, a faithful wife and a benevolent mother, who was interested in cooking and brewing liquor for the preparation of ancestral memorial services and greeting of the guests. She also hoped for a good future for her children, as that would also ensure the overall luck of the entire house as well. She conformed to Confucian standards and exemplified the preferred image of the day as a woman, wife, and mother.

However, her stance toward the education of children should be further examined in terms of her own identity.

> Reading a poem that you wrote when you parted with your friend 見爾別友詩
> There is a word from you that you want to learn from a sage 中有學聖語
> I am so happy, so in a word of praise 余心喜復嘉
> I write you a short poem, and give you it to read 一筆持贈汝

This poem was given to her grandchild Shin Geub. It shows that she was happy her grandson was trying to learn the teachings of past sages and saints (聖人). She said, "People all want to do good things. Even a child would be thrilled if someone told it that 'you are a good boy (or girl),' and be angered if told otherwise. People all favor good deeds, and that's the way they feel, so everyone should endeavor to do good things." In Neo-Confucian terms, becoming a saint means achieving the ultimate goal, a superb level of morality. Why was she so deeply interested in this subject?

The answer may lie in Neo-Confucianism, which was the only way for people to live their lives as a part of the mainstream culture. This ideology was pursued by all men during the Joseon Dynasty in order to obtain power, engage in academic studies, and build personal character. Jang emphasized this to her offspring and descendant.

Unlike Shin Sa'im-dang. who was more engaged in her own work and not deeply involved in the education of her children, Jang urged her children to be saint-like people. Also, while Shin did not think that writing poems and enjoying calligraphy were *not* for females, Jang thought such things were beyond the obligations of women and should not be pursued.

Both Shin and Jang were smart and capable women, but they concentrated their talents in different areas. Although unlike Shin, Jang quit writing poems and studying calligraphy, she did become the saint-like person, a goal initially dominated by men. So, Jang did expand the realm of objectives that a female could pursue.

However, Shin was remained in the home of her parents and allowed to pursue her own interests, while Jang had to move to the home of her husband's parents and take on the duties of a daughter-in-law. Jang actively embraced the role, determined to be faithful and loyal to the Neo-Confucian morality. Shin was allowed to live in her own childhood as a daughter, while Jang was required to live in the house of her husband as a daughter-in-law.

From the beginning, the Joseon society favored a paternal [patriarchal] society that required females to take the role of a daughter-in-law. However, it is still not certain whether full compliance to this policy was accomplished during the Joseon Dynasty. Some evidence suggests women did not completely abandon their identities as "daughters." Although Jang saw her married daughters as the daughters-in-law of other houses, she was very active and forthcoming in addressing issues that involved her birth house. When her mother died, she arranged for her father to get remarried; and, as her half-brothers and half-sisters were young, she arranged the memorial services for her ancestors. Citing filial piety for these actions, this was counter to her perspective of the duties pertinent to the "faithful daughter-in-law."

It is possible women during the Joseon Dynasty may not have truly assimilated into the role of daughters-in-law. A common phrase was repeated often during this period, "One's married daughter is no longer a member of one's house," perhaps, because females stayed "daughters" even after they married into other houses. A well-known proverb may also support this assumption, saying "In-laws should stay away." In fact, in-laws may have had close relationships, some of which may have caused problems within families. If families, even in-laws, maintained close relationships, maybe women during the Joseon Dynasty did cling to their original identity as daughters, while also becoming daughters-in-law.

References

Ebrey, P. B. (2000). *The Inner Quarters: Marriage and the Lives of Chinese Women in the Sung Period*. Berkely: University of California Press. *Junggukyeosungui gyeolhongwa saenghwal* (*The Marriage and Livings of Chinese Female*; in Korean). Bae, Suk Hui (Translation). Seoul: Samji-won.

Jang, B. I. (1997). *Joseon jeongi honinjewa seongchabyeol* (*Marriage Institutions during the Early half of the Joseon Dynasty, and Gender Discrimination*; in Korean), Seoul: Iljisa.

Jeong, Y. D. and Park, G. S. (Translation and Annotation) (1991). *Byeongja Ilgi*, in Korean, Seoul: Yejeon-sa.

Mun, S. J. (2009). *68 Nyeonui nanaldeul, Joseonui ilsangsa* (*68 years, the life in Joseon*; in Korean). Seoul: Neo'meo Books.

National Institute of Korean History. (2005). *Honingwa yeonaeui pungsokdo* (*Customs of Marriage and Love Affairs*; in Korean). Seoul: Doosan Dong-A.

Yi, S. G. (2003). Jeongbuin Andong Jangssiui sunglihakjeok sam (Madam Jang from Andong, and Her Neo-Confucian life; in Korean). *Joseonsidae sahoeui moseup* (*The Society of Joseon*; in Korean). Seoul: Jipmoon-dang.

II
Family and
Society

Chapter three

Changes in Population and Family in Korea

Eun, Ki-Soo (Seoul National University)

This chapter analyzes the transformation of the modern Korean family with respect to changes in population and society. In essence, the transformation of the Korean family is closely related to changes in population. Demographic changes arising from fertility, mortality, and migration has an immediate impact on the structure of the family. Furthermore, family norms, values, women's changing familial status, and changing gender roles influence changes in population such as fertility. Therefore, changes in population and changes in family are closely linked and cannot be regarded separately. In addition, transformations in population and family are closely linked with societal changes. For instance, a society's historical experiences throughout specific time periods have influenced the changes in population and family. As a result, analyzing the changes in population and society is a vital component for understanding changes in family. This chapter aims to examine the transformation of the Korean family during the late twentieth and early twenty-first centuries with respect to changes in population and society.

1. Changes in Population: Fertility Transition

In the early 1960s the Korean government implemented an economic development policy that introduced a strong family planning program to control the fertility rate in Korean society. The total fertility rate — the average number of children a woman bears in her lifetime — rapidly declined during this time period. In 1960 the total fertility rate equated to 6 children, but by 1970 had declined to 4.5 and later to a mere 2.8 in 1980. Just three years later in 1983 the total fertility rate declined to the replacement level fertility rate of 2 children and the fertility rate continued to recede at an astonishingly rapid pace.

Along with the fertility transition, the industry centered economic development policy of 1960 resulted in a large-scale demographic reconfiguration as people migrated from rural areas to urban areas. Urbanization in Korea was most rapidly achieved between 1966 and 1970. During this time period, the annual nation-wide population growth rate was 1.9 %, whereas the annual population growth rate in urban areas was 7.0 %. Yet in spite of the higher fertility rate in rural areas, the average population growth rate in rural regions began to decline and eventually reached a level of -1.2 % (Choi 1995: 135). The population shift from rural to urban areas would continue well after the 1960s and 1970s, which is self-evident from the increasing number of cities from 27 in 1960 to 40 in 1980 and then to 79 cities in 2000. For instance, in the year 2000, it was found that 80 % of the entire population lived in cities (Kwon and Kim 2002: 271, Table 8-9).

The immediate cause of declining fertility to replacement level rates is attributed to the use of contraceptives and the increasing marital age. Fertility began to decline as a result of delayed marriages among single men and women and the use of contraceptives by married couples as a means to control pregnancy. The success of Korea's fertility control policy was highlighted by the increasing number of married couples that use contraceptives and the subsequent rapid decline in fertility. In other words, the strong family planning program is regarded as an effective and successful policy.

Nevertheless, the introduction of a strong family planning program and the government's strict implementation of this program was not the only reason that contributed to the dramatic decline in fertility in such a short period of time. Fertility decline can be understood from the aspect of policy success, but it is important to emphasize that Koreans were eager to reduce the number of childbirths even before the family planning program was first introduced. Beginning in the early twentieth century, Korean women realized that having more children was not a blessing but a path to hardship. Therefore, women wanted to reduce the number of children they had, if they had the means to do so. However, at the time contraceptives were not readily available that enabled women to control the number of children to a desirable number. The intent to carry out fertility control — a precondition for changes in fertility — was apparent, but there was not any technology or tools to obstruct fertility. This explains the higher fertility levels prior to the introduction of the family planning program. With the introduction of the family planning program in the 1960s, new developments in tools and technology to control fertility allowed Koreans to reduce the number of children at a rapid pace. Moreover, Korea's fertility control policy was able to succeed because Korean society already possessed the preconditions to reduce fertility levels since the late twentieth century.

Demographers believed the fertility level would not decrease any further and would remain stable once fertility reached the replacement level of 2 children per married couple. In Japan, the fertility level stabilized without any dramatic changes after it reached the replacement level of 2 children per woman in the 1950s. However, fertility in Korea has continued to decline even after the total fertility rate dropped to 2 in the early 1980s. Although fertility reached the replacement level, the Korean government did not change the population policy in regards to fertility and continued to pursue the fertility control policy. In the 1970s the government used the slogan "Boy or girl, let's have only two and raise them well" to promote the fertility control policy. As fertility reached the replacement level in the 1980s, the government used the slogan "Having one well-raised daughter is no less than having ten sons." This slogan aimed to promote a one-child only policy regardless of gender by reducing the gender preference for children.

When the total fertility rate reached 1.58 in 1989 the Korean government finally abandoned the aggressive fertility control policy, which included the free supply of contraceptives. However, the Korean government did not apparently change the policy into one that would improve fertility; rather, the government simply discontinued the process of fertility control. Although fertility temporarily increased in the 1990s with the end of the fertility control policy, fertility would begin to decrease once more as people were aware of the benefits of having fewer children. For instance, in 1992, total fertility rate increased to 1.78, but by 1997 it had fallen to 1.54.

In terms of demographics, two factors played an important role

Table 1 Total Fertility Rate, Men's and Women's Age at First Marriage in Korea, 1955-2008

Year	TFR	Men' Age at First Marriage	Women's Age at First Marriage
1955	6.3 [1]	24.7	20.5
1960	6.0 [2]	25.4	21.5
1966	4.6 [3]	26.7	22.9
1970	4.53	27.2	23.3
1975	3.47	27.4	23.7
1980	2.83	27.3	24.1
1985	1.67	27.8	24.7
1990	1.59	27.8	24.8
1995	1.65	28.4	25.4
2000	1.47	29.3	26.5
2005	1.08	30.9	27.7
2006	1.12	31.0	27.8
2007	1.25	31.1	28.1
2008	1.19	31.4	28.3

Note: 1) 1955-1960; 2) 1960-1965; 3) 1965-1970.
Source: Kwon & Kim (2002: 264, Table 8-6); National Statistical Office.

in the decline of fertility until the late 1990s. First is the implementation of contraceptives and the second is the increasing marriage age. Although these two factors are equally important, we focus on the increasing age at marriage as a factor contributing to low fertility in this chapter. In Korean society there is a very strong perception that the union of a man and woman is only possible through marriage. It is only through marriage that a family can be formed. In other words, the increasing age at marriage is the contributing factor for lagging formations of families in Korean society.

As observed in table 1, the average age at first marriage for men in 1960 was 25.4 years and continued to increase, reaching 27.2 years in 1970, 27.3 years in 1980, and 27.8 years in 1990. The average age

Table 2 Total Fertility Rate in Korea, Japan and Taiwan

Year	Korea	Japan	Taiwan
1990	1.59	1.54	1.81
1991	1.74	1.53	1.72
1992	1.78	1.50	1.73
1993	1.67	1.46	1.76
1994	1.67	1.50	1.76
1995	1.65	1.42	1.76
1996	1.58	1.43	1.76
1997	1.54	1.39	1.77
1998	1.47	1.38	1.46
1999	1.42	1.34	1.55
2000	1.47	1.36	1.68
2001	1.30	1.33	1.40
2002	1.17	1.32	1.34
2003	1.19	1.29	1.23
2004	1.16	1.29	1.18
2005	1.08	1.26	1.11
2006	1.12	1.32	1.11
2007	1.25	1.34	1.10
2008	1.19	1.37	1.05

at first marriage for women also increased from 21.5 years in 1960, 23.3 years in 1970, 24.1 years in 1980, and 24.8 years in 1990. Until 1990, the increasing age at marriage for men and women has been gradual. For 20 years, starting from 1970 to 1990, the age at first marriage for men increased by 0.6 years, whereas the age at first marriage for women increased by 1.5 years. We can conclude that the age at first marriage for women increased more than the age at first marriage for men.

Fertility in Korea once again changed significantly in the late 1990s following the Asian Financial Crisis. The government's effort to discontinue fertility control temporarily increased fertility, but soon after fertility levels began to decrease again. As shown in table 1, the total fertility rate in 1990 was 1.59, but the fertility rate increased and the total fertility rate in 1995 reached 1.65. The fertility decline since the 1960s continued to decrease again after only temporarily increasing for a short period of time in the early 1990s. As indicated in table 2, in 1993 and 1994 the total fertility rate increased to 1.67 but, subsequently, began to decrease again. However, from the end of 1997, fertility decreased significantly with the advent of the Asian Financial Crisis. In 1997, the total fertility rate was recorded at 1.54, and it continued to decrease in 1998 to 1.47 and then to 1.42 in 1999. In 2000, fertility would temporarily increase due to the millennium year. Yet, in 2001, the total fertility level again reached the lowest fertility rate of 1.3. In 2005, the total fertility rate decreased to an unprecedented low fertility rate of 1.08, and Korea would, thus, become the country with the lowest fertility in the world.

As indicated in table 2, low fertility, was not a problem only for Korea. Although Taiwan recorded a somewhat higher fertility level than Korea in the 1990s, Taiwan also experienced a similar phenomenon of declining fertility. After 2005, Taiwan's fertility level plummeted below Korea's fertility level. In Japan, after the fertility rate dropped to 2 in 1950, fertility continued to gradually decrease over a long period of time. In the 1990s fertility levels in Japan were lower than Korea and Taiwan. Yet, Japan's fertility did not decline rapidly but was rather gradual. As a result, fertility in Korea and Taiwan reached a lower level than Japan by the year of 2000. After recording an all time low total fertility level of 1.26, Japan's fertility levels began to slowly increase again. Nevertheless, as fertility continues to decline, Northeast Asian countries, which include

Table 3 Age at First Marriage in Korea and Japan, 1991-2008

Year	Korean Male	Korean Female	Difference (Korean)	Japanese Male	Japanese Female	Difference (Japanese)
1991	28.0	24.9	3.1	28.4	25.9	2.5
1992	28.1	25.0	3.1	28.4	26.0	2.4
1993	28.1	25.1	3.0	28.4	26.1	2.3
1994	28.3	25.2	3.1	28.5	26.2	2.3
1995	28.4	25.4	3.0	28.5	26.3	2.2
1996	28.4	25.5	2.9	28.5	26.4	2.1
1997	28.6	25.7	2.9	28.5	26.6	1.9
1998	28.9	26.1	2.8	28.6	26.7	1.9
1999	29.1	26.3	2.8	28.7	26.8	1.9
2000	29.3	26.5	2.8	28.8	27.0	1.8
2001	29.6	26.8	2.8	29.0	27.2	1.8
2002	29.8	27.0	2.8	29.1	27.4	1.7
2003	30.1	27.3	2.8	29.4	27.6	1.8
2004	30.6	27.5	3.1	29.6	27.8	1.8
2005	30.9	27.7	3.2	29.8	28.0	1.8
2006	31.0	27.8	3.2	30.0	28.2	1.8
2007	31.1	28.1	3.0	30.1	28.3	1.8
2008	31.4	28.3	3.1	30.2	28.5	1.7

Korea, Japan and Taiwan, have shown the lowest levels of fertility in the world.

Following the Financial Crisis in Korea, fertility rates substantially declined. This phenomenon can be attributed to the increasing age at marriage. Table 3 shows that the age at first marriage for both men and women increased substantially after the 1990s. For 20 years, from 1970 to 1990, the age at first marriage increased by a little more than an average of 1 year for men and an average of 1.5 years for women, but the age at first marriage for both men and women rose to a steeper level after 1990. For men, the average age at first marriage was 27.8 in 1990, but within 5 years it increased by 0.6 years to 28.4. In the case of women, the average age at first marriage was 24.8 in 1990, but 5 years later, in 1995, the average age at first marriage increased by 0.6 to 25.4. Another 5 years later, in 2000, the age at first marriage for men increased by 0.9 years, reaching 29.3 years, and the age at first marriage for women increased by 1.1 years reaching 26.5 years. In 2000, the timing of marriage continued to be delayed. Within the 5-year period, between 2000 and 2005, the age at first marriage among men was extended by 1.6 years, and the age at first marriage among women was increased by 1.2 years.

The increasing age at first marriage among Korean men and women is the main factor contributing to the rapid decline in fertility rates as illustrated in table 2. The dramatic rise of age at first marriage in Korea is an indicator for the late formation of families. A family is formed through marriage between a man and woman, and only reproduction between married couples is recognized

Figure 1 Mechanism of Fertility Decline in Recent Korean Society

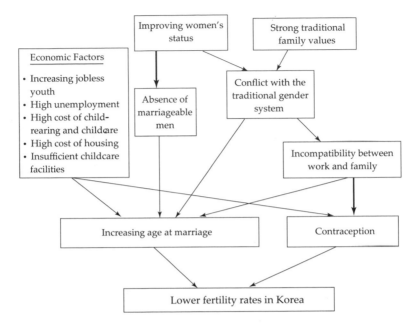

Source: Eun (2007: 56, Figure 3)

as a legitimate form of reproduction in Korea. Consequently, the rising age of first marriage means there must be a delay in the legal formation of families. This will then be followed by a delay in legitimate births. The dramatic increase of age at first marriage among men and women after the Asian Financial Crisis in 1997 does not simply delay the formation of families, but it also signifies the main cause of Korea's low fertility rate — recorded to be the lowest in the world.

2. Mechanisms for Fertility Transition

Why did fertility in Korea change significantly following the Asian Financial Crisis? Figure 1 illustrates the mechanism for Korea's low-fertility rate.

The mechanism in Fiqure 1 explains the causes of the low fertility in Korea. This mechanism displays a number of variables that influence fertility rates, while, it shows the characteristics and changes in Korean society and family.

1) Economic Factor

The reason behind Korea's significant decline in fertility rates following the Asian Financial Crisis can be revealed through three fields. One factor that directly influences fertility levels in Korea can be understood from an economic perspective. The biggest transformation Korean society underwent after the Financial Crisis occurred in the labor market. Prior to the Financial Crisis, Korea dreamed of achieving full employment and lifetime employment. Following the Financial Crisis, however, various forms of structural changes were implemented in the labor market and were accompanied by a substantial rise of unemployment. Many employees with stable jobs were suddenly exposed to great risk of unemployment, and, as a number of companies filed for bankruptcy, unemployment rates skyrocketed. The workforce became dominated by non-standard workers, such as part-time and contract workers. The traditional hiring custom of lifetime employment was no longer valid; instead, unstable forms of hiring with unpredictable layoffs became predominant. The biggest problem in the labor market rested among those seeking jobs after graduation from school. Many young people who would have entered the work force following their high-school or university graduation faced massive unemployment as the number of available jobs diminished. Since the Korean work force has a hierarchical structure based on age, those who cannot find jobs in the formal sector of the labor market within a year or a short period of time upon completing their education will have harder time in finding jobs in the labor market. As a result, many young people who hoped to enter the work force upon graduation had many troubles finding jobs and remained unemployed.

The unstable labor market greatly contributed to increases in unemployment for youngsters. Even when people found jobs, they were often unstable jobs in informal sectors. This economic problem not only influenced people's values and attitudes but also affected their daily lives. Another economic problem that influenced marriage and fertility rates was the high price of housing. Unlike Western societies, where monthly rent is the preferred payment method of residency, Koreans prefer a long-term lease or the direct purchase of houses. However, one half of the population in Korea swarmed into the metropolitan area of Seoul during the economic development period. As a result, the availability of housing for people was reduced and real estate prices skyrocketed. The rise in housing prices in metropolitan areas was followed by the rise in housing prices in non-metropolitan areas. Eventually, housing prices rose above the inflation rate, and young people had many difficulties in purchasing homes to live in upon marriage. Although young people continued to work persistently and prudently, purchasing a house to live in after marriage became a rather difficult task to achieve without support from one's parents or family.

Childbearing after marriage was not easy even after resolving the issues arising from work and housing. Despite the increasing number of women in the labor force, women had a difficult time compromising between work and family, because Korean society did not have an adequate daycare system that parents could trust with their children.

The perception that families should directly deal with problems of childbearing and childcare without the support from society is prevalent in Korean society. After the 1960s, the Korean government transferred all responsibilities of reproduction, child-rearing, and elderly care to each family as part of its campaign to promote industrialization and economic growth. In addition, the Korean government revived and reinforced patriarchal traditions descending from the late Joseon (Chosŏn) Dynasty as part of an effort to continue traditional family values. Consequently, both childcare and elderly care became the inherent duty of the family, and, the sole responsibility of women even in the late twentieth century.

Yet in the late twentieth century, the education level of Korean women rapidly increased and many of them strongly desired jobs after completing their education. Korean women's economic participation rate among OECD countries is not so high, but it is consistently increasing. However, many women often face a dilemma between childcare and work upon marriage and childbearing. Traditionally, it is common among Korean women to quit their jobs after marriage or conception in order to stay home and take care of their children. Korean women's participation in the work force is highlighted by an M-curve. This means that Korean women's economic participation is high in their early 20s but becomes low by their late 20s and early 30s. When their child-rearing duties are nearly finished, they re-enter the labor force, which raises women's economic participation rate. Although it was normal that women quit their jobs and returned to their household after marriage and conception, this trend began to change fundamentally after the Financial Crisis. Strong motivations encouraging women to work began to emerge, so that bearing a child became a relatively difficult issue as the opportunity cost of returning home for childcare exceeded their standard income.

Another economic factor impeding childbirths is the cost of childcare and children's education. After the industrialization and economic development of the 1960s, individuals and families experienced greater upward social mobility in Korean society. However, upward social mobility often required higher educational attainment. A wide wage gap exists between those with educational attainment equivalent or higher than the university education and those below the university education. Yet, simply attaining a university education is not enough in Korean society. Since Korean universities are implicitly ranked, a huge opportunity gap also exists between those who graduated from one of the few prestigious universities and those who did not. That is why Korean parents strive to send their children to one of those prestigious universities in Korea. Korean parents believe that public education is not enough to increase the probability of sending their children to a prestigious university, so they use additional means of education, such as sending their children to academies after school to increase this probability.

The 1997 Asian Financial Crisis contributed to another significant change in the educational environment of Korea. In the era of globalization, Koreans have realized that university degrees from prestigious Korean universities are not particularly useful. Moreover, they realize that English is the most important tool their children must have to be successful. Korean parents have begun to provide English education to their children, even when they are not old enough to enter school. Those parents who believed that a degree from a Korean university was not sufficient in the globalized world began to send children to schools in foreign countries to provide them with an early education in English and to have them to get diplomas from foreign schools. If the child was too young and needed at least one parent's supervision, the mother went abroad with the child for his or her education, while the father often remained in Korea to earn money. It has become a new norm that many of married couples live separately for the sake of their child's education. This results in the formation of two families, one in Korea and the other one in a foreign country, which is referred to as the "Wild Geese Family." The cost of a child's education has increased to astronomical figures as parents sacrifice everything for the sake of their child's education by providing the child with a private English education while enduring the hardships of a "Wild Geese Family."

2) The Change in the Status of Women

Not only changes in population but change in the status of women is another important factor contributing to changes in the Korean family. On the one hand, the living standard of Koreans has increased following its industrialization and economic growth. On the other hand, the number of children among married couples continued to decline to a level less than 2. When the family does not have enough resources to provide education for their children, the male-centered family system concentrates the majority of educational resources on the male rather than female child. In Korea, where the tradition of primogeniture was still strong, the education of the eldest son was considered to be of most importance. However, from an economic perspective where the standard of living improves and the number of children that requires education decreases, Korean parents are more able to provide equal and non-discriminatory educational opportunity to both their sons and daughters. Although the government's slogan, "A well-raised daughter is no less than having ten sons," did not influence this phenomenon, recent trends show that Korean parents provide education for their children without discrimination between daughters and sons. When Korean parents believe that their child has the ability to study well and possesses a passion for education, they fully support their child's education regardless of gender. As a result, the level of educational attainment by women has continuously improved. Table 4 illustrates that, since

Table 4 Changes in Levels of Education, 1975-2005

Educational Level	1975	1980	1985	1990	1995	2000	2005
Women							
Elementary school or less	77.1	67.0	54.1	43.0	35.0	30.4	25.5
Middle school completed	12.1	16.5	20.5	20.3	17.1	14.3	12.1
High school completed	8.4	12.9	20.2	28.4	34.8	37.3	37.0
Junior college completed or more	2.4	3.6	5.2	8.3	13.1	18.0	25.4
Men							
Elementary school or less	53.1	42.8	51.9	23.3	17.8	15.1	12.2
Middle school completed	17.7	19.8	20.5	17.6	14.2	12.3	10.2
High school completed	19.7	25.4	32.1	38.9	41.4	41.6	38.7
Junior college completed or more	9.5	12.0	15.5	20.1	26.6	31.0	37.8

Note: Highest level of education completed by women and men aged 25 and older.
Source: Korea National Statistical Office (2009)

the 1970s, the level of education attained by women has increased remarkably.

In 1975, 77 % of women aged 25 years and older attained education equivalent to elementary school or less. However, 30 years later, in 2005, only 25.5 % of women attained education equivalent to elementary school or less. Women with a high school education in 1975 was only 8.4 % but, in 2005, it rose to 37 %. In 1975, 2.4 % of women had completed junior college or more, and that figure increased to 25.4 % in 2005. This means that one out of four women aged 25 years and older had attained an educational level of junior college or more in 2005.

Yet, levels of education among women are still lower than the levels of education among men. In the case of men, at least 50 % attained elementary school education in 1975, and, in 2005, the percentage of men who attained elementary school education was 12. The level of education among men rapidly increased: The percentage of men with high school education rose from 19.7 in 1975 to 40 in 2005. The percentage of men with higher education also increased substantially, changing from 9.5 % in 1975 to 37.8 % in 2005.

The reason why the levels of education are lower among women relative to men in 2005 is that there is a wide difference in levels of education between middle-aged and elderly women and men. Although that the education level of women is lower than that of men, the difference is diminishing among the younger generation. Data from 2005 reveals that there is very little difference in the education levels of men and women in their late 20s. Educational attainment among women will continue to increase and, in the future, it is predicted that women's educational attainment will

Figure 2 Labor Force Participation by Sex, 1980-2005

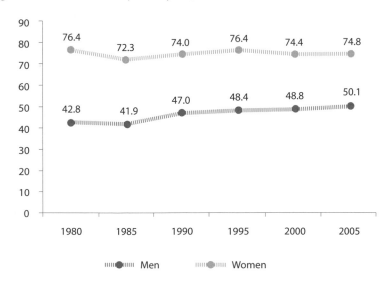

Source: National Statistical Office, *Report of Economically Active Population Survey*, Each Year.

exceed that of men.

As educational levels of women increase, their desire to enter the labor market and have their own career alongside men also increases. Korean women's participation in the labor market has been growing steadily. Figure 2 shows that the economic participation rate of men increased to 76.4 % in 1980, and, since then, it has only slightly declined. In 2005, the economic participation rate of men was 74.8 %. In contrast, the economic participation rate of women was 42.8 % in 1980. Since then, the economic participation rate of women has steadily increased and, in 2005, it reached 50.1 %.

The most significant aspect of women's greater economic participation is that women with higher education levels are primarily the active participants in the economy. Table 5 confirms that women who had completed higher education levels in the past did not actively participate in the economy. The percentage of college graduate females participating in the economy was not high. However, as time passed, the economic participation rate of women with higher education levels grew. In 2000, at least half of women who completed junior college were participating in the economy. In addition, 48 % of women with at least a junior college level of education were participating in the labor market. This trend is predicted to persist.

As briefly examined up to this point, women have achieved levels of education similar to men. Today there is almost no difference in the percentage of men and women entering universities after high school. This trend implies that Korea will follow the footsteps of the U.S. and other Western countries, where

Table 5 Labor Force Participation by Sex and Education, 1985-2000

	None	Elementary	Middle	High	Junior college	College+
Men						
1985	63.2	87.3	68.2	69.2	70.6	67.0
1990	55.5	81.2	78.6	71.5	76.1	73.5
1995	54.7	78.7	78.0	78.9	80.0	77.0
2000	53.9	72.7	71.4	75.5	75.5	76.5
Women						
1985	34.1	43.9	24.7	28.2	38.3	24.7
1990	29.8	43.4	31.4	31.9	41.6	32.7
1995	31.2	46.3	37.8	36.8	47.2	39.8
2000	33.8	49.4	47.6	44.8	52.3	48.1

Source: Min & Eun (2004: 200, Table 8.3)

the level of education attained by women exceeds the level of education attained by men.

Women who have attained higher levels of education do not wish to stay at home anymore. Participation in society was considered to be a monopolized product of men, but women are also actively engaged in activities outside of the household alongside men. Although women's economic participation level is still lower than the economic participation level of men, women's desire to actively participate in the economy is becoming stronger. The economic participation level among women has been lower than that of men, because, after marriage, child-rearing often becomes the sole responsibility of women. Furthermore, an inadequate daycare system has made it difficult for women to balance both work and family. Therefore, the economic participation rate of women in their late 20s and early 30s is relatively lower than the economic participation rate of men.

The improvement in the education levels of women and increasing economic participation by women is enhancing the social status of Korean women. The rising social status of women is an important factor contributing to both low fertility rates in Korea and transformation of the Korean family.

3) Conservative Family Values

The social environment surrounding men and women is changing at an unprecedented degree. Yet, changes surrounding the social norms and values of childbirth and family are relatively slow and incremental. The difference between values and behaviors exists in all societies, but the gap between family values and behavior of the family is greater in Korean society.

Following modernization, Korean values leaned toward individualism and Western values. However, family values surrounding gender, marriage, and family continue to remain conservative.

According to an international comparative study of family values, family values examined in East Asian countries, including Korea, Japan and Taiwan, are relatively more conservative and traditional than other societies. Unlike Western marital values, which do not perceive the social system of marriage as the only means through which a man and woman can live together, Koreans perceive the institution of marriage as the only legitimate means through which a man and woman can live together. Although other social values are becoming similar to Western values, Korean people continue to have negative attitudes towards cohabitation. An increasing number of young people practice cohabitation in many Western societies, and this has either replaced or become the accepted form of life style equivalent to marriage. Yet, Korean society is far from this reality, because negative attitudes towards men and women living together before marriage continue to exist. Even if one was brave enough to cohabitate before marriage, if the marriage partner is not the same person as the individual he or she cohabitated with, one must often hide the relationship from the marriage partner. Cohabitation is not accepted as a social norm, and, therefore, violation of this social norm is followed by negative repercussions. As a result, Koreans shy away from revealing a cohabitation.

The divorce rate in Korean society has also been steadily increasing, although a negative attitude towards divorce in East Asian societies, which includes Korea, continues to exist. An international comparative study found that many believed divorce is the best method to resolve a prolonged problem between a married-couple. Yet, in East Asian societies, including Korea, divorce was considered to be the last means by which a prolonged problem between the married couples should be resolved.

Analyzing attitudes towards marriage, cohabitation, and divorce clearly show that family values in Korea remain traditional and conservative. In contrast, attitudes towards gender roles are changing. In particular, gender roles in regard to family succession are not as traditional or conservative. A survey conducted in 2003 and 2006 indicated that attitudes towards gender roles is changing in Korea. Koreans no longer perceive men as the sole provider of the family, and the role of women is no longer limited to child-rearing and housework. Attitudes toward gender roles across different age groups also indicate that the older age groups no longer cling to traditional gender roles. This change in attitudes toward gender roles — especially regarding the attitude that income should be earned by both men and women — was strengthened following the 1997 Financial Crisis in Korea. Due to the Financial Crisis experience, Koreans realized that if the man is the sole source of income for the family, the entire family will be in trouble should the man lose his job. As a result, attitudes towards traditional gender roles have significantly weakened.

Nevertheless, family values regarding marriage, cohabitation, and divorce, in general, have continued to remain conservative and traditional. Moreover, the burden of housework remains the burden of women. Data from a 2004 time-use survey reveals that the number of hours married men participate in housework is very low. Even in dual-income families, the number of hours that men participate in housework has been very low, while women continue to be responsible for housework and child-rearing.

Despite the continued instability in the labor market and the increasing economic participation of women, family values continue to remain male-centered and traditional. Thus, women are reluctant to get married. Fertility in Korea continues to decrease as marriages are delayed and has reached a point where Korea's fertility is the lowest in the world.

3. The Changes in Family in Korea

As mentioned, the results from fertility transitions and other social changes indicate that the Korean family is changing rapidly. This section discusses a few of the specific characteristics of change that the modern Korean family is experiencing.

1) Small Family and Changes in Family Structure

After the 1960s, Korean society experienced a high level of urbanization in addition to reaching a low-level of fertility — slightly over one child per woman's lifetime — that has transformed the structure of the Korean family.

Table 6 shows that the average number of people per household is decreasing significantly as a result of the low fertility rates. In 1960, there was an average of 5.5 persons per household. However, the average number of persons per household continued to decline, and, by 2005, the average number of persons per household reached less than 3 persons or 2.9.

In 1960, 48 % of all households had an average of at least 6 members in the family. Yet, by 2005, only 2 % of all households had at least 6 persons in a household. From 1960 to 2000, the percentage of four-person households has increased. However, in 2000, the percentage of households with at least 4 persons per family began to decrease. In contrast, the percentage of one person and two person households in the population continued to increase. In 1960, 7 % of all households consisted of two person households, but the percentage increased to 10.5 % in 1980, to 13.8 % in 1990, and to 22 % in 2005. Increases in the percentage of one-person households are even more astonishing. In 1960, a mere 2.3 % of all households consisted of one person households; however, in 2000,

Table 6 Household Size, Household Structure, and Family Structure, 1960-2005

	1960	1970	1980	1990	2000	2005
Total Number of Household (unit: 1000)	4,361	5,576	7,969	11,355	14,312	15,887
Average Size of Household	5.5	5.2	4.5	3.7	3.1	2.9
Household Size (%)						
One Person Household	2.3	-	4.8	9.0	15.5	20.0
Two Persons Household	7.1	9.7	10.5	13.8	19.1	22.2
Three Persons Household	11.8	13.3	14.5	19.1	20.9	20.9
Four Persons Household	14.7	15.5	20.3	29.5	31.1	27.0
Five Persons Household	15.9	17.7	20.0	18.8	10.1	7.7
Six or more Persons Household	48.2	43.8	29.9	9.8	3.4	2.2
Family Structure (%)						
Nuclear Family	-	71.5	72.9	76.0	82.0	82.7
Stem Family	-	19.9	11.6	10.6	8.0	6.9
Other	-	8.6	15.5	13.4	10.0	10.4
Generation Structure (%)						
One Generation	7.5	6.8	8.3	10.7	14.2	16.2
Two Generations	64.0	70.0	68.5	66.3	60.8	55.4
Three Generations	26.9	22.1	16.5	12.2	8.2	6.9
Four or more Generations	1.6	1.1	0.5	0.3	0.2	0.1
Other	0.0	0.0	0.3	10.5	16.7	21.4

Note: 1) Total number of households in 1960 does not include collective household (15,015) and the uncertain (1,534).
2) One person households and non-blood related households are excluded from calculation of family structure.
3) Family structure is defined as follows:
Nuclear family: Couple only + a couple and unmarried child(ren) + One parent and unmarried child(ren)
Stem family: Couple and parent(s) + a couple, parent(s), and (un)married child(ren)
Other: Families not included in the above nuclear or step family
Source: Census, each year; Kwon & Kim (2002: 91, Table 3-6)

the percentage increased to 15.5 % and then to 20 % in 2005.

From a family structural perspective, the structure of the traditional family known as the stem family comprised 20 % of the population in 1970 but declined to 7 % by 2005. In contrast, the percentage of nuclear families continue to increase.

Finally, if we examine the generational structure of each household, the two generation household is the most common household structure. In 1960, two generation households comprised 64 % of all households, and, by 1970, it grew to 70 %. It began to gradually decrease to 55.4 % by 2005. On the other hand, one generation households, which reflect the one person household, have continued to increase. In 1960, 7.5 % of households were one generation households, but, by 2005, the percentage grew to 16.2 %. Furthermore, three generation households have continued to decrease from 26.9 % in 1960 to a mere 6.9 % in 2005.

Urbanization, declining fertility, changing attitudes toward living arrangements, and other factors have contributed to a decreasing household size and the emergence of small families in Korea.

2) The Decline of Son Preference

One characteristic of the Korean family is the neo-Confucian principle that emphasizes the importance of family succession through the eldest legitimate son. In other words, in order to continue a family's line, there needs to be at least one son born by a legitimate wife. During the traditional period in Korea, fertility was high, but mortality was also high; therefore, it was often difficult to have a son that lived until adulthood. Since the legitimate son was the only one who could carry on the family line, the ultimate goal of each family was to have a son who lived until adulthood. The idea of son preference during the traditional era did not imply that a family needed to have many sons. Rather, son preference only implied that family succession required at least one legitimate son in the family.

Son preference — the notion that family succession required having at least one legitimate son in the family — continued to be a strong value in Korean society following modernization. Even during modernization in the 1960s and 1970s, it was common in Korean society to adopt a son who could succeed the family line if one could not give birth to a legitimate son. However, child mortality and adolescent mortality declined and the need to adopt a son for family succession decreased, whereas the possibility of having one's own son increased. Nevertheless, Koreans faced a dilemma when fertility declined as the number of children per family decreased from 4 to 3 to 2 and, finally, to 1. The probability of giving birth to a son declined with the reduction in number of childbirths. Families with two children would try to have a third child if both of the previous children were daughters. They would even try to have a fourth child if all three of the prior children were daughters. Although the total fertility rate decreased to 2 childbirths, the sex ratio among the third, fourth, or higher birth was very high. The traditional strong preference for male children is reflected by the high sex ratio at natural birth.

In cases where son preference remains strong, people prefer to have at least one son, if they have either one or two children. Considering there is a low number of childbirths, having at least one son is not an easy process. As a result, once it was possible to identify the sex of the fetus through sonograms, people who wished to have a son relied on abortion if the fetus was a daughter. As a result, in the 1990s, the sex ratio at birth was considerably skewed. When the fetus was identified as female, many relied on abortion and, from a social perspective, this result skewed the sex ratio at birth.

Skewed sex ratios at birth became a serious social problem, and the Korean government made it illegal to identify the sex of the fetus. Furthermore, they began to punish those who violated this law. The skewed sex ratios at birth began to normalize after the implementation of this government regulation. At the same time, the sex ratio for third births or higher gradually reached the normal sex ratio. In other words, people no longer had third births or higher in order to have a son.

In 2010, the sex ratio at birth has recovered to the normal sex ratio. This indicates that the strong son preference in the past is declining in Korean society.

Why does the deeply rooted tradition of son preference suddenly decline in Korean society? The first reason is the change in inter-generational relations. In the past, family succession was carried out by the son, especially the eldest son. When parents became older, the eldest son was responsible for taking care of them. On one hand, migration after modernization became frequent and as urbanization took its course the rate of children, living with parents, including the eldest son living with parents, decreased substantially. On the other hand, improvements in living standards increased and the number of years parents had to support their children also increased. Therefore, despite the decline of fertility, the cost of child-rearing increased. In Korean society, the quality of care for the child has become more important than the quantity of children. Thus, as the time and cost of supporting unmarried children increased substantially, taking care of elderly parents became more difficult. Consequently, as Korean parents reached old age, they realized they could not depend on their children after retirement. As inter-generational relations changed and the belief that sons should support his parents declined, the need for a son weakened as well.

Secondly, the family system in Korea is strictly male-centered, and even in the modern family, life is traditionally centered on patriarchy or the father's side. In reality, however, the family life is centered on the mother's side and the wife's family. Daily life routines, such as taking care of children, spending leisure time together, taking care of sick parents, and other family relations, are not patri-centric but centered on the mother's side. The male-centered perspective of family indicates that the traditional social norms are weakening and, in reality, the daily lives of families have a closer relation to the mother's side. This can also weaken son preference and underscore the importance and utility of daughters.

Thirdly, Korean society has a long history of calling for gender equality through women's rights movements. Although gender equality was a difficult concept to accept by the traditionally male-centered Korean society, women's rights movements and promotion of universal human rights have contributed to the acceptance of gender equality in Korea. In 2000, the Ministry of Gender Equality was founded against the backdrop of a progressive political party, institutionalizing gender equality. Furthermore, the family register system, which allowed women to be identified only through their relationship to men, was abolished in 2005, further enhancing the institutionalization of gender equality. As the concept of gender equality became prevalent in Korean society, values towards sex preference and son preference also changed. As a result, Korean societal values no longer reflect a specific sex preference for children. Although one may find other reasons to explain the decline in son preference, the family system perspective highlights the usefulness of daughters and can be an important cause of the decline in son preference.

3) General Changes in Family Life

Changes in economic conditions, population, and culture, including value changes, have resulted in the general transformation of family life. This section will introduce a few general changes in family life.

First, increasing age at marriage is the main cause of low fertility and, as fertility declined, the family structure has changed significantly. On the other hand, the increasing age at marriage indicates an important change in the life course of an individual. The change in the life course of an individual is again closely related to changes in family. We can discuss transition to adulthood from three different aspects: leaving home, transition to marriage, and transition to parenthood. Unlike traditional life transitions in Greece, Italy, Spain, Portugal and other Southwestern European countries, where children live an independent life separate from their parents during their youth prior to living with a partner, this pattern is relatively rare in Korean society. Regardless of gender, a Korean youth often lives an independent life style concurrent with marriage. Furthermore, Korean society still perceives the institution of marriage as the only legitimate means by which a man and woman can live together. In Western societies, including the United States, marriage is not the only method for transition into adulthood. However, in Korean society, transition into adulthood is only understood as being accomplished through marriage. Yet, the age at marriage in Korean society continues to increase. This trend indicates that the transition to adulthood continues to be delayed among the Korean youth. If children do not become independent from their parents, the time they live with their parents is extended and the time parents have to spend supporting their children is also extended. In Korean society, child-rearing, childcare, and support for elderly parents are all considered to be a responsibility of the family. As a result, as the period of transition into adulthood in Korean society continues to be delayed, the burden of supporting their children continues to increase among Korean parents.

Secondly, divorce and remarriage among Korean families are increasing. Yet from an international perspective, attitudes towards divorce among Koreans are relatively conservative. In Korean

Figure 3 Marriage and Divorce Rate in Korea, 1990-2009

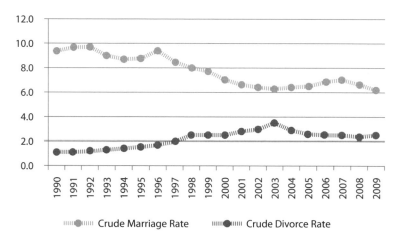

IIIII●IIIII Crude Marriage Rate   IIIII●IIIII Crude Divorce Rate

society, the belief that divorce is not the best solution for marriage-related problems is relatively high. However, if we examine this from the perspective of actual behavior in regards to divorce, Koreans no longer brand divorce as taboo. If we examine the crude divorce rate — the number of divorces per 1,000 persons in a population — we can observe that on a global scale Korea's divorce rate is high. The divorce rate increased significantly in the 1990s and, after the Asian Financial Crisis in 1997, the divorce rate soared at a rapid pace. In 2003, divorce rates again soared and reached the crude divorce rate of 3.4 but subsequently began to decrease. By 2005 Korea's crude divorce rate was between 2.4 and 2.6.

Why do divorce rates continue to grow in Korean society, while attitudes toward divorce remain relatively negative? Is it because problems in families among married-couples have increased today compared to the past? The increase in divorce rate after 1990 does not indicate that there is an increase in the number of problems within the family or married-couples. Even if women want to divorce, it is difficult to implement in a male-centered society that has a strong negative attitude towards divorce. Women cannot pursue divorce even when they are faced with problems, for instance when a husband is engaged in extramarital affairs. However, cultural changes, including overall changes in values, have led to the decline of negative attitudes toward divorce. Furthermore as the level of education increased among women and as they became economically independent, women began to perceive divorce as something that was possible and as a new start in their lives. After the 1997 Financial Crisis, the role of men as the sole source of income declined, and many women who were dissatisfied with their economic condition chose divorce as an alternative. In a "painful and unhappy marriage," divorce became an "alternative to the unhappy married life." (Han 2009: 59).

As negative attitudes toward divorce declined, the approval of remarriage increased. During the traditional era, the attitude towards remarriage among women was especially negative. This attitude remained until the modernization period of the late twentieth century. However, respect for an individual's privacy, increase in the status of women, expansion of gender equality, and the improvement of women's social status emerged after modernization. Thus, separation, divorce, and remarriage for women were no longer a subject of importance. Not only women but men as well became more autonomous in the decision to remarry, and the rate of remarriage among men and women increased.

In 1999, 87 % of marriages among men were first marriages and 12.8 % were remarriages. In 2009, the percentage of first marriages decreased to 82.6 % and the percentage of remarriage increased to 17.4 %. In the case of women, 85.8 % of marriages were first marriages and 14 % were remarriages. In addition, the percentage of first marriages among women in 2009 decreased to 80.9 %, and the percentage of remarriage increased to 19 %. In other words, among married women in 2009, two out of every 10 women were remarried.

The decline in the negative attitude towards remarried women can also be confirmed by analyzing the partner of the remarried woman. In 1999, 4.7 % of all marriages consisted of remarrying women and men who were marrying for the first time. This

Figure 4 Remarriage Rate in Korea, 1992-2009

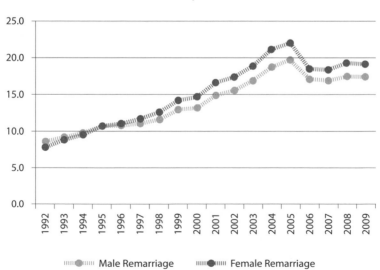

Source: National Statistical Office, Vital Statistics, Each Year.

percentage increased to 6.4 % in 2005, and, in 2009, it increased to 6.1%. In contrast, the percentage of first-time marriages for both women and men was 82.3 % in 1999 but decreased to 76.4 % by 2009.

The increase in divorce and remarriage observed in Korea also indicates that marriage and family life in Korean societies are in the process of transformation. The increase in divorce and remarriage is a transformation in the family, resulting from the rise of women's social status in a male-centered Korean society.

The third big change in the Korean family is the increase in international marriages. The societal composition in Korea and Japan is relatively homogenous. In other words, Korea and Japan avoided interracial marriages and, for a long time, lived in

Figure 5 International Marriage in Korea, 1992-2009

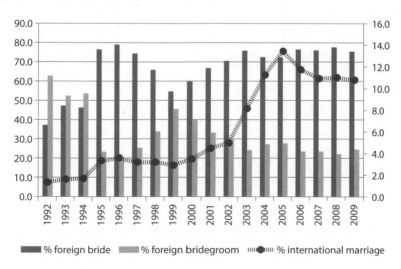

Source: National Statistical Office, Vital Statistics, Each Year.

a closed society. However, globalization has made it impossible to avoid contact with other racial groups. Not only do different races interact through work in their daily lives, but exchanges at an individual level are also inevitable and sometimes lead to love and even marriage. In the past, Koreans had a strong abhorrence for interracial marriages. However, Koreans today have a more positive attitude towards interracial marriages.

As shown in Figure 5, the distribution of international marriages in Korean society is very low. In 1994, less than four out of every 100 marriages were international marriages. However, in 1995, the percentage of Korean men marrying foreign women suddenly increased and the share of international marriages in Korean society also increased. Then, for the first time, in 2004, at least 10 out of 100 marriages were international marriages. By 2005, the percentage of international marriages reached an all-time high of 13.5 %. Since 2006, the distribution of international marriages in Korean society remains at the minimum of 10 %.

Most international marriages prior to the significant growth of international marriages were between Korean women and foreign men. However, international marriages started to grow at a rapid pace as Korean men began to marry foreign women. Normalization with China in 1992 resulted in the increase of marriage between Korean men and Chinese women. These women were nationals of China, but, racially, they were ethnic Koreans living in Northeast China. As the percentage of marriages with foreigners grew, many men living in rural areas began to actively search for foreign brides, because Korean women avoided marrying men from rural regions unless their level of education increased and their economic status improved. The consequence of this trend was that it became difficult for men living in rural areas to find Korean women as marital partners. The only choice for rural men who exceeded the average marital age was to find a bride from a foreign country. The mate-matching industry developed as Korean society began to introduce foreign wives to men who exceeded their marital age. International marriages surged in a short period of time, because Korean men were able to marry young foreign brides and foreign women were able to enjoy improved living standards by marrying Korean men.

Finding a suitable marriage partner in a short period of time was a difficult process for mate-matching companies. Therefore, many social problems emerged from international marriages. The marriage was not based on love but was closer to a transaction. Consequently, the risk of marital dissolution was high in international marriages. Many marriages ended because of the lack of cultural understanding. Korean society is not accustomed to accepting other racial groups, and, as a result, these married-couples often have trouble overcoming the challenges of marriage. Foreign brides and grooms often face discrimination in their daily lives due to a lack of acceptance in Korean society. In addition, interracial children often face prolonged prejudice in Korean society. The history of international marriage in Korea is very short. Although international marriages do not impose a great influence on Korean families, the increasing number of international marriages indicates that international marriages will have a significant affect on parent-child relationships, inter-generational relationships, and kinships.

As a result, international marriages will have a significant influence on Korean society and its transformation to a multi-cultural society.

4. Summary and Conclusion

Korean society has been changing at an astonishing level since the late twentieth century. Changes in population have significantly influenced this change. In particular, fertility transitions reflect the changes in Korean society, influencing the transformation of Korean families.

Fertility in Korea reached the replacement level within a 20 to 30-year time period, and, since then, fertility has continued to decrease. As a result, Korea has the lowest fertility rates among all countries in the late twentieth century.

Controlling pregnancy and fertility using contraception is one of the most important factors contributing to the low fertility rate. Yet another important cause of lower fertility is the increasing age at marriage. Women and men are seeking a high-level of education in order to find stable jobs before marriage. Although they want to marry, difficult economic conditions make this wish very difficult to achieve. Society has transformed into a consumer society abundant with products of leisure, but the labor market continues to be unstable and prone to irregular jobs.

The most significant contribution to the lower fertility rates is the improvement of women's social status. Korea has been one of the most male-centered societies in the world. Yet for the past 20 to

30 years, the level of education and economic status achieved by women has been remarkable. Although women generally achieve a lower level of education than men, today's levels of education attained by women are almost equal to the levels of education attained by men. As education levels for women increase, their desire to enter the labor market to have their own career alongside men has also increased.

Although change in the status of women is a cause of low fertility, it is also an essential factor in changes in the family. Korean families have experienced many changes as fertility declined, while the status of women improved. The size of the family has changed more than anything. The average number of persons in a household is less than three, and two generation households have taken center stage in Korean society. In addition, one person households are also increasing. The formation of small families, the increase of one person households, and the decline of stem families have changed the size of families in Korea.

Traditional family values have influenced the characteristics of modern families in Korea. The preference for a son, which necessitated a legitimate son for family succession according to traditional Confucian society, has remained strong in modern Korean family values. However, in the past 20 years, the spread of Western values, including women's rights movements and gender equality, has resulted in a decline of son preference. Today, some families even prefer having a daughter to a son.

Korean families have experienced many changes. This chapter also analyzed the effects of increasing marital ages on the transition to adulthood, as well as the rise of divorce and remarriage in Korean families. The negative attitudes toward divorce and remarriage have declined, and, today, Korean society experiences a relatively high divorce and remarriage rate compared to the past. There is a new awareness that views "divorce and remarriage as a better alternative" and that an "unhappy marriage" should come to an end.

Finally, this chapter analyzed the increase in international marriages in Korean society, which has remained relatively homogeneous and racially exclusive. The marriage between a Korean man and a foreign woman is a unique phenomenon in a homogeneous society such as Korea. As Korean women's expectations for a marital spouse has increased, Korean women began to have trouble finding suitable men who can meet their expectations. In addition, the skewed sex ratio at birth as a result of son preference may be another reason why Korean men cannot find suitable Korean women to marry. In rural regions, it has become very difficult for men to find Korean women as marital partners. Against this backdrop, Korean men have sought foreign women as wives through mate-matching companies, and the proportion of men marrying foreign women has increased. Consequently, there has been a significant transformation in Korean families. Husband-wife relationships, parent-child relationships, kinship, adaptation problems for interracial children, and other problems have emerged from international marriages as a cause of transformation in Korean families.

Changes in the Korean family can be understood from many

different perspectives. Nevertheless, one can better understand changes in the Korean family, if one can understand the changes as an interaction between changes in population and family. In addition, these changes should be understood with respect to the social changes that have influenced both the changes in the population and changes in the family, as was presented in this chapter.

References

Choi, J.-H. (1995). Population Distribution by Region. In *Population and Family in Korea*, ed. Tai-Hwan Kwon, Tai-Hun Kim and Jin-Ho Choi, 127-235. Seoul: Ilsinsa.

Chung, W. and Gupta, M. D. (2007). The Decline of Son Preference in South Korea: The Role of Development and Public Policy. *Population and Development Review* 33(4): 757-783.

Eun, K.-S. (2007). Lowest-Low Fertility in the Republic of Korea: Causes, Consequences, and Policy Responses. *Asis-Pacific Population Journal* 22(2): 51-72.

Kwon, T.-H. and Kim, D.-S. (2002). *Inguui ihae (Understanding Population*; in Korean)*. Seoul: Seoul National University Press.

Min, K.-H. and Eun, K.-S. (2004). Labor Force Participation, Occupation and Industry. In *The Population of Korea*, ed. Doo-Sub Kim and Cheong-Seok Kim. Korea National Statistical Office.

Park, C. B. (1983). Preference for Sons, Family Size, and Sex Ratio: An Empirical Study in Korea. *Demography* 20 (3): 333-352.

Park, C. B. and Cho, N.-H. (1995). Consequence of Son Preference in a Low-fertility Society: Imbalance of the Sex Ratio at Birth in Korea. *Population and Development Review* 21(1): 59-84.

Chapter four

Compressed Modernity and Korean Families: Accidental Pluralism in Family Ideology[1]

Chang, Kyung-Sup (Seoul National University)

1. Introduction

South Koreans are well known for their family-centeredness in personal and social life (Chang 1997b, 1997c). However, their notions and attitudes about family are extremely diverse. In particular, mutually distinctive family ideologies (inclusive of family values and norms) are expressed, reflecting rapid changes in economic, social, and cultural systems. As South Koreans have compressively experienced within four or five decades what had been experienced by Westerners over two or three centuries (Chang 1999a), they have

---

1 This is a slightly revised version of the author's article which appeared as "Compressed Modernity and Korean Family: Accidental Pluralism in Family Ideology," *Journal of Asian-Pacific Studies*, number 9 (September 2001), pp.31-39.

been exposed to different economic structures, social relations, and cultural environments depending on different times of birth and a host of other social factors.[2] While South Koreans' familism (gajokjuui) is often pointed out as an enduring trait, their family relationship and domestic life cannot but be affected seriously by the rapidly changing social environments.[3]

As a result, different generations have developed strikingly dissimilar family ideologies, so that frequent intergenerational conflict and animosity are pronounced concerning family relationship and domestic life. Educational, regional, and gender differences also interact with rapid social change so as to produce serious differences in family ideologies. Consequently, the more South Koreans pursue a family-centered life, the more psychological burden they have to confront within the family because of the differences in family ideologies engendered from generational and other differences. Such differences in family ideologies are often controlled in an authoritarian manner through the familial power relationship or, even worse, induce serious diminution in familial conversation and contact.

Of course, the existence of diverse ideologies in the family is not necessarily a social problem. On the contrary, it could offer

---

2 In recent years, the South Korean government has proudly published numerous statistical compilations of social, economic, cultural, political, and other changes since the Liberation (from Japan) or the beginning of the Republic (in 1948). For instance, see National Statistical Office (NSO), 1998, *Tonggyero bon daehanminguk 50nyeon-ui gyeongjesahoesang byeonhwa* (*Economic and Social Change in the Fifty Years of the Republic of Korea in View of Statistics*; in Korean).

3 I define familism, or *gajokjuui* in Korean, as all the values, norms, attitudes, and understandings concerning family-oriented personal and social life.

a valuable resource for generating lively family culture. But the generation of diverse family ideologies in South Korea has been a highly accidental process contingent upon macro-level economic, social, and cultural transformations. For instance, when young generations are exposed to Western family relationships and domestic life through mass media and pursue their life accordingly, their family ideology lacks any systematic relationship with the conventional family ideologies and, thereby, leads them into a situation of irresolvable intergenerational conflict. In South Korean families, four main family ideologies exist— namely, Confucian familism, instrumental familism, affectionate familism, and individualistic familism. The dilemma is that these diverse family ideologies came into existence accidentally due to abrupt social changes and, thus, do not necessarily reflect any democratic or liberal family culture among South Koreans.

Until recently, the main approach to the psychological and ethical dimensions of family change in South Korea has accepted the modernization theory (Cho and Lee 1993; cf., Shorter 1988). It proposes that most of the problems in family life and relationships emanate from the tension between tradition and modernity (Chang 1997a). But the critical trait of South Korean society is that the coexistence of traditional, modern, and even post-modern cultures results in serious tension and conflict among different generations who have been exposed to such diverse cultures in varying degrees. Furthermore, the interaction between traditional and modern cultures and between traditional and post-modern cultures leads to new hybrid elements. These tendencies are directly reflected in family norms and attitudes, so that the complexity of family ideologies of South Koreans is unparalleled and complex. As their family life and relationships embody the complex family ideologies, a new line of theoretical approach is indispensable.

2. Compressed Social Change and Family Ideology

Despite the explosively rapid social change in the last several decades, the family-centeredness of South Koreans is known as an enduring trait. During the tumultuous processes of colonization, war, military rule, and industrialization, South Koreans could not turn to the state or communities for material, physical, and psychological protection. Instead, they have coped with various crisis situations, explored new opportunities, and maintained social identities only through familial support and cooperation. Thus, the familism of South Koreans is a crucial mechanism for digesting rapid social change. In a sense, the twentieth-century social history of South Korea may be best studied by aggregating family histories of grassroots and elite groups.

However, the family-centered life of South Koreans does not necessarily presuppose a certain line of common family ideology. On the contrary, the values and norms of South Koreans about family are more diverse and complex than those of most other nations. South Koreans have been exposed to Confucian familism, instrumental familism, affectionate familism, and individualistic familism. Different generations, regions, genders, and educational backgrounds have been responsible for different degrees of accommodation to each of these family ideologies. Consequently, not only the entire society but also each family has to confront the tension and conflict ensuing from the maladjustment among contradictory family ideologies. The more individuals rely on their families to meet personal and social needs, the more intense such tensions and conflicts become. Unfortunately, such differences in family ideologies are often controlled in an authoritarian manner thorough the familial power relationship or, even worse, induce serious diminution in familial conversation and contact.

The existence of diverse family ideologies in a family does not necessarily constitute a social problem. It could rather serve as a valuable resource for producing lively family culture. However, the emergence of the diverse family ideologies in South Korean society has been an accidental outcome of rapid macro social, cultural, and economic changes. Thus, the family ideologies of South Koreans reflect a sort of accidental pluralism. Originally, pluralism is a political philosophy of Western democracy for pursuing a progressive coexistence of different or competing social elements on the basis of mutual tolerance and recognition. The diverse family ideologies of South Koreans are not based upon pluralism as a progressive principle of social and familial integration. Their diversity in family ideology is the result of individual experiences of a long and abrupt series of historical incidents and social transformations including colonial rule, war, Westernization, industrialization, urbanization, commercialization, informatization, as well as traditional revival. Although some of these processes have been voluntarily pursued, the overall nature of the ideological transformation of South Korean families is far from harmonious or stable.

Besides the explosive and complex social changes, the rapid lengthening of life expectancy has facilitated the plurality of family ideologies. That is, the family ideologies emphasized by old generations, such as Confucian familism and instrumental familism, have extended social life spans thanks to the impressive expansion of old age (Chang 2001). Simultaneously, affectionate familism and individualistic familism have rapidly spread among middle agers and youth, so that South Korea has become an arena for coexistence of the family ideologies of traditional, modern, Asian, and Western origins.

3. Major Types of Family Ideologies

In the following, let me briefly explain the characteristics and backgrounds of Confucian familism, instrumental familism, affectionate familism, and individualistic familism.

1) Confucian Familism

The kernel of Confucian familism consists of the modern inheritance of the traditional family values and norms of the Joseon era (Choe 1991). This family ideology, centered on the moral hierarchy and support relationship between different genders and generations, still exerts the most dominant influence on contemporary South Korea. Despite various significant symptoms of weakening and deterioration, its influence on the relationship between parents and children and between husband and wife is critical.

There are two historical factors that make the influence of Confucian familism pervasive but problematic: first, Confucianism, including its family ideology, was a limited class phenomenon monopolized by the Yangban aristocracy, and, second, its modern sustenance has not been in par with the nature of macro social change. As the Confucian family rituals and relationships required heavy cultural and material resources unbearable for ordinary and lowly classes, it enabled learned and landed aristocracy to legitimize their morally coated class domination. Interestingly, Confucian familism was universalized society-wide after the traditional class system was dissolved in the nineteenth century. This trend reflected the aspiration of previously ordinary and lowly people for assimilating the exclusive class culture of their old day masters (Kim 2001). After colonial devastation and war, Confucianism was utilized in promoting social integration and stability on the basis of familial unity. As the state and local communities were in disarray due to repeated political and military conflicts, private families were entrusted with full responsibility for protecting and controlling individuals.

While a sort of re-traditionalization or yangbanization took place in family life and relationships, the political, social, and economic changes outside the family necessitated abrupt secession from tradition. Japanese colonial rule, American military rule, war, and labor exploitive industrialization forced grassroots people to break away from the traditional social and cultural environments of life and production and undergo hardship and deprivation. Consequently, the material difficulty of grassroots people has betrayed their cultural aspiration for practicing Confucian family rituals and relationships. Also, the gender and age hierarchy of Confucianism has caused alienation and discrimination to women and young people who, otherwise, would have critically increased their social role in accordance with the modern social and economic trends (Chang 1997c).

2) Instrumental Familism

Instrumental familism is a sort of life philosophy that has evolved out of various family-reliant survival strategies of South Koreans in the turbulent twentieth century. As the dissolution of the traditional order, the successive colonial rule by Japan and the United States, and the Korean War destroyed stable state governance and communal order, South Koreans had to turn to their families only for personal protection and social achievement (Chang 1999b). Even after the initiation of full-fledged industrialization, South Koreans have developed and managed their industrial system in a family-reliant manner. For instance, the formation of educated and skilled labor forces has been possible not because of active governmental and corporate investment in human capital but because of ordinary citizens' excessive zeal in their own and their children's education. A majority of the widespread small-scale commercial and industrial operations are family-funded and/or family-staffed ventures. *Chaebol*, the largest business organization, is also family-controlled both in ownership and management (Cho 1991).

South Koreans have mobilized their family resources and kin networks for their social advancement, material achievement, and even political success. A good family is one that can meet such social, economic, or political needs of its members. That is, they came to develop an ideology that the family has to function as an instrument for its members' social competition for status, wealth, and power. If a family fails to serve that purpose, it becomes embarrassing evidence of inferiority. As an inevitable cost of instrumental familism, many South Korean families tend to sacrifice normal domestic life for the sake of their members' success and achievement in society. As family relationships are confirmed not through harmonious and gentle domestic interaction but through strategic support for social competition, home has been reduced to an empty shell. On the other hand, the mobilization of family resources and kin networks often infringes upon fair social, economic, and political order by nurturing corruption, speculation, and collusion in various areas of society (Chang 1997c).

3) Affectionate Familism

Affectionate familism was originally established as the psychological protective function of the family in the process of capitalist industrialization of Western countries (Lasch 1977). The emergence of large-scale industrial capitalism, in which production was fulfilled in big factories and management in big offices, resulted in the economic and social demise of many bourgeois entrepreneurs who used to depend on familial economic organizations. This trend triggered a social effort for reestablishing the family as an arena for the emotional protection of people (Zaretsky 1973). They began to expect the family to provide psychological buffers against rampant suppression, exploitation, and alienation in industrial society. Women were supposed to harbor the emotional integrity of the family. Afterwards, the prohibition of child labor and the protection of maternity made children and women stay home, and the improved income level of male providers stabilized the material condition of domestic life. These trends facilitated the spread of affectionate familism as a family culture of the middle class proletariat.

In South Korea, rapid industrialization and economic growth allowed a speedy expansion of middle class workers who accepted affectionate familism as a main family ideology. Also, as most of the highly educated women remained home after marriage, they were exposed and accustomed to the Western affectionate familism disseminated by mass media (Chang 1997c). When affectionate familism is compared with Confucian familism, the former concurs with the latter on its emphasis on women's domestic status and homemaker role but differs from the latter on its emphasis on the emotional union between parents and unmarried children, excluding elderly grandparents. When affectionate familism is compared with instrumental familism, the former differs from the latter on its emphasis on the quality of domestic life as the core standard of a good family. These differences of affectionate familism from Confucian and instrumental familism often lead to intergenerational and spousal conflict.

4) Individualistic Familism

Individualistic familism in South Korea is hinged upon two social trends, namely, social democratization nurturing the development of individuality in regards to women and youth and commercialization of domestic life amid the rapid expansion of consumer capitalism (Chang 1997c). While individualist familism was initiated in the West, it has spread rapidly into South Korean society under the compressed processes of economic growth, democratization, Westernization, and even economic and cultural globalization.

Both in the West and in South Korea, the status of women has fundamentally altered due to the intense feminist critique of the women's role in the nuclear family of the middle class as an emotional protector and provider and also the increased partici-pation of women in the labor market under constant economic restructuring and destabilization of family income sources (Chang 1998). These circumstances led to a growing awareness of the need for a gender-equitable role and status arrangement both at home and in society. Furthermore, more and more women consider marriage merely one of the compromisable options in life and postpone it until very late or even avoid it altogether.

On the other hand, modern families and homes have become

the target of boundless attacks by commercial capital as individual tastes and preferences are touted for every familial matter — from wedding to daily life. Money does it all for commercialized home life, as it can purchase various electronic equipments, home video movie, instant meal, and even delivery party cuisine. This deterioration of family culture has a particularly spoiling effect on the youth, who are often described by mass media and academia as an asocial and unspiritual new generation indulged in commercial consumption (Ju 1994). For many of them, the utility of the family consists mainly in the provision of commercial goods or money for purchasing them. Since even the adult generation is increasingly immersed in commercialized daily life, they cannot exercise strict moral pressure on the attitude of youth.

4. Predicaments of Accidental Pluralism

The essential trait of family culture in South Korea is not a sustained shift from Confucian and/or instrumental familism to affectionate and/or individualistic familism but the coexistence of such diverse family ideologies with varying distributions according to age, generation, gender, region, education, class, etc. The entire society, each family, and even each individual has to uphold the diverse family ideologies simultaneously and live complicated and delicate everyday life. Accidental pluralism in family ideology is responsible for everyday struggle in personal, familial, and social life as family-centeredness dictates not only families but also individuals and society.

Let us briefly examine the distribution of different family ideologies across various individual characteristics. In general, those who are young, better educated, urban resident, and female are inclined towards affectionate and individualistic familism, whereas the opposite groups are bending towards Confucian and instrumental familism (Chang 2000). Among these differences, the age and/or generation-specific differences are the most distinct. It is, of course, because different generations and/or age groups have been exposed and accustomed to vastly different social, cultural, and economic environments in this compressively changing society. When young children pursue individualistic family life as a result of their exposure to Western individualistic familism through mass media and commercial promotion, it has hardly any systematic relationship with local family values and norms and easily leads to irreconcilable conflict with strongly Confucian parents. On the other hand, when parents imbued with instrumental familism try to drive their children's marriage as a means for elevating social and/ or economic status (cf. Kong 1990), it may baffle many children who idealize affectionate familism of the Western nuclear family.

Accidental pluralism in family ideology does not necessarily imply that the existence of each family ideology itself is accidental. Confucian familism, instrumental familism, affectionate familism, and individualistic familism all have some significant historical or social reason to be here. Although it is true that affectionate and individualistic familism have spread rapidly on the basis of sudden public exposure to Western culture through mass media, there has been a simultaneous process of compressed social and economic restructuring commensurate with the new family cultures. Consequently, the material and social basis for affectionate and individualistic familism has been established and made these family ideologies realistic and practical in daily life. Of course, the social and economic restructuring itself has been pursued after the Western model to a significant extent. Even when Western family ideologies and Western social and economic structures are brought in separately without considering what Parsons dubs "functional fit" between cultural and material elements, their coexistence in South Korea may ultimately result in the functional linkage of one kind or another.

In addition, there are some logical unions between different family ideologies. For instance, Confucian familism and affectionate familism concur on the emphasis of the moral quality and psychological function of women as the homemaker. This accordance provided a crucial cultural background under which South Korean upper class families, many of them still heavily Confucian, accepted Western affectionate familism so easily. On the other hand, as Confucianism tends to extremely oppress women's domestic and social status, it serves as the critical backdrop against which feminist voice and individualistic family ideology from the West are highly appealing.[4] Some feminists may even deny

---

4 The most notorious evidence of women's oppression is, of course, the skewed sex ratio. Merciless abortions have been done to female fetuses causing one of the highest sex ratio (boys vs. girls) in the world (Han 1994). Recently, the ratio is constantly declining toward the biologically normal level.

the plurality in family ideology itself, arguing that instrumental, affectionate, and even individualistic familism are all subordinate to patriarchal Confucian familism and, thus, do not prove any plurality of South Korean society, whether accidental or systematic.

Despite these possibilities and arguments, it is an undeniably accidental phenomenon that many mutually dissimilar and even contradictory family ideologies coexist in South Korean families and society. This is a direct reflection of the accidental coexistence of diverse macro-social trends — traditional, modern, post-modern, Korean, East Asian, Western, etc. It is this accidental pluralism that determines the most fundamental dilemma of South Koreans' family life and relationships. The disharmony and contradiction among diverse family ideologies impose various psychological difficulties on the family life and relationships of South Koreans on top of the burdens and pains each of the family ideologies cause separately.

5. Family Ideology and Social Policy

In South Korea, a comprehensive set of public policies and programs are urgently needed in order to deal with various social problems accumulated in the wake of the rapid industrialization and economic growth since the 1960s. The new policies and programs can be realistic and creative only by systematically reflecting the concrete social conditions and cultural environments, not by copying the Western examples uncritically. In this milieu, it is necessary to develop a welfare system in harmony with various functions and roles of the family, since most South Koreans tend to live extremely family-centered social and economic lives. Numerous scholars and policymakers have already proposed to establish a family-centered welfare model (e.g., Chung 1991). Even before these propositions, the South Korean government maintained a highly family-dependent social policy system (Chang 1997a).

Undeniably, public welfare services and benefits will produce maximum effects on family-centered South Koreans when they help to facilitate family life and relationships. However, a critical problem in the governmental pursuit of a family-centered welfare system is that they promote welfare policies and programs by accepting several simplified family norms, not by concretely analyzing the basic values and attitudes of people concerning family life and relationships. Even if most South Koreans live family-centered lives in reality, it does not warrant that they maintain a coherent and enlightened moral commitment to family support. Furthermore, since rapid and abrupt changes in social, cultural, and economic life spawn diverse family ideologies according to age, generation, gender, region, education, class, and many other factors, a policy or program presupposing a certain line of family ideology is unlikely to achieve comprehensive success. Therefore, the pursuit of a family-centered welfare system should not include any effort at extolling a certain type of "normal," "standard," or "model" family. What appears normal or universal is the complexity of family ideologies and the ensuing cultural diversity. Any policy or program that ignores this fact and demands a particular type of family life and relationship is certain to cause more harm than benefit.

Until recently, the South Korean government has devised and implemented numerous social and economic policies by endorsing a particular type of family from the Confucian perspective (Chang 1997a).[5] As an inevitable consequence, many social groups in desperate need of welfare protection have been rather systematically alienated from public welfare benefits (Rhee, et al. 1989; Cho and Cho 1992). In addition, many conservative figures in academia, government, and social organizations have proposed to designate a certain type of model family and guide people's family life and relationships towards that direction. No visible social impact or repercussion were generated from this moralist initiative. Since an effort to compulsorily unify diverse family values and norms even within a family can cause serious conflicts and problems, a similar effort at the societal level may well cause even worse conflicts and problems. From now on, new policies and programs should be developed by clearly acknowledging the complexity of family ideologies and the related diversity in family relationship, domestic life, and household structure. To this end, a comprehensive and systematic nation-wide survey of family life, relationships, and structure should be done on a regular basis.

---

5 A similar trend is observed in contemporary China, where market-oriented economic changes demand private families to strengthen their self-support function predicated upon the Confucian tradition (Chang 1993).

6. Prospect

In the twenty-first century, South Korean society will undergo even more rapid and abrupt social changes amid informatization, globalization, and other new social trends. Since these changes are at an incipient stage, it is hard to systematically diagnose or predict their impact on individual life and social order. However, one thing is clear — South Koreans will still lead highly family-centered lives and cope with such changes even when they have to juggle with various contradictory family ideologies.

For instance, the recent economic crisis, an obvious result of economic globalization, induced most South Koreans to seek various family-centered survival strategies (Chang 1999b). When the national economic crisis turned into a familial economic crisis for grassroots South Koreans, South Korean families became both stronger and weaker. Stronger when family members were able to unite and cooperate in spite of economic hazards; weaker when the accompanying economic burdens and pains drove them beyond their capacity of endurance and austerity. Also, cultural globalization and informatization, on the one hand, accelerate the exposure of South Koreans to American, Japanese, and other cultural elements, and, on the other hand, encourage them to award higher value to indigenous cultural elements. These tendencies are likely to directly affect the subjective basis of family life and relationships, so that the complexity of family ideologies will grow even further. In sum, the family-centered life of South Koreans and the complexity of their family ideologies are not going to be replaced by various new social trends but interact with them to produce even newer modes of individual life and social order.

References

Chang, K.-S. (1993). "The Confucian family instead of the welfare state: Reform and peasant welfare in post—Mao China." *Asian Perspective* 17(1): 1169-1200.

Chang, K.-S. (1997a). "The Neo-Confucian right and family politics in South Korea: The nuclear family as an ideological construct." *Economy and Society* 26(1): 22-42.

Chang, K.-S. (1997b). "Modernity through the family: Familial foundations of Korean Society." *International Review of Sociology* 7(1): 51-63.

Chang, K.-S. (1997c). "Everyday conditions of authoritarian politics: Familial forms of social conflict and political control in South Korea." Paper presented at the International Conference on Democracy and Social Contentions in South Korea, the Center for Korean Studies, University of Hawaii at Manoa, Honolulu, November 1997.

Chang, K.-S. (1998). "Yeoseong, sijang, gonggonggajokeuroseoui gukga: Jaesaengsan sahoehwawa seongjilseo (Women, market, and the state as public family: Socialization of reproduction and gender order; in Korean)." *Sahoebipyeong* 18: 298-327.

Chang, K.-S. (1999a). "Compressed modernity and its discontents: South Korean society in transition." *Economy and Society* 28(1): 30-55.

Chang, K.-S. (1999b). "South Korea society in the IMF era: Compressed capitalist development and social sustainability crisis." Pietro P. Masina, ed., *Rethinking Development in East Asia: From Illusory Miracle to Economic Crisis*. London: Routledge Curzon.

Chang, K.-S. (2000). "Gajokinyeomui wubaljeok dawonseong: Apchukjeok geundaeseonggwa han-guk gajok (Accidental pluralism in family ideology: Compressed modernity and Korean families; in Korean)." Paper presented at the Winter biannual meeting of the Korean Sociological Association, the Academy of Korean studies, December 2000.

Chang, K.-S. (2001). "Apchukjeok geundaeseonggwa noinmunjeui jaeinsik: 'Sinsedae' rosseoui noin (Compressed modernity and reconception of the aging issue: Aged people as a new generation; in Korean)." *Gajokgwa Munhwa (Family and Culture)* 13(1): 1-29.

Cho, D.-S. (1991). *Han-gukjaebeolyeon-gu (A Study of the Korean Chaebol*; in Korean). Seoul: Maeil Economic Daily.

Cho, S.-N., Lee, D.-W. (1993). "Towards relevant scholarship: Family sociology in South Korea." *Current Sociology* 41(1): 25-39.

Cho, U., Cho, O. (1992). *Dosi binminui salmgwa gong-gan (The Life and Space of Urban Poor*; in Korean). Seoul: Seoul National University Press.

Choe, H.-K. (1991). "Yugyowa gajok (Confucianism and family; in Korean)." *Gajokhaknonjip (Journal of the Korean Family Studies Association)* 3: 207-228.

Chung, D.-C. (1991). "Han-gugui gajokbokjijeongchaek (Korean family welfare policy; in Korean)." Han-gukgajokbokjijeongchaek-yeon-guso, ed., Han-gukgajokbokjijeongchaekgwa noinmunjae (Korean family welfare policy and elderly problem), Seminar proceedings.

Han, H.-J. (1994). "Unwelcome daughters: Son preference and abortion in South Korea." Judith Mirsky and Marty Radlett, eds., *Private Decisions, Public Debate: Women, Reproduction and Population*, 33-42. London: Panos.

Ju, E.-W. (1994). "90nyeondaewa han-gugui sinsedaewa sobimunhwa (The new generation and consumption culture of South Korea in the 1990s; in Korean)." *Gyeongjewa Sahoe (Economy and Society)* 21: 70-91.

Kim, S.-J. (2001). On naraga yangbandoegi (Yangbanization of the entire country; in Korean). Paper presented at the Summer biannual meeting of the Korean Sociological Association, Chonnam National University, June 2001.

Kong, J.-J. (1990). Jaebeolgaui honinyuhyeong (The marriage patterns of chaebol families; in Korean). Yeoseonghan-guksahoeyeon-guhoe, ed., *Han-gukgajongnon (A Study of the Korean Family)*, 37-59. Seoul: Kachi.

Lasch, C. (1977). *Haven in a Heartless World: The Family Besieged*. New York: Basic Books.

National Statistical Office (1998). *Tong-gyero bon daehanminguk 50nyeonui gyeongjesahoesang byeonhwa* (*Economic and Social Change in the Fifty Years of the Republic of Korea in View of Statistics*; in Korean).

Rhee, K.-O., et al. (1989). *Noindandokgagu siltae-e gwanhan Yeon-gu* (*A Study of the Real Situations of Elderly-Only Households*; in Korean). Seoul: Korea Institute for Population and Health.

Shorter, E. (1988). "Grand theories of family change: Modernization theory." Paper presented at the seminar on 'Theories of Family Change,' International Union for the Scientific Study of Population.

Zaretsky, E. (1973). *Capitalism, the Family, and Personal Life*. New York: Harper & Colophon Books.

III
Family, Change, and Space

Chapter 5

Economic Roles of Women and Men in Korean Rural Families:
Between 1930 and 1980

Chapter 6

Urban Family Relationships in the Rapidly Industrializing Korean Society

Chapter 7

An Evaluation of Older Less-Educated, Lower-Class Working Women

Economic Roles of Women and Men in Korean Rural Families: Between 1930 and 1980[1]

Park, Boo Jin (Myongji University)

1. Introduction

South Korean society has experienced rapid socio-economic changes for the last half a century. Especially in the 1970's and 1980's when rural areas experienced radical changes.[2] Traditional rural society, which was organized on the basis of small-scale, self-sufficient agricultural production and land as an important means of production, transformed itself to an industrialization-oriented

---

1　This study is based on the data collected for my Ph.D. dissertation. I conducted a fieldwork in a village called *Golma-eul* in *Gangwon* Province for one year between 1987 and 1988, and revisited the field in 1991 and 1992. Discussions of this chapter are partially dependent on my dissertation (Park 1994a).

2　Several studies (Byun 1993; Cho 1998; Kim 1992, 2006; Son 2002, 2007) demonstrate that Korean rural areas began to change in the 1970's, mainly due to Five Year Economic Development Plans, the first of which was launched in 1962.

enterprise. The increasing availability of wage labor and diverse employment opportunities in the countryside and the migration of villagers to urban areas had an impact on rural families as basic units of production and reproduction.

Many studies exist regarding the changes Korean families have experienced and can be categorized into two groups. One group of studies emphasizes the nuclearization of the family associated with the industrialization process,[3] while another group of studies argues that Korean families have maintained traditional relationships and continue to cling to conventional family roles despite changes in the family form.[4] These two contrasting views reflect the fact that in a period of rapid social change families adopt new cultural components while maintaining traditional ones in order to maintain stability.

The most notable changes, which occurred among rural families in the late 1980s, were the decrease in family size and nuclearization of the family. In the past parents did not have a chance to accumulate wealth for their children, while maintaining their families with agricultural activities. Even when they had land to bequeath to the eldest son,[5] land did not increase the family's wealth because its value decreased so much.

Educated children did not want to follow in their parent's foot-

---

3 This group of studies include Choi (1966), Han (1985), Kong (1987), and Kwon (1992).
4 The second group of studies (Chang 1993; Lee 1971; Park 1994b) stresses traditional characteristics found in contemporary Korean families, especially the ways in which family members maintain relationships with each other and how they categorize family members cognitively.
5 Korean society practiced primogeniture until the Family Law was revised in 1991.

steps tilling the land and forming stem families in the countryside, but preferred to migrate to urban areas to find new employment opportunities. Parents who could not provide better options for their children allowed them to emigrate. Young people believed they could make more money in the city when they adopted a career strategy and formed independent nuclear families. Thus, the number of small families and families of elderly parents without children has been increasing in Korea in recent years. The changes in economic conditions and family forms in cities and villages have resulted in not only spatial separation between parents and grown children but also transformation of interaction patterns among family members.

In this study I examine the changes that Korean rural families experienced between the 1930s and 1980s, focusing on the economic roles of women and men based on interviews, which were conducted with the residents of *Golma-eul* between 1987 and 1988 and again in 1991 and 1992. *Golma-eul* is a valley village located near *Gangneung* city in northeastern part of South Korea.[6] This study will demonstrate how the changing national economy and social conditions have influenced lives of families in the Korean countryside. In addition, the implications of gender division of labor and roles in the rapidly industrializing society will be explored.

---

6 *Gangneung* is a medium-sized city and center of education, culture and economy for adjacent villages.

2. Backgrounds of Research Site

1) Population Distribution and Household Composition

There were 73 households and 271 inhabitants in *Golma-eul* as of December 1987. Distribution of inhabitants by age is shown in Table 1. There is little difference in the distribution of villagers by sex, and population distribution of *Golma-eul* is not much different from other Korean villages in the late 1980s.[7] Table 1 shows a relatively small number of children under the age of 10 as well as people in the 30s age group, which is a normal age bracket for childbearing and childrearing. The Korean government implemented aggressive family planning programs in the 1960s and 1970s, which dramatically lowered the nation's birth rates. Although some villagers left for education or mandatory army service, they remained residents of the village according to registration records. These were primarily young people in their teens and 20s and potential migrants to eventually move out of the village.

In *Golma-eul* the majority of the households were headed by the eldest man of the family, as were other Korean villages. Sixty-two households listed the eldest man of the family as the head of the household, while the rest of the households were headed by women. Two of the male head of household families were three-

---

7 Composition of the Korean rural population changed drastically in the late 1980s. The proportion of young population (under the age of 20) accounts for 40 % of the total rural population in 1980s and decreased to 20 % in the early 2000s. The older population (over the age of 65) changed from about 10 % to 30 %.

Table 1 Distribution of *Golma-eul* Inhabitants by Age

age	9≦	10's	20's	30's	40's	50's	60's	70's	80's	total
N	32	59	31	28	31	35	31	16	8	271
%	12	22	11	10	11	13	11	6	3	99

generation stem families, where two men of different generations reside in the family together.[8] The 60 remaining households were headed by men and were nuclear families.

2) Occupation of Women and Men

As Table 2 shows, the majority of heads of household in *Golma-eul* engage in agriculture. Although the main source of income for heads of households is agriculture, young or middle-aged heads of households tend to work at construction sites or factories in the city of *Gangneung* and adjacent areas to earn extra money during the off-seasons of agriculture. Young villagers, who are not heads of households, help their parents with agriculture or work in construction, sales, or as drivers in the city. Heads of households, who depend on rent from their land or monetary support from their children for their livelihood, are all women.

None of the married women in *Golma-eul* families were full-time homemakers. Almost every wife in the village engaged in agricultural activities with her husband or alone when her husband

---

8 Since the elderly heads of older generation in these stem families were too old to actively engage in economic activities, I interviewed men of younger generation (47 and 56 years old) although they were not the heads of households.

Table 2 Occupation and Livelihood of Heads of Households

Occupation /Livelihood	Agri-culture	Sales	Driver	Construc-tion Worker	Public Employee	Rent	Support from Children	Total
N	61	1	3	2	2	3	1	73
%	84	1	4	3	3	4	1	100

Table 3 Occupations of Women

Occupation /Livelihood	Agri-culture	Sales	Factory Worker	Day Laborer	Unemployed	Total
N	·53	1	1	6	10	71
%	75	1	1	8	14	99

was away for trading or working for other people. Although the wives thought of their agricultural activities as a part of home-making, those activities were included as an occupation in this study, because they contributed to the family economy. Table 3 shows the various occupations of women in *Golma-eul* families. In Table 3, two widower households and 11 households headed by women were excluded, examining only the 60 households with both a wife and a husband. Both a mother-in-law and a daughter-in-law were included when they lived and engaged in agricultural activities together. Eleven households fell into that category.

Village women actively engaged in economic activities as long as their health allowed them to do so. During non-agricultural periods, women took part-time jobs, such as drying persimmons or shedding dried fish; and, even during peak agricultural seasons, they took work on other people's land for additional income. In

Table 3, day laborers are those who work on a day to day basis, such as wallpapering or painting at construction sites. Among ten unemployed women, four women under the age of 40 did not work even though they were capable of working, while the six other women were too old or too sick to work.

3) Educational Level of Inhabitants

The overall educational level of *Golma-eul* residents is similar to that of other rural villages in South Korea. Men tend to have attained higher education levels than women and younger people more so than older people. While men over the age of 40 rarely graduated from junior high school, most men in their 30s and younger have completed junior high school and above. While most women in their 30s and above only graduated from primary schools, women in their 20s had at least a junior high school education or above. Parents in the village were more concerned about their children's education than in the past, and many could afford to send their children on for higher education. However, some discrimination did exist in that sons were more likely than daughters to receive educational opportunities, especially if there was a limited amount of money for education.

4) Ownership of Family Property and Economic Activities of House-   holds

The major economic activity in *Golma-eul* is agriculture, and 84 %

of the households engage in agricultural activities. In order to understand the economic status of the households, the ownership of family property was surveyed, as demonstrated in Table 4.

The ownership of a rice field is considered an important indicator of the economic status of a household in Korean villages. Thirty-eight households owned rice fields, ranging between 800 *pyeong* and 1,000 *pyeong*.[9] According to the residents of *Golma-eul*, they need 800 *pyeong* of rice fields and 500 *pyeong* of dry fields in order to feed a family of five and provide the basic necessities. Often, in order to provide extra income for educational expenses, the head of a household will work on other people's land during agricultural peak periods or work as day laborers in slack periods for extra money.

There are six types of households in *Golma-eul*, determined by the agricultural activities in relation to the ownership of land: 1) self-cultivating households, headed by relatively young men without paid jobs; 2) households of self-cultivation and cultivation by tenants, headed by relatively old men; 3) households of cultivation

Table 4 Ownership of Family Property

Ownership of Property	House	House+ Dry Field	House+ Rice Field	House+ Dry & Rice Fields	House+ Dry & Rice Fields+ Forest	None	Total
N	26	4	7	22	9	5	73
%	35	5	10	30	12	7	99

---

9 *Pyeong* is a unit of area, used in Korea. One *pyeong* is equal to 3.954 square yards.

by tenants only, headed either by very old men or men with paid jobs; 4) households with three income sources, that is, self-cultivation, tenant farming, and support from migrated children; 5) landless, tenant households; and 6) landless households that survive on paid agricultural work only. The distribution of households by patterns of agricultural activities illustrates that most rice fields in the village were not cultivated by owners but by tenants or agricultural workers.

Landlords had a set of principles or norms in selecting tenants, which were not always easy to follow. They prefer to lease land to relatives in the village, especially diligent and skilled ones. They also attempt to maximize rent and reach an agreement with potential tenants before a contract is signed. When they are not able to lease land to relatives, they seek tenants who are reliable. Despite these concerns and preferences regarding tenants, the number of possible tenants has been decreasing, while the number of landlords has been increasing in the village, leaving the landlords with fewer choices than the prospective tenants.

There were 53 cases of tenant farming in the village, and the land was owned either by village residents (15 cases) or by outsiders (31 cases).[10] The outsiders are usually people who left their own land and migrated to other areas. In only 14 cases (30 %) of tenant farming cultivation were the tenant farmers relatives of the landlords.

---

10 The number of cases of tenant farming is larger than the households that employ them. For example, in three cases, one household cultivated the lands owned by three different landlords.

The cost of leasing land differs, depending on the quality of land and the relationship between the landlord and the tenant, ranging between 30 % of the harvest (nine cases), 40 % of the harvest (25 cases), and 50 % of the harvest (19 cases). For example, when a male sibling cultivates land for another sibling who has migrated away from the land, rent is relatively low compared to land rented to strangers. In a later visit to the village, the author found rent had decreased to the range of 10-30 % between 1988 and 1992, because the ratio of landlords to tenants was imbalanced in addition to a decreasing interest in agriculture and an increasing wage for agricultural workers.

Until 1988, agricultural products produced in the village were sold through consignment with an agricultural co-op or an urban middleman. Village women occasionally took their products to the market in the city of *Gangneung* city, but they were interrupted by shop owners at the market. Furthermore, the village women could not afford the market tax nor spend all day at the market to vend their products, since they had to work on the land in the village. After several years of repeatedly filing complaints about the situation to the county office (*guncheong*) and at *Gangneung* city hall, villagers were allowed to sell their products directly to consumers in an early morning market, called "lightning market,"[11] at higher price than what they could get from middlemen. Villagers learned to compare the prices of different markets and diversify their

---

11 It is the market which opens between 5 a.m. and 8 a.m. in the morning before the regular *Gangneung* market opens.

marketing strategies. For example, they could take rice and beans to the agricultural co-op, where they got a higher than market price for their products, and they could take other products to the lightening market and sell them directly to the consumers.

Village women actively engaged not only in marketing their products but also wage labor. In addition, the overall shortage of labor in the village pushed women to work not only on their own land but on other people's land as well. Because the village was located near *Gangneung* city, the villagers had better opportunities for wage labor, which helped to increase the family's income, than people who lived in more remote areas.

3. Changing Economic Roles of Wives and Husbands

Social roles include the rights and duties of individuals who occupy certain positions in a society and reflect the expectations of members of the society as they relate to those positions. Social roles lead to certain patterns of behavior, which are defined by the cultural codes of the society, and similarities exist in the behavior of people who carry out the same social role. In this section, the conjugal roles of *Golma-eul* families in different periods are compared, and how characteristics of those roles have changed over time is investigated. Based on the assumption that conjugal roles are related to the division of labor within the family, three major activity areas — production, management, and consumption in the household — are explored.

1) Division of Labor in Production Activities

(1) 1930s and 1940s

Until the 1940s, the household economy in rural areas was solely dependent on agricultural activities. It was the man's job to cultivate grains and vegetables, which provided the major income for the family. Women did not engage in agricultural activities, except during the harvest when extra help was needed. Women were occupied with homemaking and childrearing and rarely had the extra time or energy for agricultural activities. In addition, most households had small pieces of land, which did not require outside labor to cultivate.[12]

Many of the villagers recollected that most households had a small parcel of land, and the workload was not heavy in the 1930s and 1940s when they were young. Because of the shortage of land, they would borrow a small piece of rice paddy for tenant farming and planted millet, bean, and potato in dry fields on a small scale. Households formed stem or extended families for many years, which provided plenty of male labor, with 2 to 4 adult men per household.

During this period, households with a small amount of land had to find opportunities to tenant farm within the village, which were primarily given to relatives in the village. There was little opp-

---

12 While male labor was available in the household in the 1940s more than in 1980s, in *Golma-eul*, most households had less than one jeongbo (a unit of area equivalent to about .99 acres) of agricultural land, which did not require the labor of every male member of the household cultivate.

ortunity for paid agricultural work at that time, and people were content with food in exchange for wages when they helped others.

Since the family's survival was dependent on the man's role as a food producer, grains such as rice and barley, which were produced by men, were more valuable to the family than wild greens and vegetables, which were collected or cultivated by women. Therefore, adult men, as valuable family members, received respect from other family members and, enjoyed authority and power in the family. Although women carried out a variety of productive activities and duties for the family, they were viewed as nonproductive, as well as "food-consuming" family members. Most of the work done by women was related to the production of consumer goods and was considered more for the comfort of family life rather than as income for the family's survival. When there were food shortages, the men's diet was differed from the women's. Men "who worked so much" got to eat rice, while women, "who did only house chores," had to survive on wild greens, wormwood, and porridge made with dried greens. Women often had to skip lunch, "because they did not do agricultural work."

Because of their low status in the family, women were recruited as wives for specific purposes, that is, for housework and son-bearing. Furthermore, in the patrilineal family and society of the period, they could be easily replaced, if they did not accomplish those purposes. Wives were often compared to other wives and criticized for their attitudes and behaviors. They were constantly pressured to make sacrificial acts. The ideal wife was someone "who worked hard but ate little" or "who sacrificed herself for the family."

In contrast, the male head of the household was considered the "pillar of the family" and irreplaceable.

A woman's day was filled with a series of tasks from early in the morning until late at night, pounding barley in a mortar, cooking for the men, transforming ashes into lye, washing clothes, mending clothes, and weaving hemp into cloth for family members. Still tired from yesterday's work, women woke each day to repeat the same tasks all over again. Furthermore, women often worked three to four hours longer than men. Hunger and lack of sleep was a common experience many women shared during this period. Furthermore, although women worked longer hours, their labor was not taken as seriously as that of men. In fact, they were often viewed as "someone who only consumed food without doing hard work." Even elderly women in the village interpreted their role in the family negatively, believing they did not help support the family, even though they were physically exhausted by the end of each day. One village woman resents that "she was ignorant about how the real world worked back then, and she did not think about doing something for the family like trading eggs or vegetables for grains at the market when the family was short of rice." Since elderly women thought they were not help in the family's survival, they also believed they could not raise their voices in the family.

(2) 1950s

In the 1950s, when the Korean War (1950-1953) broke out and the economy was in chaos, the primary task for the villagers was survival. Every adult member of the family, male or female, was mobilized to find ways to feed the family. Several *Golma-eul* villagers remember that there wasn't any land for tenant farming in the 1950's or that there weren't any rice paddies, any men (they were drafted in the army), or any rice.

However, the imbalance between the labor needed for farm production and the available labor in the workforce in the 1950s was not unlike previous decades. Farming was still dependent on the labor of men, while the major tasks of women were centered in the home. In smaller, self-sufficient farming households, the men worked not only on the rice paddies but also on the dry fields, plowing and planting vegetables. Women were also engaged in productive activities, such as raising pigs and chickens, and collecting acorns and wild greens. In the event of a labor shortage, women helped the men with planting, weeding, and carrying manure or compost. Moreover, when a bride moved into the house of her husband's family, she was expected to help with agricultural work as well as housework.

By end of the Korean War in 1953, the country began to be stabilized. As the country began to recover, public education programs were established, and families began to invest heavily in their children's education, especially their son's. Young married couples, who lived in stem families, were pressured to contribute a portion of their income to the education of the husbands' brothers or nephews. A common belief in the 1950s was that in order for the family[13] to achieve social status, the eldest son's family had

---

13 Here "the family" means extended families. From the family head's (i.e., the father-in-law's)

to be prosperous, and everybody in the family was responsible for achieving that goal. Education was highly valued, and, thus, everyone was expected to make significant personal sacrifices to ensure that children, especially boys, were afforded the best available learning opportunities.

Even when married couples moved out of the stem family's house and established an independent household, they maintained economic relationships with the husband's family of origin (called *keunjip*, meaning "big family"). They also continued to be responsible for helping the husband's parents and eldest brother with agricultural work or contributing to family events, like birthdays and marriages. Once children of branch families (i.e. younger brothers' families, called *jageunjip*, meaning "small family") were married, members of the "big family" were no longer considered family members but relatives, and, economic and familial commitments and obligations became focused on the members of one's own extended families.

(3) 1960's

In 1962, the Korean government announced the first Five Year Economic Development Plan and began to implement a wide range of economic reform programs, emphasizing self-reliance and modernization. As the Second Five Year Economic Development Plan was launched in 1967 and focused on industrialization, life in rural villages began to change. According to a villager, by the end of

---

point of view it includes married children and their families.

the 1960s, "things were getting better."

The economic and technological growth during this period not only improved the standard of living for people but also expanded their employment opportunities. Many villagers left to look for jobs elsewhere, especially in the rapidly growing industrial and commercial sectors in surging urban areas. Women began to fill the labor shortage created by the migration of villagers and engage in rice cultivation, formerly the domain of men. Although agricultural labor was available for hire, it was more beneficial for families to recruit female family members for agricultural work than pay hired workers. Women worked alongside husbands in both rice and dry fields; however, plowing was still considered men's work.

Industrialization also freed women from weaving hemp and grinding grain, giving them more time for farming. Factory-manufactured clothes made of synthetic fabrics began to replace Korean dresses made of hemp or cotton, and synthetic, western-style clothes were much easier to take care of than Korean dresses. Power-driven grain mills eliminated the time and energy necessary to grind grain.

Women entered the agricultural workforce at different times, depending on their family. Women, who formed nuclear families upon marriage in the 1960s, helped husbands with various kinds of agricultural work right after marriage. Women, who moved in with their husbands' families, however, did only housework as brides, while male members, mothers-in-law, and older sisters-in-law engaged in farming. After the first several years of marriage, brides would begin to participate in agricultural work alongside their mothers-in-law and sisters-in-law.

(4) 1970s and 1980s

In the 1970s, as young people migrated to cities for education or employment nuclear families without children began to increase and villages began to experience a labor shortage. Women became the only additional and available family member who could contribute labor to the family farm. Wives and husbands had to work together in order to optimize the family's means of production and reduce production costs without having to depend on hired agricultural labor.

Moreover, agricultural open-door policies and subsidized grain policies, which the Korean government implemented in the 1980s, hurt rice growers (Bae 2008). Income from rice cultivation decreased dramatically, and villagers switched to growing cash crops in dry fields. Income from cultivating dry fields, which used to be women's work, became more profitable than rice farming, and some men began to actively participate in dry field cultivation.

New agricultural machinery was introduced to *Golma-eul* that helped to solve the labor shortage problem and encourage a more flexible gender division of labor, narrowing the gap between the hours women and men worked in agriculture by the 1980s. The distinction of type and place of agricultural work done by women vs. men disappeared, and only differences in the intensity of labor remained. Although the men were still in charge of plowing fields, which required intense labor, and women still grew vegetables and weeded dry fields, gender division of labor was not strictly followed as previous decades. For example, a husband would weed and take care of the vegetables when the wife was busy with the children. Women began to have a voice, and, if her husband did not work hard, his wife would demand that he weed the rice paddies or plow the dry fields until they finished the work together.

Women also became actively involved in agricultural work to help with the cost of education for their children, which was viewed as an important investment in human capital for the family's upward mobility. Village women said they were willing to plant anything that could be sold at the market, because they needed money to send children to "good schools in *Gangneung* city." The increasing labor shortage and need for cash pushed women to engage in more agricultural work and the double burden of homemaking and farming.

Women were more active than men in marketing agricultural products, and especially young women, who made more money by selling their agricultural products directly to consumers rather than to a middleman. An important activity for young women became taking their products to the early morning market in *Gangneung* city. Now, they were managing money from their sales and expressing opinions to their husbands when making decisions on a range of agricultural activities, for example, the kind of vegetables to grow, the purchase of agricultural machinery, and the plans for detailed agricultural activities. Women carried out these roles not simply as a supporter of her husbands' agricultural work but as an agricultural worker and manager.

2) Division of Labor in Property Management and Consumption

The properties of rural households consist of two kinds, real estate (for example, rice paddies and dry fields) and movables (for example, savings, agricultural products, and domestic animals). In order to explore the division of roles between women and men in managing family properties, this study surveyed family members who participated in selling or buying properties for the family and those who managed money related to those activities. Regarding the consumption activities of the villagers, three aspects were examined: those who made consumption decisions, those who managed expenses, and those who went to the market for the family. .

(1) 1930s and 1940s

After interviewing nine women who lived with in-laws as newly wedded brides in the 1930s, division of labor between the married couple in property management and household duties depended on the life stage of the family. At the time, Korea was under the colonial control of the Japanese, and the patriarchal characteristics of the Korean family system were reinforced by the Japanese system. While women did not have inheritance rights, the male head of the household controlled the ownership of the family property. Seven women in the village said the oldest man of the family (i.e., the father-in-law) was the head of the family and managed the family's properties. Two other women said, since their father-in-law died, the oldest brother-in-law managed the family's property as the head of the family. In nuclear families, the husband took care of the household property, income, and sales of products.

In the 1930s, the father-in-law was also the decision maker for the sale of domestic animals or harvested agricultural products and the manager of household income (six cases). Only when the father-in-law died or was ill did the oldest brother-in-law (two cases) or the mother-in-law (one case) took over the father-in-law's role. It was also the man's job to go to the market. The daughter-in-law did not have the right to dispose of domestic animals or vegetables not even for household consumption without her mother-in-law's permission. In almost everything, the daughter-in-law had to ask for permission or simply follow latter's commands.

The situation in the 1940s was not much different from that of the 1930s, according to fourteen women in the village who were young brides during this period. Women were still excluded from the ownership and management of the family property. While the father-in-law was alive, he owned and managed the family property. When he died or the married couple formed branch families, the husband took control of the family property. When the husband died, if there was a son, he inherited the family property, and the wife could only express her opinion to the son when he decided to sell them.

Through the 1940s, the only way to obtain cash in village life was through the sale of domestic animals or agricultural products. Since women were not allowed to engage in marketing activities, even for the vegetables they grew, they did not have "a chance to touch cash with hands," according to women in the village. One woman said, when she had to sell products from her dry field in order to educate her son, she had to go to the market in secret early in the morning before any villagers woke up to spot her. If any of the elderly members of her deceased husband's family learned about her marketing activities, they would feel she had damaged the family's grace.

(2) 1950s

Changes in the management of family affairs and the family roles began to change in the 1950s. According to the interviews with fifteen couples who married in the 1950s and lived in extended or stem families, not only the fathers-in-law (five cases) but also the mothers-in-law (five cases) managed family finances, product sales, or purchases of commodities. In the case of branch families (two cases), the wife rather than the husband managed the family finances. However, the male head of the family, such as the father-in-law, oldest brother-in-law, or husband, still controlled the ownership of family real estate.

In the case of fourteen other women, who had been married longer than the previous group, in stem families (six cases), the father-in-law (three cases) owned and managed the family estate while he was alive. When he died, either the mother-in-law (one case) or the husband (two cases) took over those rights. As for marketing agricultural products and managing cash, not only the father-in-law (two cases) or the husband (two cases) but also the wife (two cases) participated. In branch families (eight cases), either the husband (five cases) or the wife (three cases) engaged in marketing products and managing cash; however, the family real estate was still managed by the husband. Thus, it was in the 1950s that the right to manage the household economy began to be handed down to younger generations or middle-aged women.

This was due, in large part, to the outbreak of the Korean War in 1950. The villagers began to have more contact with the outside world through refuges or people from other villages who sought shelter in the southern provinces. The *Golma-eul* people also began to take more trips outside the village, unlike in the past when they were economically self-sufficient and carried out most of their daily activities within the village. Women also became free to go to the market for the purchase of consumer goods, such as clothes, soap, and containers.

(3) 1960s

In the 1960s, rural villages experienced drastic socio-economic changes, as people migrated to the city, wage labor became available, and the income of rural households increased. The wife's responsibilities expanded to include agricultural work, such as the production of grains, formerly the work of men, in addition to housework. However, women were still not given ownership or management rights over the family property. Among eleven women, who began their married life in the 1960s, eight women said their father-in-law (six cases) or eldest brother-in-law (two cases) were in charge of the family property as was their right as head of the stem or extended family. In three branch families, the husband had ownership and management rights for the family property.

However, as the agricultural activities of women increased,

women also began to manage the household income, and their influence within the family increased. After one or two years of marriage, most women actively participated in both agricultural production and management of the family income. The contributions to the family income by women were finally being recognized as a benefit for the family.

Women, especially mothers-in-law and older sisters-in-law, freely made trips to the market for the purchase of commodities, although men still purchased goods directly related to rice cultivation, such as agricultural machines, seeds, and fertilizers. Among six women, who lived with married children in three-generation families, two women stated that they managed the cash for the family, and one woman said that her daughter-in-law took that role in the family. In branch families with children, wives (six cases) rather than husbands (three cases) managed the household income. The strict gender division of roles in purchasing consumer goods was disappearing, especially among young couples who formed branch families.

In the 1960s, young couples began to move out of stem or extended families and form nuclear families after two or three years of marriage, shortening the period their income from agricultural activities went to members of their stem or extended families. Once young couples formed branch families, wives rather than husbands managed the household income. Sometimes arguments erupted in branch families when couples disagreed on how much economic support they should give to the members of stem or extended families. Younger sons tended to feel less responsible for his family of origin than the eldest son.

(4) 1970s and 1980s

In the 1970s women's participation in agricultural production expanded even more. According to the interviews with thirteen women, who married in the 1970s, women were now responsible for managing the family economy and making decisions on consumption for the family, although men still owned and managed the family real estate.[14] In six of the seven nuclear families, the wife was in charge of managing the family finances, and, in five of the six stem families, the mother-in-law was responsible. Among eleven women who were married by the 1970's, nine women said they managed family's finances.

By the 1980s, management of family finances became the woman's responsibility, except the sale of agricultural products for a large sum of money. In general, men were in charge of the consignment of products with the agricultural co-op and managing the money it earned. However, after one woman's suggestion on the sale of potatoes at the market brought more money than her husband's plan for consignment with the co-op, the village women began to raise their voices in more decision-making processes and resented that their husbands did not listen to their advice

---

14 The definition of family as a unit of production and consumption differed, depending on the position of family members. From the wife's point of view, "the family" meant the husband's family of origin, if he was the eldest son of the family. If the husband was a younger son, the family included only members of his nuclear family. From the eldest son's point of view, however, the family included his parents and members of his nuclear family, even when he formed branch families.

because they were women. The behavior of one woman created the momentum for change in the sale of agricultural products in the village when she did not follow the traditional norm that "the wife must follow the husband's opinion."

Young women increasingly participated in agricultural work, and assumed responsibility for managing the household economy earlier in their marriage. Even when they lived in stem families with their parents-in-law, the wife began to manage the household economy and to assume homemaking responsibilities after two or three years of marriage. Daughters-in-law believed they worked harder when they were responsible for running the household, because their own livelihood depended on them. Mothers-in-law also preferred to hand over the household responsibilities to their daughters-in-law, believing that "younger people were better than older people in thinking and working." In nuclear families, wives took the responsibility of managing the family's economy as a matter of course and actively engaged in a full range of activities, including production, consumption, and management of income.

As the Korean society moved into a stage of full-fledged industrialization and economic development, the overall economic situation of families improved and parents began to pay more attention to their children's welfare and future. One village woman said, "Parents did not feel tired from strenuous agricultural work when they thought about children's wellbeing." Parents believed their children's future was crucial to the family, and they were committed to sacrifice for them. Mothers especially tended to invest large amounts of energy and money in their children, who could give them emotional comfort and security in old age. It was important for women in a patriarchal society like South Korea where a woman's access to economic resources was limited (Browner 1986; Wolf 1972).

In most families of the 1980s, the wife and the husband managed various incomes separately and respected each other's right to do so. The wife usually managed the savings from the sale of rice and potatoes, which brought the largest sum of money to the family, and cash from the sale of vegetables, such as cucumber, young radish, cabbage and red pepper. The wife and husband usually made decisions on expenditures together, although the wife had increasingly more rights in managing the family economy as she managed the living expenses for the entire family.

4. Conclusion

In traditional Korean families, men were valued as agricultural producers and were responsible for the family's livelihood. They had an important role in determining family succession, who should continue the family line. Women were excluded from the production of valuable grains and engaged in the production of goods for everyday consumption. The husband, as the head of the family, produced and controlled important resources to maintain and develop the family's status, and he had more authority in the family than the wife. He had a range of rights regarding the family's economy, including production and consumption of goods, ownership and management of real estate, and absolute power over family members.

Traditionally, the husband was considered the protector of the wife, and the wife was dependent on and subservient to the husband, following his commands and living "under his shadow." The wife was recognized as a social being only by the husband, and was referred to as someone's wife rather than by her given name. Even when a husband was unable or too lazy to carry out his role as the primary income earner for the family, he still expected respect from his family members. In contrast, if the wife was negligent or unable to carry out her role as a homemaker, she was criticized as "a lazy woman who was ignorant about homemaking."

Both the wife and the husband worked hard to support the family, and they did not question their roles. The wife was expected to practice feminine virtues, such as hard work and sacrifice for the family, while the husband was immediately rewarded for his work with respect from and authority over his family members. Evaluation of and compensation for a woman's work occurred later in her life, many decades after she had devoted and sacrificed herself for her children, husband, and in-laws.

In the 1980s, changes occurred in rural areas in the sphere of agricultural production and family life. Nuclear families became more common, and both the husband and wife engaged in agricultural production due to a labor shortage. The couple worked as partners in agricultural activities and took complementary roles in daily family life.

Crops, which could be exchanged for cash, were not limited

to grains, such as rice and barley, but included a variety of dry field crops as well. The diversification of agricultural production increased the need for women to participate in the labor force, and the production and marketing of vegetables by women was valued as much as men's work in rice production. New marketing methods of agricultural products increased the income of rural families, and women's marketing activities, i.e., taking products to the daybreak market (*saebyeoksijang*), became a valued source of additional income.

As younger generations began to make more income from non-agricultural economic activities, the status of the male head of the household as an agricultural producer weakened. The husband's role changed from "a hard-working agricultural worker who supported the family" to "someone who did both good agricultural work and good homemaking." The wife now demanded the husband's participation in housework, while she was expected to be "a good income earner" more than "a good housewife."

The hierarchical structure of the family did not change in form, and the husband still occupied the top position as head of the family. In reality, however, the power and authority of the husband weakened, while the wife's status was strengthened in the family. As the wife began to have opportunities to work in a factory or a service industry as a wage worker outside the village, she was regarded as "someone who worked the hardest in the family" or as "someone critical for the family's survival." Women were proud of their contribution to the family economy through wage labor.

With the double burden of homemaking and agricultural work, women in rural areas contributed to the family income, which brought additional benefits to the family members. Although women's work became valued and their status improved in the family, women were still excluded from the ownership of immovable family properties and did not have the right to manage them. Furthermore, women's agricultural activities were still not considered an occupation but more an extension of housework or a wife's duty to her husband, the agricultural managers in the family.

Today, the double burden of homemaking and agricultural work does not appeal to many young Korean women, and many avoid marrying men from the countryside. An increasing number of these young or middle-aged men have trouble finding life partners who are willing to accept the rigors of village life, and so many look for women outside Korea, especially Southeast Asian countries.

References

Bae, Y.-D. (2008). Han-guk nong-eop geundaehwa-e ttareun nong-chonmun-hwaui byeondong (Changes of rural culture in the modernization of Korean agriculture; in Korean). *Studies in Agricultural History* 7(1): 49-79.

Browner, C. H. (1986). Gender Roles and Social Change: A Mexican Case Study. *Ethnology* 5(2): 89-106.

Byon, W. S. (1993). Han-guk nongchongajokui gujowa kineung byeonhwa (Changes in Structure and Function of Korean Rural Families; in Korean). *Nongchonsahoe (Rural Society)* 2: 127-155.

Chang, H. S. (1993). Han-guk sahoeneun haekgajokhwahago inneunga: gajokjeongchaekui baljeoneul wihan gichoyeon-gu (Are Korean Families Nuclearized?: A Study for Development of Family Policies; in Korean). *Han-guk geunhyeondae gajokui jaejomyeong (Reflections on Modern and*

Contemporary Korean Families; in Korean), pp. 42-80. Seoul: Munhak kwa jiseong-sa.

Cho, S.-Y. (1998). Nongchon gajok guseongui byeonhwawa gajoknong saengsanhyeongtae (Change of Rural Family and Forms of Production of Family Farm; in Korean). *Korean Cultural Anthropology* 31(1): 151-187.

Choi, J. S. (1966). *Han-guk gajok yeon-gu (A Study on Korean Families*; in Korean). Seoul: Minjungsokwan.

Han, N. J. (1985). Han-guk gajokjedoui byeonhwa: Gajokyuhyeonggwa gajokyeokhaleul jungsimeuro (Changes in Korean Family System: A Study on Family Patterns and Familial Roles; in Korean). *Han-guk sahoeui byeonhwawa baljeon (Change and Development of Korean Society)*, pp. 411-430. Seoul: Bommunsa.

Kim, H. S. (1994). Nong-gaui saengsan-gwa jaesaengsaneseoui yeoseongnodong (Women's Labor in Production and Reproduction of Rural Families; in Korean). *Han-guk sahoehak (Korean Sociology)* 28(winter): 139-161.

Kim, J. H. (1992). *Pumassiwa jeongui ingangwangye (Pumatsi and Warm-Heartedness in Social Relationships*; in Korean). Seoul: Jipmundang.

Kim, J. H. (2006). Nongchongaguyuhyeong-ui byeonhwawa gajoksaengjonjeollyak: Gyeonggi-do Sanjinma-eul-e daehan jaejosagyeolgwareul jungsimeuro (Changes of Household Patterns and the Family Survival Strategy in a Rural Korean Village: A Re-Study of Sanjin Village in Gyeonggi Province; in Korean). *Nongchon sahoe (Rural Society)* 16(2): 119-150.

Kong, S. K. (1987). *Han-guk gajok jeongchaek-ui byeonhwa (Changes in Korean Family Policies*; in Korean). Seoul: Research Center for Population and Public Health.

Kwon, T. W. (1992). Ingu byeondonggwa nongchonsahoeui byeonhwa (Changes in Population and Rural Societies; in Korean). *Nongchonwahoe (Rural Society)* 1: 39-56.

Lee, H. J. (1971). *Dosiui chinjokgwangye (Kinship Relations in Cities*; in Korean). Seoul: Korean Research Center.

Park, B.-J. (1994a). Han-guk nongchon gajokui munhwajeok uimiwa gajok gwangyeui byeonhwae gwanhan yeon-gu (Changes in Cultural Meanings and Family Relationships of the Korean Rural Family; in Korean). Ph. D.

Dissertation, Seoul National University, Seoul.

Park, B.-J. (1994b). Jeonhwangi han-guk nongchon sahoeui gajok yuhyeong (Family Structure in a Changing Rural Village in Korea; in Korean). *Han-guk munhwa inryuhak (Korean Cultural Anthropology)* 26: 157-201.

Son, H.-S. (2002). Jeonnam jiyeokui nongchon nodongnyeok byeonhwa-e gwanhan yeon-gu (1982-2002) (A study on the Rural Labor Change in *Jeonnam* Region (1982-2002); in Korean). *Han-guk jiyeok gaebal hakhoeji (Korean Regional Development)* 14(3): 43-60.

Son, H.-S. (2007). 24 nyeon dong-an nongchon nodong-nyeok byeonhwa siltaee gwanhan josa yeon-gu (A Study on the Rural Labor Change in *Jeonnam* Region for Twenty Four Years; in Korean). *Nong-eop jeongchaek yeon-gu (Korean Journal of Agricultural Management and Policy)* 34(4): 887-908

Wolf, M. (1972). *Woman and the Family in Rural Taiwan.* Stanford: Stanford University Press.

Chapter six

Urban Family Relationships in the Rapidly Industrializing Korean Society[1]

Kim, Myung-hye (Chonnam National University)

1. Introduction

The South Korean economy has experienced rapid and intense industrialization, since the government launched the first Five Year Economic Development Plan (hereafter referred to as FYEDP) in 1962. The Korean society has transformed itself from an agriculture-based to a dynamic industrial economy within one generation and has been praised internationally for its accomplishment of an "economic miracle" in such a short period of time. The effects of late-industrial capitalist development have been immense not only economically

---

1 Discussions of this chapter are dependent on the author's previous works (Kim 1992, 1993, 1995, 1996).

but also culturally. The development of industrial capitalism, however, did not eliminate patriarchy, which was well-established before the introduction of capitalism in Korea. Family ideologies based on patriarchy were carried over into capitalist forms of labor and transformed underlying structures of gender and age.

This chapter deals with class and gender relationships, which have been affected by Korea's industrialization during an intense period in the 1970's and 1980's. Specifically, it explores the effects of industrial capitalist development on upper-middle-class families in Seoul, and the dynamic interrelationships among their members. With systematic attention to gender and age variables, it investigates the ways in which the structure of upper-middle-class families have been transformed, compared to their low-class counterparts, as industrial capitalism has progressed in the Korean society. There has been little research conducted on upper-middle-class families for various reasons, yet, they have been highly visible in urban South Korea. They have been economically and culturally dominant, have been identified as a symbol of the nation's economic progress, and have been considered as role models for lower-class families.

The chapter examines family structure and relationships and investigates how families of the upper-middle class have functioned as holders of patriarchal ideology and "shock absorbers" in a rapidly industrializing, capitalistic society. It demonstrates how industrialization has not destroyed the Confucian foundations of patriarchy but has transformed them by the spread of wage labor and public education. Industrial capitalism has developed conditions for the decreasing importance of kinship structures, but these structures have nonetheless remained in a modified form. And, those modified patriarchal structures are manifested differently, depending on the class position of the family.

This chapter analyzes three major relationships of upper-middle-class families, which include wife-husband, child-parent, and daughter-in-law and mother-in-law relationships. It pays special attention to the power structure of families and diverse strategies through which gender and class ideologies are represented in interactions among members. This chapter also examines specific forms and contents of patriarchy, which lie in relations of reproduction located within upper-middle-class families in urban South Korea.

The discussion of this chapter is based on the ethnographic research of seventy-two upper-middle-class families and intensive interviews with the wives of those families, which the author conducted in Seoul in 1990.[2] While the sample may not be fully representative of families of the same social class, they share a range of socio-economic indicators, such as husband's income and occupation, ownership of property, residence size, monthly household budget, wife's educational level, and family lifestyle. Narratives of the women interviewed also reveal their class positions, family ideology, and the nature of their work.[3]

---

2 This chapter discusses the situation Korean families encountered up to 1990 when my ethnographic research was conducted. Considering that the speed of economic and cultural changes in South Korea has accelerated in the last two decades, I added discussions on some of the more recent changes among Korean urban families throughout the chapter.
3 For detailed discussions on the family backgrounds of upper-middle-class families and narratives of the wives of these families, refer to Kim (1992, 1993).

2. Late-Industrialization, Families, and Classes in South Korea

Intense and rapid late-industrialization in South Korea began after colonial industrialization under the Japanese rule (1910-1945) was abruptly ended and economic chaos followed the Korean War (1950-1953). The government launched the first FYEDP in 1962 and began to aggressively engage in developing urban-centered, export-oriented manufacturing industries. Through a series of FYEDP,[4] the authoritarian interventionist state provided subsidies for private firms in order to stimulate their economic activities, while, at the same time, it exercised its influence over areas from productivity standards to managing labor.

The nation's rapid industrialization mobilized and incorporated a large proportion of labor into the export sector of production for the maintenance of international economic competitiveness. As the manufacturing sector of the national economy increasingly contributed to the gross national product, both the proportion and number of industrial workers increased faster than those in the tertiary sector between 1960 and 1990.[5] Women, in particular, have been incorporated into the export-oriented, labor-intensive

---

4 Between 1962 and 1981, 4 FYEDP's were implemented. After 1982, FYEDP was renamed as Five Year Economic and Social Development Plan, and incorporated social components into the development plan in order to narrow a gap between the rich and the poor. South Korea's GNP per capita has grown from 62 US dollars in 1962 to 6,757 US dollars in 1991, more than 100 times in three decades. GDP per capita is 27,169 US dollars in 2009.

5 For detailed discussion on the characteristics of South Korea's industrialization, which are contrasted to other developing countries, refer to Kim (1992).

industrialization process at a faster rate than men. Young, un-married women, who migrated to the city from the countryside in order to "give their younger brothers an education" or just relieve the economic burden of their parents, were recruited for ultra-long working hours, yet low pay (Kim 1992).

Industrialization has increased not only the number of factory workers but also that of office workers, yet with heterogeneity and differentiation of status among workers. Female workers have rapidly been recruited in business firms related to light manufacturing for low-level clerical work, while male workers have moved into higher level white-collar jobs. Well-educated men have occupied a large proportion of white-collar jobs for economic innovation and execution as managers or engineers. In contrast, highly educated women, however, have persistently been excluded from those well-paid, high-status jobs. The Korean government has generously rewarded educated managers and engineers, who have been successful in raising shop-floor productivity, for their contribution to the nation's economic expansion. And, the majority of male heads of upper-middle-class families were beneficiaries of the government's generosity.[6]

South Korea's industrial capitalism has been based on a patri-archal, segmented labor-market structure and prevailing cultural prescription that a woman's primary responsibility is to serve the family. Marriage has been a barrier to women's participation

---

6 They are managers or executives of private companies (47 %), professionals (14 %), high-level government officials (7 %), entrepreneurs (26 %), and other (7 %).

in the formal sector of the national economy and has led them to involuntary resignation from wage labor under the pressure of employers or family members.[7] Contrary to the argument of human capital, women's educational background has been considered as important, not so much for their potential wage earning capability or economic independence but for the social grace they bring to their husbands and the social status they bring to the family. Especially in upper-middle-class families where resources are relatively abundant, the wife's employment is assumed to contribute little to the family finances. Rather, the important role for women, which is to maintain the harmony and integrity of the family, is stressed, and their employment after marriage is even viewed as a stigma to the family status.[8] Well-educated wives are pressed to engage in supporting the labor activities of other family members and concentrate on household management.

The process of export-driven, industrialization penetrates families of different social strata and constantly deepens the gulf between social classes. Upper-middle-class families are the suppliers of well-educated managers or engineers for the export sector of large, private companies and public enterprises in the national economy. Male heads of upper-middle-class families are generously rewarded for their successful management and productivity by the

---

7 While 79 % of college-graduated women in upper-middle-class families identified themselves as full-time housewives at the time of the interview, 71 % had white-collar jobs, as office administrators (49 %), schoolteachers (39 %), and the like (12 %) prior to marriage.

8 Wives' employment can be translated as a sign their husbands do not make enough money to afford having their wives stay at home.

state or by private enterprises in terms of job security and salary. Low-class families, on the other hand, are constantly excluded from full participation in building the mainstream national economy and suffer from low wages, unstable employment, and work-related diseases and accidents (Kim 1995).[9]

3. Upper-Middle-Class Families in Seoul

Many scholars suggest that as a society experiences industrialization, families no longer carry out production functions and become nuclear. Scholars are divided into two groups in characterizing the process of nuclearization of families: one emphasizes negative aspects and the other stresses positive aspects (Kim 1996). Marxist scholars like Engels (1985 [1884]) and Kuhn (1978), for example, argue that the industrial, capitalistic economy is based on a particular gender division of labor within the nuclear family, where women who do unpaid household work depend upon men who do paid work outside the home. Scholars of modernization theory, on the other hand, emphasize the positive effects of industrialization on family life, and posit a natural evolution from the complex family to the nuclear family and from male-dominated to egalitarian values in the family (Jaquette 1982; Rosen and LaRaia 1972).

Whatever the reason is, this scheme of nuclearization of the

---

9 For more detailed comparison between the families of different social classes in urban South Korea, refer to Kim (1995).

family in industrial societies appears to be applicable to South Korea in terms of an overall statistical distribution of family forms. The proportion of nuclear families in a sample of the upper-middle-class is 85 %, slightly larger than the national average (80 %). Although there is a trend toward nuclearization of the family in South Korea, its dynamics require much more attention, compared to Western counterparts.

In the following sections, this study will address three major relationships among the members of upper-middle-class families: relationships between the wife and the husband, between children and parents, and between the daughter-in-law and the mother-in-law. It will examine the changing family dynamics brought on by recent industrialization and urbanization processes in South Korea and present specific forms in which patriarchal principles are manifested in contemporary, industrializing South Korea. It will explore the ways in which patriarchal ideologies interplay with late-industrial capitalism by focusing on the three sets of family relationships (Kim 1996).

1) Wife-Husband Relationship

During the Yi Dynasty (1392-1910), when patriarchal ideology became firmly rooted, Korea was a society organized on the basis of patrilineal descent groups. The stated purpose of marriage was to guarantee the uninterrupted continuation of the lineage retrospectively by securing ancestor worship services and prospectively by bringing forth male offspring (Deuchler 1992).

Marriage was an institution that weakened the conjugal bond and accorded particular importance to the parent-son relationship. The marital union was arranged by relatives or matchmakers and was asymmetrical. The man was the successor of the family, while the woman joined him as a newcomer in order to help him carry out his role as a representative of the family (Kim 1996).

The ideology of marriage changed as the society became industrialized and "modernized." In the upper-middle-class families of urban South Korea, love-marriage, based on egalitarianism and companionship between the couple, is replacing arranged marriage by matchmakers or relatives. And, marriage is viewed as a process where individual attributes, such as occupation and educational level, are negotiated in order to determine and maintain the social status of the future family partners form together (Kim 1993). Although family backgrounds and parents' opinions are still considered as influencing factors in marriage decisions, individual attributes, personality, and feelings of companionship between potential lifetime partners are emphasized as more important. The paradoxical reality is that woman's education is valued as a means to maintain social grace for husbands and to provide quality education for children rather than to enhance mutual understanding with the spouse or self-development for women themselves (Kim 1992).[10] Educated housewives are in turn provided with economic security by their husbands. In the contemporary upper middle-class

---

10 There is a popular notion that the degree requirement for women who want to marry lawyers or medical doctors has been upgraded from a B.A. to M.A. in recent years.

families of urban South Korea the new form of patriarchal family co-exists with the ideology of egalitarian, companionate marriage (Kim 1993).

The family has different meanings for husband than wife in the upper-middle class. While the husband believes that the family is important for his emotional comfort, the wife sees the family as a site where she can obtain economic security through her service work to other members (Kim 1992). Contrary to the arguments of the human capital model and modernization theory, upper-middle-class women do not show a positive relationship between educational endowment and labor-force participation. Nor do they show an inverse relationship between fertility rate and labor-force participation. Although they have college diplomas and relatively small numbers of children to care for, they do not participate in the paid economy as much as their lower-class counterparts (Kim 1992).[11]

Upper-middle-class women are encouraged to stay at home and take full responsibility for social reproduction, by supporting labor activities for workers (husbands) and future workers (children) and providing personalized services to them, in and out of the home. While men are responsible for providing the main income for the family, women carry out a range of tasks as housewives. Their major tasks include child education, "status-production" work, and personalized services to family members.[12] They tend

---

11 Only 21 % of the women have full time (8 %) or part-time (13 %) jobs. This labor force participation rate is much lower than the national average for the entire female population (47 %) in 1990 in South Korea.

12 For more detailed discussions on upper-middle-class women's work, refer to Kim (1992).

to devote themselves to socializing their children and supervising their studies as highly educated, "education mothers." Women engage in unpaid labor activities, which affect the ability of the family to maintain and enhance its status, such as gift exchange, informal economic activities, and social activities for gathering and disseminating information. They also provide various personalized services to family members in the name of homemaking and home management. Those services include big and elaborate feasts, which they prepare for their husbands' employees throughout the year,[13] and an occasional help for their husbands'.[14]

Wives of upper-middle-class families took this act of laboring for family members at home with ambivalent attitudes. On the one hand, they felt relieved and lucky that tradition had not yet changed to impose on them demanding income-earning responsibilities in an increasingly competitive public sphere (Kim 1992). On the other hand, they were resentful that they had lost self-confidence as potential professional workers after they had been pressured to carry out the traditional roles and responsibilities of decent wives, mothers, and daughters-in-law at home. Wives believe their knowledge from college was obsolete after several years of childbearing and

---

13 Korean lifestyles have changed so rapidly since 1990 that it is more common to invite people out to restaurants than to provide them with homemade dishes. Housewives resist having feasts at home, considering them too labor-intensive and too much of a burden on themselves.
14 Some women are recruited frequently for their husbands' businesses on an informal basis to do administrative work at home, to help out in offices or factories when there are labor shortages, and to manage their husbands' moonlighting jobs. In these cases the importance of women's role as "a good wife" and team player of the couple are emphasized (Kim 1993).

childrearing and reentry into the labor force or systematic job-training provisions are limited or simply unavailable for married women like them (Kim 1992).

Many women believe their husbands are dedicated, hard workers, and think it is unreasonable to ask their husbands to be involved in housework when they come home exhausted from work. The men's neglect of homemaking responsibilities is justified by their need, as primary income earners, to support families, while women's dependence on men and their dedication to running a smooth household is emphasized (Kim 1993). This allows men to concentrate on wage-earning and career-building without interrupting the rapid process of industrialization in the South Korean economy.

Patriarchal, late-industrial capitalism assumes that consumerism and affluence can replace, or at least reduce, women's work. Upper-middle-class husbands compare their economic capabilities for paying housemaids' fees and providing luxurious labor-saving devices with sharing homemaking responsibilities with their wives. They felt that the little bit of housework left over by housemaids and household appliances would give their "idle" wives something to do (Kim 1992). Women take this act of laboring for family members at home as a victory rather than a defeat in responding to the impersonal processes of industrialization (Turnaturi 1987).

In a rapidly industrializing society, good family administration and fulfillment of private life are not only useful to the national economy but also complementary to it. As impersonal industrial capitalism requires the transformation of the older order and social structure and as the paternalistic state increasingly intrudes into every area of life, the family becomes a haven from the competitive, external world of male workers. In South Korea, a long tradition of Confucian sex segregation still remains to the extent that the responsibility for providing emotional and moral support to family members "naturally" falls to women. Working long hours with heavy responsibilities for national-economy building, as professionals and high-level executives of large companies, husbands of the upper-middle-class families felt they deserved to be free from other trivial responsibilities, such as homemaking and childrearing (Kim 1992). In the meantime, the state secures dedicated, high-level, white-collar workers for the development of the national economy by giving the men and their families high salaries, social recognition, and prestige (Amsden 1989).

Although upper-middle-class men exercise their authority as major wage earners by not allowing their wives to work outside the home, women establish their own domains of autonomy and influence in the management of family finances, socialization of the children, and maintenance of the family status. Sexual segregation of white-collar husbands and housewives among upper-middle-class families does not necessarily mean that women are confined to private roles and men to public roles. Unlike in traditional Korean society, where the male head of household dealt with public institutions as representatives of the family, contemporary upper-middle-class women take care of such matters with household registrars offices, tax offices, and banks almost on a daily basis. They also participate in communal activities, all in the name of homemaking and household management. It is a paradox that the importance of women's work is recognized by family members and the society, yet only as complementary to men's work (Kim 1993).

2) Child-Parent Relationship

Upper-middle-class families are child-centered and mother-dominant. Highly educated mothers have ultimate control over the children — their discipline, education, and achievement — and bear the burden of child socialization and education. In contrast, fathers believe that their responsibility to the children ends when they hand over their monthly salary to their wives for the children's educational expenses as the primary wage earner.

Daily schedules of the mothers of upper-middle-class families are organized around the children's education. As described in detail in Kim (1992), those "education mothers" gather information about various educational materials, including books and audio and visual materials, and purchase them for the children as early as just after the children are born. They believe that those materials provide "a natural environment" for children to learn basic skills and a second language like English. They organize private lessons for their preschool children and send their older children everyday to three or four different kinds of extracurricular tutoring, such as piano, swimming, martial arts, and calligraphy, in addition to advanced lessons for regular school subjects like math, science, and language.[15] While children are in school or with private tutors, mothers are busy spending time with other "education mothers" at restaurants, shopping centers, or health clubs, maintaining and strengthening relationships with them. They believe that social networks among mothers of the same social class are crucial for the children's success in school in order to exchange valuable information on schools, teachers, grades, tutors, and other child-education methods, as well as ensuring proper future marriage partners for children (Kim 1992).

Upper-middle-class mothers are keenly aware of the importance of schooling for their children's economic futures, because they themselves have achieved their present social status partly through formal-educational attainments. Credentials from prestigious colleges, especially for boys, have led to a fast track of good and secure employment and have offered possibilities for leadership positions in the national economy. Given a labor market segmented by sex, credentials for girls have been related to their value in the marriage market, more than in the labor market. Thus, for either boys or girls, education has contributed to the competitive advantage of upper-middle-class families, in terms of greater access to resources as future workers or lifetime partners (Kim 1992).

The mother's role as thorough planner and organizer of the children's education seems to work against paid work and self-development. Once a mother's daily schedule is filled with activities

---

15 Parents believe that children, who master the subjects one year or so ahead of schools' regular schedules have a competitive advantage in entering prestigious colleges.

for children — preparing snacks, taking children to various tutors, extracurricular activities, and so on — little energy and time are left for wage-earning activities or career development. Moreover, mothers are discouraged by their husbands, who are concerned that working mothers would not have enough time for the children and, then, the children would not do well in school (Kim 1992).

The upper-middle-class families adopt a traditional ideology of motherhood, which emphasizes the role of married women as a wise and caring mother. In the contemporary late-industrial society, mothers invest their wisdom and care mainly in helping their children excel at school and guiding them for future economic and social success (Kim 1992). Many mothers stretch their physical and mental abilities to their limit in carrying out these roles, yet they are not supposed to disengage themselves from this maternal labor, which is viewed as valuable yet invisible (Papanek 1989). With little help from their husbands, mothers take over the increasing burden of socializing future workers, which is now shared less with other institutions such as a wider kin group or the government. Mothers are often caught between their husbands' un-involvement in childrearing and child education and the lack of state support for children's education in an increasingly competitive capitalistic world.

In the past, a mother's sole joy in life was for her son to grow up and support her, guaranteeing her comfort when she was old (Lee 1975; Yim 1987). The mother had a responsibility to work hard for the welfare of her son, who depended upon her support and help for his future success and status. In the industrial Korean society, the ideology of motherhood has expanded, and the mother is expected to be dedicated not only to the son's but also the daughter's socialization and education. However, unlike in the past, the mother is not automatically rewarded by children's filial piety or her old-age security. Furthermore, working for the children is not necessarily related to her self-esteem or postponed gratification (Kim 1993).

Changing forms of families accompany shifting relationships among family members in such a way that the interdependency between parents and children decreases, and the bond between mother and son, based on mutual emotional support, weakens. The mother's influence over the son decreases, as he chooses his own spouse instead of by arrangement of the parents. The mother's sense of security also diminishes with the likelihood that the eldest (or even the only) son will not stay with her, as individualism grows stronger among the younger generation. Now, many eldest sons and their wives refuse to form a stem family with their parents and negotiate to live with the parents only for a year or two if the parents insist, as discussed in a later section (Kim 1993).[16]

Both parents and children are calculative in the arrangement of parents' old age. Even when they have only one son, parents of upper-middle class families prepare themselves with savings, so they can be independent from him economically as well as

---

16 Emotional bonds between the mother and the daughter has been strengthened in recent years, and young professional women prefer their mothers to their mothers-in-law for help with childrearing and family management.

emotionally in old age (Kim 1993). Parents postpone passing their money or property to their children until they die, fearing the children would refuse to support them once they received their inheritance.

Unlike parents in lower-class or rural families, who tend to equate child education with the investment in land (Yoon 1989), upper-middle-class parents are keenly aware of the irony of the changing processes that tend to undercut the collective ideology of the family. While they have successfully achieved economic and social status as beneficiaries of the rapid industrialization and modernization of society, they have also become practitioners of modern values in family life, such as individualism, free choice, and mutual agreement. Although parents are able to invest in their children's education, they do not have expectations for their old age security or a sense of collective identity from their children (Kim 1993).

The ideology of continuity and harmony in upper-middle-class families is emphasized for the maintenance of social status, which is viewed as dependent upon sharing resources among extended kin. Inheritance has a broader meaning in upper-middle class culture and includes not only handed-down family properties but also education, individual ability, and hard work, because individuals are able to gain those resources with the guidance of parents and the support of other extended kin members (Kim 1993).

Similar to Rapp's study on American families (Rapp 1991), sharing is a norm of kin behavior in South Korea, but it is a hard norm to live by. To comply with the demands of the extended family completely is to lose control over material and emotional resources of the nuclear family. To refuse is very dangerous, as family members lose face, especially in a society with a long tradition of intricate patronage. In this process, upper-middle-class women become the nodal points in extended family networks that the nuclear family utilizes as resources for the maintenance and enhancement of its social status. The image of dependent and weak wives co-exists with the image of socially motivated mothers who have a strong influence over family matters, including children's education and the maintenance of extended kin networks (Kim 1993).

3) Daughter-in-law and Mother-in-law Relationship

The relationship between daughter-in-law and mother-in-law has changed in contemporary South Korea compared with the traditional relationship based on patriarchal Confucian ideology, which was adopted as a state ideology during the Yi Dynasty. In the traditional patriarchal, patrilineal Korean family system, the son was regarded as "property" of the family, while the daughter was viewed as an outsider as she married (*chulgaoein*). The son was to maintain the family name, honor, and values transmitted by the father. The son was expected to repay his debt of gratitude by being dutiful to the parents (*hyo*) and accepting the father's authority and the mother's love. Especially the eldest son had the responsibility to sustain an unbroken patrilineal family link by carrying out ancestral worships, supporting aging parents, and providing male heirs to the family (Yim 1987). In contrast, the bride, who married into her husband's family, occupied the lowest position in the family and was expected to obey all of the family members. She was pressured to conform to the husband's family customs and, most importantly, give birth to a son who would be a future successor of the family (Lee 1975).

The traditional, patriarchal family was a site where domination and exploitation of the mother-in-law over the daughter-in-law occurred. According to the Confucian rule of hierarchical order by age, the mother-in-law had a right to supervise the daughter-in-law's domestic activities and even punish her wrongdoings. At the same time, the mother-in-law felt threatened by the daughter-in-law, as she viewed the latter as a competitor for her achieved status in the family, an invader in her territory of daily homemaking activities, and an attacker of her cherished bond with the son. *Sijipsari* was an open form of conflict and tension between the two women in the family and had many forms of abuse and coercion, which have provided a rich repertoire for Korean folktales, novels, axioms, and testimonies (Kim 1996).

Upper-middle-class families in contemporary South Korea show a strong tendency toward neolocal, post-marital residence patterns, unlike traditional high-class families. A small number of newly wedded couples move into the groom's parents' house, and they live with the parents during an early stage of marriage and later move out to form a branch family. In this case, the groom is usually the eldest son of the family and creates a stem family similar to a traditional one, yet only for a couple of years, unlike in the past when he lived with the parents until they died (Kim 1996).[17] Eldest sons, who live with parents in the early stage of marriage, consider these living arrangements as temporary and stay with them for convenience, not so much because of filial obligation. For example, newly married couples, who do not have adequate places to live right away, stay with the man's parents until their new homes are built or until their contracts on condominiums are effective. Some daughters-in-law, who have full-time, professional jobs, prefer to rely on their dedicated mothers-in-law, rather than hired housemaids, for childrearing and family management and live with in-laws until their children start school (Kim 1996).

As discussed earlier in the upper-middle-class, the term, family (*jip*), has at least two levels of meaning. One is normative: husband, wife, and children live together and form a nuclear family. The other meaning includes a more extended network of kin relations that people may activate selectively. Living apart does not necessarily mean autonomy and independence for a married son and his family from his parents. He and his wife still feel responsible for the parents' well-being and provide emotional and material support for them. Nuclear families are under cultural constraints to appear as both autonomous and independent and, simultaneously, private and communal. The ideal autonomy of an independent nuclear

---

17 Among the families I interviewed in 1990, only 34 % of the married eldest sons lived with both (9 %) or one parent (25 %). Some daughters-in-law accept co-residence with an elderly, widowed parent-in-law in their later stage of marriage. In this contemporary stem family power dynamics among members differ from traditional stem family, and it is considered as the son's family rather than the parent's, because it is the elderly parent who moves into the son's family and receives care from them.

family is constantly being contrasted with the realities of extended kin networks, in which resources must be shared and faces must be saved (Kim 1993). The daughter-in-law, not the son, is the one who facilitates the ties among existing patrilineal extended kin through frequent visits and gift-exchanges.

Sometimes it is more troublesome and expensive for daughters-in-law to travel to visit parents-in-law across the city than to serve them on site by living together in a stem family. Yet many daughters-in-law prefer separate living arrangements. They believe it is still "better for everyone in the family" than having the tension and little privacy that results from co-residence out of a superficial acceptance of filial responsibility (Kim 1996). Contemporary daughters-in-law devise strategies for kin work in different ways than their mothers and grandmothers, who felt destined to serve parents-in-law as daughters-in-law.

The image of the tyrannical mother-in-law mellows as younger women acquire an achieved authority based on education over the ascribed authority of mothers-in-law.[18] Although a college education does not necessarily link young daughters-in-law to the labor market, it can be an important basis for their domestic power, especially in dealing with in-laws and defending themselves from harassment or unfair treatment by in-laws. Daughters-in-law use reasoning in their interaction with mothers-in-law, and

---

18 In recent years the educational difference between younger and older generations has narrowed, especially among the upper-middle-class, as many of the college-educated young wives interviewed for this study in 1990 had become mothers-in-law by 2010.

they are more concerned with achieving individual comfort than with conforming to public expectations. They know how to postpone or negotiate the favors requested by the mothers-in-law. In contemporary families mothers-in-law seem to be afraid of the increasing bargaining power of their daughters-in-law. Mothers-in-law exchange ideas with friends about how to manage relationships with daughters-in-law, while the latter discuss how to deal with the former at class reunions and other social occasions. Objectives for both parties are the same, that is, to avoid direct confrontation and maintain peaceful, effective extended family relationships. Neither woman can afford the negligence of traditional values, which would lead to familial ostracism and the danger of ruining the family's face (Kim 1996).

When they form stem families, contemporary daughters-in-law do not wait long after their marriage to take over the rights and roles of the housewife from the mother-in-law, unlike the case of their traditional counterparts. Some women assume their roles of housewife as soon as the first child is born. Daughters-in-law control and manage the family economy with little consultation with their mothers-in-law and even take over the *anbang* (inner room) from mothers-in-law. Contemporary mothers-in-law lose a source of great satisfaction when they lose recognition of their competence as homemakers by sons and daughters-in-law (Kim 1996).

The recent late-industrialization and modernization have not lessened the roles of homemaking but have transformed the nature of homemaking and the relationship between the daughter-in-law and mother-in-law. Modernized living conditions, such as condominium units where upper-middle-class families reside, are equipped with modern household appliances and allow women to save time and energy compared to the traditional modes of homemaking and childrearing. However, as activities of consumption and education for children expand, younger women spend more time in managing and organizing activities around the family than in the traditional family. In other words, as roles and activities for the mother-in-law shrink and those for the daughter-in-law expand, the mother-in-law loses her privilege of commanding the labor of the daughter-in-law so as to lighten her own work-load in the family (Kim 1996).

Mothers-in-law and daughters-in-law have experienced different stages of economic development and have enjoyed different fruits of social change. Less-educated mothers-in-law have been busy managing the household and working hard for the upward social mobility of the family. Daughters-in-law, on the other hand, have received higher education, with parental support, and have expanded their social networks via classmates and friends, sharing activities in art, sports, and hobbies (Kim 1996). College-educated daughters-in-law do not blindly follow their "uneducated" mothers-in-law's advice or life styles, including childrearing practices, home decor, furniture arrangement, diet, and laundry methods. Instead they are critical of them and insist on their own ways of doing things, even when they are advised to change them by their mothers-in-law.

Not all daughters-in-law are successful in their task of peace-keeping with their mothers-in-law, and conflicts between them are not simple "women problems" or women's jealousy over a man. Rather, the conflicts are complicated social issues that are derived from interaction among patriarchy, class ideology, and industrial capitalism. The economy continues to develop as it keeps highly educated, upper-middle-class women in their roles as professional homemakers who support workers (husbands) and future workers (children); it also maintains patriarchal ideology through the women's kin network.[19] In a development-oriented society, young, educated daughters-in-law are likely to take a leading role in carrying out that historic task, more so than their older and less-educated mothers-in-law. Daughters-in-law of the upper-middle-class families can not only afford to concentrate on reproductive work at home but also to present themselves as a role model for women of the lower class (Kim 1996).

4. Summary and Conclusion: Class and Gender Processes in South Korean Families[20]

The process of export-driven, late-industrialization has influenced South Korean families in diverse ways and has changed the

---

19 There has been a "silent revolution" by young, educated women in recent years, who postpone marriage or choose not to get married at all in order to develop professional careers or to not to be confined within the traditional role of homemaker and caretaker in the family. They have reduced the national birth rate to the lowest level among OECD countries. The birth rate of South Korea was 1.22 in 2010.
20 Discussion of this section is dependent on Kim (1995). Refer to Kim (1995) for more detailed comparisons of urban Korean families in different social strata.

dynamics of relationships among family members. In the late-industrializing wage-economy, it is economically possible, if not advantageous, for families to set up independent nuclear families as soon as the son marries. Urban South Korean families show an increasing tendency toward nuclearization. In contrast to Western societies (Rapp 1991), however, old kin networks co-exist in the form of virtual stem or extended families and compete with the nuclear family in the late-industrializing society. The upper-middle-class families maintain the nuclear family as a base for social status and power within the traditional gender division of labor and loyalty of its members. At the same time, they keep the boundaries of the family flexible and maintain their family status and class position through constant exchange of resources among the extended kin. On the other hand, lower-class families, which lack the resources to share with members of the wider kin group, maintain more rigid boundaries and emphasize familial loyalty and economic contributions by the nuclear family members rather than the extended kin (Kim 1995).

In industrial capitalism, families function to absorb the conflicts, contradictions, and tensions generated by the material, class-structured relations they hold to resources (Rapp 1991). Families devise diverse strategies to deal with these forces, which are potentially destructive to the welfare and existence of the family, depending on their social positions. Women, rather than men, have an important role in carrying out these strategies in urban South Korean families. In upper-middle-class families, women, as professional homemakers, provide personalized services for family members and engage in various "status production" activities for the family (Kim 1992). In lower-class families, women contribute to the family economy as income-earners, as well as managers of the family economy, and concentrate their psyche and energy on maximizing the chances for the family's survival (Kim 1995).

In the late-industrializing society, families may function as shelters for exhausted workers in the national economy, yet they represent different family ideologies and gender relations, depending on their class positions. In upper-middle-class families, in which the male is formally the head of the family and primary wage earner,[21] patriarchal ideology is transformed into a situation where women become specialized in reproducing quality workers and socializing future workers for the further development of industrial capitalism. In lower-class families, in which every able-bodied family member, including the wife of the male head of the family, is sent to work outside of the home for the reproduction of the unit, the patriarchal authority of the male family head is threatened (Kim 1995).

South Korean families represent different ideologies, not only by social class but also by gender, because classes and genders stand in different material relationships to one another (Rapp 1991). In upper-middle-class families, where economic resources allow for the preservation of the traditional gender ideology, women exchange unpaid domestic work for economic security and family

---

21 In upper-middle-class families, wives engage in various informal economic activities and help the family maintain social status. For more detailed discussion, refer to Kim (1992).

status. In lower-class families, women carry the burden of working outside the home in addition to homemaking. As a result, they both challenge and accept the patriarchal norm whereby the male head of the family is the primary wage earner and the wife is the homemaker. Women in both types of families seek to achieve a degree of independence and autonomy through their work inside and outside of the family, but they do so in different ways (Kim 1995).

A patriarchal, patrilineal family system is not outmoded in the late-industrial capitalism, but, rather, it is complementary to it. Conflicts between daughters-in-law and mothers-in-law or between nuclear families of the married son and his parents threaten not only the status of the family but also the stability of the society. In a prospering economy, survival is not a major concern of upper-middle-class families, but the maintenance of the family's status through good family management and intricate kin work is, which in turn contributes to stable functioning of the society. Educated housewives begin to question the traditional virtue of endurance and devise strategies that will not directly challenge a patriarch, the father-in-law or the husband, but to manipulate him in seeking their own independence and welfare.

Gender politics of upper-middle-class families are critical in shaping the direction and content of social change, because they have been major actors in framing dominant ideological discourses in late-industrializing South Korea (Kim 1996). Upper-middle-class families have been a mechanism to perpetuate class cleavage and gender hierarchy in the society. Socio-cultural formations of late-industrialization have made the existence of two systems of social classes and gender classes, or late-industrial capitalism and patriarchy, possible as an integrated process in families. These two structures interact and accommodate each other and determine the course of historical change in the society (Kim 1992).

References

Amsden, A. H. (1989). *Asia's Next Giant: South Korea and Late Industrialization.* New York: Oxford University Press.

Deuchler, M. (1992). *The Confucian Transformation of Korea: A Study of Society and Ideology.* Cambridge, MA: Harvard University Press.

Engels, F. (1985). *The Origin of the Family, Private Property and the State* [1884]. New York: Penguin Books.

Jaquette, J. S. (1982). Women and modernization theory: A decade of feminist criticism. *World Politics* 34(2): 267-284.

Kim, M. H. (1992). Late industrialization and women's work in urban South Korea: An ethnographic study of upper-middle-class families. *City and Society* 6(2): 156-173.

Kim, M. H. (1993). Transformation of family ideology in upper-middle-class families in urban South Korea. *Ethnology* 32(1): 69-85.

Kim, M. H. (1995). Gender, class, and family in late-industrializing South Korea. *Asian Journal of Women's Studies* 1: 58-86.

Kim, M. H. (1996). Changing relationship between daughters-in-law and mothers-in-law in urban South Korea. *Anthropological Quarterly* 69(4): 179-192.

Kuhn, A. (1978). Structures of patriarchy and capital in the family. In A. Kuhn & A. M. Wolpe (Eds.), *Feminism and Materialism: Women and Modes of Production* (pp. 42-67). London: Routledge and Kegan Paul.

Lee, K.-K. (1975). *Han-guk gajogui gujo bunseok* (A Structural Analysis of Korean Family; in Korean). Seoul: Ilji-sa.

Papaneck, H. (1987). Family Status-Production Work: Women's Contribution to

Social Mobility and Class Differentiation. In M. Krishnaraj & K. Chanana (Eds.), *Gender and the Household Domain: Social and Cultural Dimensions* (pp. 97-116). New Delhi: Sage Publications.

Rapp, R. (1991). Family and Class in Contemporary America: Notes toward an Understanding of Ideology. In E. Jelin (Ed.), *Family, Household and Gender Relations in Latin America* (pp. 197-215). London: Kegan Paul International.

Rosen, B., & LaRaia, A. (1972). Modernity in Women: An Index of Social Change in Brazil. *Journal of Marriage and the Family* 34(2): 353-360.

Turnaturi, G. (1987). Between Public and Private: The Birth of the Professional Housewife and the Female Consumer. In A. S. Sassoon (Ed.), *Women and the State: The Shifting Boundaries of Public and Private* (pp. 255-278). London: Hutchinson.

Yim, D. (1987). Yeoseonggwa gajok gwangye (Women and Family Relationships; in Korean). In Yim, Dawnhee (Ed.), *Yeoseonghakui irongwa silje* (Theory and Practice in Women's Studies) (pp. 357-390). Seoul: Women's Study Curriculum Committee, Dongkuk University.

Yoon, H. (1989). Kinship, Gender and Personhood in a Korean Village. Ph. D dessertation, University of Michigan, Ann Arbor.

Chapter seven

An Evaluation of Older Less-Educated, Lower-Class Working Women

Cho, Oakla (Sogang University)

1. Introduction

Korean Society has experienced radical changes since it had adopted highly driven economic policy for industrialization. Since the middle of the 1990s, Korean society has adopted a policy of "globalization" and the changes have affected most areas from work to everyday life (Lee 1992). These trends have contributed to the restructuring of economic and social organizations. Postmodern jobs and social relations have slowly penetrated to the lives of most people. Deindustrialization of the manufacturing sector and the expanding service sector seems to have affected many people in terms of rising unemployment and job instability. These changes have highlighted the widening differences in wealth among the classes. Divorce rates are also rising.

Women laborers seem to have suffered the most, especially after the financial crisis in 1998. Women laborers lost their jobs more easily than men; their positions disappeared and were replaced by part time jobs. Moreover, the labor condition of lower class female workers was more seriously affected (Shin, et al. 2004: 131).

Often women in the lower class are considered to be engaged in marginal areas of employment with lower aspirations. Or, they tend to be regarded as victims of the patriarchal family system. These interpretations seem to be derived from the assumption that lower class women have to work harder to survive, which may not allow them to find any meaning in life. This chapter argues that these assertions have not reflected the women's own perspective of their work and family. Other studies have started with the nature of labor for lower class women and its linkage to their family situation. This chapter deals with the working condition of lower class women, especially relatively older and less educated women. It also analyzes "how women of the lower class connect their work with their family role." The data for this study was collected by in-depth interviews of 15 women, whose job varied from domestic helper to a worker in small factory.

The women that were interviewed have many similarities. Most were brought up in the rural areas of South Korea as daughters of poor farmers, who came to urban centers after they graduated from primary school to find a job and who returned home to marry through an arranged marriage. These women started working at home when they were quite young. The jobs they found in cities were also quite simple ones from a domestic helper to an office assistant to a bus driver. Most send their income home to help their families and to accumulate a fund for marriage. Their stories from this early period are full of suffering, but they seem to have accepted their role as a part of their life as the daughter of a poor rural family. Their married life was another development that brought hardship to them. After marriage, the women had to again assume work within the family, traveling from one job to the other in each turn of their family life. These women continued to work hard all their lives, but they were all proud of themselves for their role in the family and for their strong identity as a worker.

The women's interpretation of their job and family, in some sense, differs from previous conceptions of poor women as victims of the capitalistic labor structure and patriarchal family system. Their identity seems to be formed on their early experiences in childhood and their first job in an urban center. They want to see themselves as a successor rather than a victim of society. This chapter describes how these women conceptualize their work and family and argues that an inside point of view has to be reconsidered in order to understand these women.

The previous studies on lower class women (Park 1994; Chung 2001; Cho, Uhn 1990; Cho, O. 1990) tend to emphasize how the economic needs of lower class families affect the women's work, analyzing survival strategies within the family (Cho, U. 1990). In that sense, the family system with its patriarchal ideology can limit women's life (Cho, O. 1990). These arguments indicate that the patriarchal family structure and women's work are closely interrelated. However, there have not been many studies on the condition of women's work and their own interpretation of their work and family relations.

This chapter will focus on less-educated, older working women based on their oral stories of their working conditions and family life. The data was collected in Seoul and Ch'ungch'ongnam-do, South Korea, from 2003 to 2004. Fifteen women interviewees are divided into four categories for analysis: 1) those engaged in salary-based employment in the formal sector; 2) those holding hourly-based jobs in the informal sector, usually domestic-related work; 3) those working in urban small shops and on rural farms; and 4) those with part-time employment with social activities. The categories demonstrate the diversity of working conditions for these women. They are categorized in terms of organizational structure and labor relationships. Women in the first category are employed by formal organizations. The second is women working in the private sector, such as a restaurant or private home. The third represents women working as small, independent shop owners or wives of rural farmers. The final category is those engaged in social activity groups in addition to their outside jobs work.

All the interviewees were married at the time of this research and were 40 to 66 years old. All were born in rural areas and had worked in Seoul before marriage. Most had gone to home to marry and returned to Seoul a few years after marriage. All but one are daughters of rural poor families and have worked all their life. All families but two are nuclear families. Two farmers live closely to or with their mothers-in-law.

Table 1 Characteristics of Interviewees

Categories	Education	Place of employment	Length of employment	Age
1) Formal sector	1. Middle school	University	20 years	58
	2. Drop-out in primary school	IT company	10 years	66
	3. Middle school	IT company	10 years	56
	4. Drop-out in primary school	factory	5 years	52
2) Informal sector	5. Primary school	Restaurant	3 years	45
	6. Middle school	Private house	3 years	53
	7. Primary school	Private house	1 years	57
	8. High school	Private house	10 years	45
3) Urban small shops and rural farms	9. Middle school	Laundry shop	10 years	54
	10. Middle school	Milk delivery shop	3 years	60
	11. Middle school	Farm	20 years	45
	12. high school(middle school, husband)	Farm	3 years(orchard)	41
4) Labor related to social activities	13. High school	Insurance com.	3 years	40
	14. High school	Restaurant	3 years	48
	15. Primary school	Garment com.	9 years	49

2. Employment Characteristics

Women in the formal sector seem satisfied with their working environment. They said their working place was clean, and people in the company tended to be kind and greet them nicely. The working hours were fixed, and they received health insurance. These conditions were far better than their previous jobs, such as piece-work at home, a small shop keeper, and various other part-time jobs in the private sector. However, their income level was relatively low, around 700,000 won (approximately US$700 at the time of this research), which was lower than the average income for an informal sector, part-time worker. However, these women thought they were lucky to work in a formal organization, as not many stable jobs are available to older women. All of them thought that they would not be able to secure a similar position, if they quit. One woman, who was 52 years old, worked as a factory worker for an automobile parts plant, and she said she intends to stay in the job as long as the factory does not fire her. She thought her job was easy, because it was a simple repetitive job, compared to her previous work in a restaurant, which demanded various roles from peeling onions to serving clients and to dishwashing.

Women in the informal sector, the second category based primarily on hourly, part-time jobs, were engaged in odd jobs related to domestic activities. Three women worked in a private home, while another woman worked in a restaurant for charity. They felt the flexible work hours were one of the advantages of being a domestic worker. They also chose this job, because it was relatively easy for them. Two women started working when their husbands' businesses failed: one just being in debt and the other cannot continue working due to injuries from car accident. The women intended to work until the family's finances improved. A woman (53 years old) said she wished to have at least the blessing of work, if she does not have good fortune in her life. All the women in this category did not demonstrate any devotion to their job. Rather, they saw it only as necessary, although they did not explain why they would not prefer to work as a domestic helper, which is a relatively higher paying job.

Women in the third category included two self-employed small shop keepers and two farmers. The first self-employed woman was managing a small milk delivery shop, and the other worked in a laundry shop. Both worked with their husbands without any staff. They had the heaviest workload, because of their outside work and their housekeeping burdens. They said it was difficult to separate their work from their daily life, which left them with little time of their own. However, they were very sure about their contribution to family economy. Both of them began working after their husbands went into bankruptcy. Working with their husbands stifled the women's autonomy. They also had to play the role of wife both in their place of work as well as at home.

The two female farmers in this category also revealed similar problems. However, they lived with their mothers-in-law, who helped them with the housekeeping. Both of the female farmers were eager to adopt new farming techniques in order to improve their profit. One grew apples, and the other opened a sundry shop near the highway. They wanted to try other things to expand their income, but they said they had to negotiate with their husbands and mothers-in-law on every proposal. In fact, during the first interview with one female farmer, her mother-in-law insisted on staying in the room during interview, so she was interviewed again when the mother-in-law was not present.

The women in the third category seemed to suffer with both the heaviest workload and a lack of freedom in the workplace. In that sense, of all the women, they were affected the most by the patriarchal family system, because their job environment was inseparable from their family life. This contradicts previous arguments that posit the sharp division of labor by gender causes gender inequality (Rosado 1974). The vague division of work between home and the work place seems to produce more physical and emotional suffering for these women.

Women in the fourth category engaged in income-generating work devoted to social activism. Three women in this category were interviewed in order to understand how these less educated, older female workers connected their lives to social issues. One woman was the secretary general for the wives association, representing the poor, in her apartment complex. She also worked for an insurance company, but she was not able to recruit enough clients to keep her job stable. She was an instructor of home fashion and embroidery for a welfare center as well. Even though she helped organize a weekly market and festival for the senior residents in her association, she was so busy with her other income-generating activities that she had little time to devote to the association. She wanted to spend more time helping her neighbors, but she was still struggling to pay the debts of her husband. However, due to her endeavors, she has developed a wide range of social networks, which was rather rare among lower-class women.

Another woman (48 years old) was a radical activist who had fought against the redevelopment of her residential area, a shanty town and had obtained a right for a flat in newly builted apartment complex in 1993. She was one of many activists whose efforts resulted in a new apartment complex in the area. Although she does not participate in social movements anymore, she has opened a small restaurant that has become a center for former activists.

Interestingly, she made an excuse for her family not being actively involved in social movements anymore.

Another 49-year-old woman had also fought against redevelopment of her poor residential area in 1990s. Her participation in social activism started with a hunger strike in a garment company in the early 1980s and continued with a community movement of 'one rice-pot' in 2000s. At the time of this research, she had been working for the last nine years as a contracted part-time supervisor in a garment company that manufactured modernized Korean dress. She said the flexible work schedule enabled her to attend to her child-rearing duties at home. She also said she was willing to share her talent as a garment technician with her neighbors once her family obligations lessened.

The women interviewed in these four categories had various job experiences. All but two female farmers had held five to six jobs. The women in the first category seemed the most satisfied with their jobs despite the relatively low wages. The stability and formal recognition they received from their jobs influenced their decision to stay in the job. The second group of women tended to consider their present positions as temporary. Informality and a high turn-over rate were common characteristics in this type of work. However, both these groups held similar positions, such as janitor, dishwasher, or domestic helper (part-time maid). The main differences between the two categories were the differing degrees of stability and fringe benefits, such as health insurance. Women in the third category worked with their husband, which indicates their family role is closely intertwined with their role as an outside worker. The women in this category had the heaviest workload. Although the women in the fourth category were poor, they were actively engaged in social change, struggling to juggle their concern for the poor with their need to earn a wage. However, they seemed to link their income-generating activities to their social activities.

Few of the women, except those in the third category, complained about their job situation. Most tended to accept the job opportunity as it was and made a sincere effort in the job. They seemed content to follow orders and were more concerned about keeping their jobs than changing them. In that sense, the sustainability of a job was a more important factor than its nature or condition.

3. Employment Networks or Routes for Employment

Most women, as well as the women interviewed for this study, seek employment through informal networks, usually friends or neighbors. However, the women in the third category, who were self-employed in either a small shop or farming, differed from the other categories. The two female farmers became rural workers after their marriage to rural men. One female farmer had three different jobs: mill assistant, apple orchard laborer, and small shop keeper. Her workload expanded after she married. In the beginning, she worked as an assistant to her husband. Then, her mother-in-law retired from the mill, and she took over her position. At the time of the interview, she had recently opened a stall on a highway to sell her produce, because she can get a better price for their apples. She said she preferred outside work instead of domestic tasks. In fact, she said her mother-in-law handled all the household tasks. She also said this division of labor helped to avoid potential conflicts between family members. Another female farmer, who was 41 years old, started farming when she discovered her husband was wasting money gambling and carousing. Instead of asking for a divorce, she decided to increase her efforts at farming her own land, which she obtained from her husband. She had also moved to a house close to her parents-in-law.

Another woman, who was 54 years old, became a full-time worker in the laundry shop of her husband's brother, after her husband lost money for the business. To secure additional income, she also became the seamstress for the shop. Another woman started a small milk delivery business after her husband's business lost money during the financial crisis in 1998. She eventually persuaded her husband to work with her in the business.

These four unlikely women found a solution to the financial problems of their families, which were due, in large part, to their husband's financial failures. They were not unpaid family workers. Rather they initiated new business or farming and became a co-worker in the family business.

All of the women, except those in the third category, found their various jobs through neighbors, relatives, and friends. In particular, those with experience in similar jobs were very helpful to the job-seekers. Five out of the 11 women obtained their present job by following a neighbor's recommendation after letting their friends and neighbors know they were looking for work. Their past job experience did not seem to help them find new jobs. Only two of the women, one who works full-time at a factory and the other who works part-time at a garment company, found their jobs based on their job history. The factory worker was able to secure her job, because she had five years of experience. Apparently, she was familiar with the factory's past labor shortages and could negotiate well. The garment worker, on the other hand, had a good reputation for her ability to supervise young staff workers and executives. The workers call her "teacher."

4. Social Interaction and Employment

Most of the women interviewed for this study were not socially active. Only the women in the fourth category had been or were involved in social movements. The women's work and lives were so intertwined that they did not have time to develop social networks, although neighbors and friends help one another find jobs or lend money. In this sense, the women in the third category suffer the most from the lack of a social life. The lives of these women revolve around home and family both at work and at home. The woman in the laundry shop works all day with her husband. She said even at home they live like old friends all by themselves. She also said she rarely speaks to customers, preferring to read books or watch television when no customers are around. She seems accustomed to her social isolation. The woman with the milk delivery business starts her work at 2:00 am. After she delivers the milk, she eats breakfast and does housework. Her husband rarely helps with the housework. She also takes care of her daughter's baby in the afternoon when she has to work. She has little time to rest. After she broke her leg last winter, she felt extremely tired. During the interview, she said she was not sure how much longer she could continue her job. Although, she was a member of *ch'in mok-gye*, a rotating credit club for friendship that arranges seasonal tours, she had not been able to participate so far. Furthermore, she worries whether she will be able to travel in the future, because she was already 60 years old in 2004.

The female farmers work mainly in the apple orchard. They joined *chak mok-ban*, a work group for a special crop that is composed of approximately 10 households, to learn special farming techniques and employ labor for special tasks like trimming trees, weeding, and harvesting. This group also travels together. However, this group is composed of households of apple growers, so the women are considered as the wives, rather than farmers. Only household heads, men, have an official membership.

For women in the third category, their lives at work and home are closely linked, and they are very dependent on other members of the family in their work. Women in this category are the most socially isolated.

The women who have developed a wider social network belong to the fourth category. The woman working as the president of the wives association in the low-income apartment complex has the ability to influence people, fight for common causes, and offer advice to neighboring apartment complexes. This woman is also struggling to pay her husband's debts, taking on additional jobs. It must be very difficult for this woman to juggle her employment responsibilities and her social obligations at the same time. However, she said she took the association position after strong encouragement from neighboring wives and the former president of the association.

Another woman interviewed, who had also fought against redevelopment of this neighborhood, has played a significant role as an advisor to residents' association. Her small restaurant near the apartment complex hosts many local residents and former activists. This is a very different position for her than her role as a mother and restaurateur. The third woman in this group also has a large social network. Although she was not as active as she used to be, she still has a keen interest in the social movement. She has even considered contributing her expertise as a garment worker to the community movement.

All three of these women manage to blend their wage-earning work with their social movement activities. They see the community movement as an important interplay of work and life, fellow workers and neighbors and region and community. Their activities have the potential to improve not only their lives and status but also their community as well.

Women in the first and second categories either do not care or do not have the time for social activities. The first group of women, who work in formal organizations, has few complaints. They cited two reasons for their satisfaction. One reason is that they should be able to stay in this job until they were quite old. The other reason is they do not have to worry about personal or hierarchical relationships. In fact, they can start work early and finish early, because most of these types of jobs, such as janitorial work, must be done before the formal work day begins. Therefore, they do not have to interact with other employees. These women prefer this more isolated situation. The women usually eat lunch and drink tea together, often bringing food to share. They have built their own relaxed, informal community and tend to act indifferently to others in the former sector. When asked if they knew the purpose of the formal institute or who worked there, they bluntly said, if they knew everything, then, they would not work there as a janitor.

The three domestic helpers also said they prefer to work in an environment where they can work independently without worrying about interacting with other employees or management, different houses each time if possible. They all agree that building a good relationship with a housewife will result in more referrals for more jobs. However, recently, short-term positions, such as once or half-day a week have increased, making it more difficult to develop a long-term relationship with the employer.

Therefore, the social interaction in the workplace varies, according to the nature of work and to the worker's commitment to family and community. The first two groups, engaged in "traditional" manual labor, were not particularly concerned about social relationships. They preferred to separate the job from social relationships. The second two groups differed sharply in their emphasis on social interaction. Those who worked closely with their husbands, either in a shop or on the family farm, preferred to limit their social relationships to the family. However, those in the fourth group were more likely to link their jobs and social activities, especially if they had a personal interest in the social activity.

5. Employment and Pride

The women in this study worked in various places: rural farms, small shops, factories, corporations, universities, private homes, and small restaurants. This research wanted to understand how these women regarded their work in terms of place, income, family, and social relationships. According to the data gathered through interviews, most of the women seemed satisfied with their accomplishments. In order to evaluate their positive conception of their work, it is important to consider their economic situation as well. Fourteen of the fifteen women interviewees were born and raised in poor rural families. Most came to Seoul to get a job. They had worked in various occupations as a maid, a shop clerk, a factory laborer, as an assistant driver, and others. Although they returned to their native village to marry through an arranged marriage, they eventually moved back to Seoul. Many of them had expected to be relieved from outside work after marriage, but they soon realized they would need to earn money to supplement their husband's income. They had tried various odd jobs from peddler to dishwasher to piece work at home. Therefore, for most of the women, this was their fifth or sixth job. They said their life is much better now than their early days in the rural village. Since many of the women had only received minimal education, it was very important to them to keep their children in school as long as possible. They were proud that they could provide a better education and better living conditions for their children than their parents were able to do. They felt they had contributed significantly to the family income and hoped their hard work had laid the groundwork for a peaceful life in their old age. In that sense, they believed their efforts had been successful.

All of the women hope to continue their income-generating activities as long as their health is good and a job is available. They do not have any sense of how the changing industrial and technological advances may affect their job conditions. However, according to their accounts of the current working conditions, it appears they have experienced some changes. The women who work for an information technology (IT) company like its environment, less authoritarian atmosphere. They prefer the elastic and autonomous atmosphere, and they are committed to staying there.

There are changes in domestic jobs too. The women, who worked as domestic helpers, liked the hourly-based wage positions. They preferred situations where they did not have to get "personally acquainted" with their employers. They seem to be afraid that they may come across old social stigma between maids and noble ladys. The separation of work and self frees the women from social connotations attached to the job. Women workers no longer have to feel any lack of self worth from working as a janitor or a domestic helper. Furthermore, few, if any, young women are competing with these women for the job, so the older women enjoy some job security.

6. Employment and Economic Needs

Previous studies on relationships in lower class families have emphasized the sacrifices made by women in order to improve the family's economic situation (Cho, Uhn 1990; Cho, Oakla 1990; Ok and Sung 2004). In this context, they have tried to find evidence that would suggest poverty and its stigma are hereditary; that is, they are passed from one generation to the next, possibly from mother to daughter (Cho, Uhn 1990). As discussed previously, the patriarchal family system has imposed a heavy burden on women (1990), there appears to be a connection from the mother and to the daughter in families of the urban poor. For example, if the mother refuses to perform her role at home, the family system can be demolished. However, in other research, such as that by Ok and Sung (2004), it has been found that lower class women believe that the refusal to act subservient at home can benefit the family. These different interpretations regarding the role of women in the South Korean family may reflect variances in data collected during different periods of the country's change and rise to economic power. This research seems to support the perspective of Ok and Sung. Of the fifteen women interviewed all but one were very positive about their economic role in their family. This positive attitude can be analyzed in three ways. First, in that the data is a compilation of narratives from older, married women, holding a job well into old age may indicate the positive reflection of a survivor in hindsight, someone who overcame the hardships of poverty with perseverance, industry, and dignity. Second, the women's positive attitude may be the result of a developed and expanded Korean society that has "naturally" improved the lives of its members. Finally, it illustrates the different points of analysis: the women's own voice and the socialist feminist point of view. At this stage it is still too early to credit one interpretation over the other to explain this phenomenon. Rather, as the Korean culture continues to become more modernized and urbanized, further research will be required to see how family system changes and affects the lives of women and how, in turn, these women give new meaning to the family through their increasing participation in the workforce.

All the women interviewed for this study began working out of economic need. They had worked before marriage in shops, factories, farms, and at home. Those who migrated to Seoul, either with friends or alone, had come to earn money, to get away from farming, or to avoid housework. Furthermore, they came to accumulate funds for their future marriage expenses. Most sent money home to help their natal family. One of the women sent money for her brother's education, to compensate her unfulfilled aspiration to receive an education. She was very proud she was able to help her younger brother, who has become a teacher because of her financial support. This sense of family responsibility, as well as their own needs, pushed them to work hard and to save their money. Moreover, these incentives to work hard did not lessen after marriage. In fact, after marriage, the women's obligations only increased their income generating activities. The fragility and instability of the lower class family structure left these women with little choice but to work and work hard. One 60-year-old woman started delivering milk after her husband's business failed and he was in a car accident. Five or six years later, her husband started a new business and she was able to stop working for awhile. However, her husband's business failed again during the economic crisis of 1998, and she was once again forced to work. Another woman, who was 57 years old, opened a peddling business after her husband had several car accidents. She later worked as a dishwasher in a restaurant and started a snack shop. At the time of this research she was working as a part-time domestic helper. This pattern was typical of most of the women interviewed. The women's husbands were unable to provide stability because of debt, accidents, or loss of work.

Another factor influencing the women's decision to work has been their children. Initially, the women would try to balance their work and raising their children. Women in their 40s emphasized the need for flexible work hours and a job in close proximity to their home. A 45-year-old woman took at a position at a restaurant, because the hours were compatible with her daughter's school hours. Another 49-year-old woman quit her full-time job to work part-time, because her son was having difficulties in school. All of the women over 50 had experienced some type of job re-adjustment, sometimes several times, in order to better provide for their children as well as to supplement the family's income.

None of the women regretted the sacrifices they had made for their family and children. They continue to adjust their lives and their work when faced with each new crisis. They remain flexible in order to overcome the varying challenges and obstacles. Rather than stilling their resolve, their experiences have made them steadfast and proud. They are proud women. They and their families have survived, due, in large part, to their ability and willingness to work hard.

7. Employment and Identity

All of the women interviewed for this study, except one, intend to continue working well into old age. Being a productive worker and provider has instilled a strong sense of identity in them. They were not only concerned about the welfare of their husband and children but also their own welfare, especially as they aged. The women still working in their 50s and 60s enjoyed some autonomy, although their children tried to discourage them from working on a regular basis. Two of the women said they could save money for the future by keeping a job.

This study suggests that the meaning of a job, at least for women, has been changing as the needs of the family change. Furthermore, the work or job itself has become important to them. Throughout their lives, they have sought employment that would best serve the family's needs. Throughout the process, factors, such as working conditions, work hours, and location, affected that decision. In all likelihood, careful consideration of these factors has contributed to a more stable and solid foundation in their families. Furthermore, their contributions have solidified a more valuable presence for them within the family. Finally, the older women, especially those over the age of 55, appeared to be satisfied with their new role in the family.

For some, their fulfillment came from their ability to be self-sufficient as an income earner and their sense of independence. Others believed they would have been bored, if they had stayed at home. This should come as no surprise. After all, these women had been working all their life and had never been dependent on someone else. One woman said, "I have struggled to survive in all my life, and I do not want to be a burden to my children." Although economic conditions compelled these women to work initially, now they justify working on their own terms. One woman said, "Even though we are still in economic difficulties, I go to job to make use of my time within limited short hours, which differs from old days when we did not have enough food and lodging." That explains why three busy working women of the 40 among interviewees take classes in nearby community center.

Therefore, many of these women continued working for personal reasons, viewing it as the cornerstone of their independence and, thus, security. Some of the women also felt their identity was intertwined with their outside employment. Working gives women a role in society, even as they continue to support their children and family. One woman said it makes her feels good to have the ability to help her son. Another woman was willing to support her daughter and take care of her children, so her daughter could pursue a professional career. The women's positive perspective of "their labor" is a sharp contrast to more conventional analyses of labor relationships of the working class in order to understand conflict or inequality in general. The increasing link between their personal identity and their work identity appears to be related to their optimistic evaluation of their contribution to family. The cultural construction of their work to the welfare of the family extends to the self-identity of these older women. They value the "job" because of its function in supporting the family. As family demands lessen, their self-esteem as a worker becomes greater. The women perceive that their growing status is due, primarily, to their job. In that sense, they develop pride both in themselves and in their job as they become older. After years of struggling, they remain in their job for their own satisfaction and security in their old age. Recognition of this positive outcome among working, older lower-class women should broaden our understanding of these women, who are often described as victims due to their economic status and the patriarchal family system. This data clearly indicates that women workers, regardless of status, income, education, or age, can recreate both their familial and societal roles and claim their own space.

8. Conclusion

The women interviewed for this study gave an oral history of their personal development as they migrated from rural villages to urban cities. Their stories provide valuable insight into the effect of Korea's socio-economic development on the personal lives of older, working, lower-class women. Their stories also highlight their struggles to ensure the survival of both themselves and their families. Compelled to work for one reason or another, they were able to find work that still allowed them to carry out their responsibilities at home and care for their children. Through it all they became self-sufficient and self-reliant and, in turn, gained a sense of self-worth and pride in their accomplishments.

Family was always important to these women. Thus, each woman carefully considered how their income generating activities would affect their family before accepting a job. In fact, every decision was based on the needs and obligations of the family. In this sense, while the family system may be viewed as "oppressive," the women seemed to enjoy their new influential position within the family and the new identity they had gained as a worker. Their working experience, then, is less a burden than a source of economic independence and self-esteem. The women's stories illustrate how a job, even in combination with family responsibilities, can be a powerful base as women reach for a better future. They are determined to succeed for themselves, their children, and their family. Finally, how well will these women survive in the post-industrial era? On the surface, their working conditions appear to be the same. They are still a janitor, a dishwasher, a peddler, or a piece worker. However, due to technological advances, increased automation, and globalization, organizational structures are changing. Many companies, small businesses, and, even, private employers hire manual workers indirectly through an employment agency. Therefore, many jobs are part-time, temporary, or contractual forms of employment, and there is little, if any, contact with the "formal" employees and management of an organization. They may only communicate with an agent or a responsible staff member who is in charge of "indirectly employed workers." Even when working in a private home, there is minimum contact with the employer these days, as domestic service is often arranged through an agent.

These new conditions affecting hiring practices and employment for temporary, part-time, or contractual workers may hinder their organization as a workforce, but, on the other hand, it may allow these workers more choice when choosing employment than the former system. Surprisingly, women do not appear to be resisting this changing environment. Rather, they seem to be more comfortable under less personal conditions, which allow some autonomy and anonymity. Finally, the number of jobs for these women is not shrinking but growing. Therefore, they can be optimistic about their future. However, only future studies will be able to evaluate how the post-modern society and the ever-changing conditions of their work environment have affected their status and identity as a woman and a worker.

**This paper has been rewritten based on an earlier paper — Cho, O. (2006). Labor of middle-aged women workers: The meaning of labor and family among less-educated, middle-aged women workers, *Journal of Social Science* 14(2): 220-261.

References

Cho, O. (1990). Dosi binmin gajokgwa nongchon yeongsebinnong gajokui bigyo (Comparative Studies on Family between Urban Poor and Rural Farmers; in Korean). Yeoseonghan-guksahoeyeon-guhoe, ed., *Han-gukgajongnon (A study of the Korean Family,* in Korean), 283-299. Seoul: Kachi.

Cho, O. (2004). Jeohakryeok goyeonryeong yeoseongdeului gajokgwan: Saengjonui geungeoimyeo, anjeongseongui gibaneuroseoui gajok (Family Studies of Low-educated Aged Women Workers: Family as Basis of Survival and Stability; in Korean). Annual Meeting of Korean Association of Family Studies, keynote speech.

Cho, O. (2005). Jungjangnyeon yeoseong nodongjadeului salm sokeseoui bingon (Poverty and Middle-aged Women Workers; in Korean*). Dosiwa bingon(City and Poverty)* 72: 45-63.

Cho, O. (2006). Jungjangnyeon yeoseong nodongjaui nodonggyeongheom: 21 Segi han-guk sahoeeseo jeohakryeok, goyeonryeong yeoseong nodongjadeului nodonggwa gajokgwan (Labor of Middle Aged Women Workers: the Meaning of Labor and Family among Low-educated, Aged Women Workers; in Korean). *Sahoegwahak-yeon-gu (Journal of Social Science)* 14(2): 220-261.

Cho, U. and Cho, O. (1992). *Dosi binminui salmgwa gonggan (Life and Space of Urban Poor*; in Korean). Seoul: Seoul National University Press.

Cho, U. (1990). Dosi binmin gajokui saengjonjeonryakgwa yeoseong (Survival Strategy of Urban Poor Families and Women; in Korean). In *Han-gukgajongnon (A Study of the Korean Family),* ed. by Yeoseonghan-guksa-hoeyeon-guhoe, 178-206. Seoul: Kachi.

Kim, M., et al. (2002). *Je 4cha yeoseong-ui chwieop siltaejosa* (*The Forth Survey on Women Employment*; in Korean). Seoul: Korean Women Development Institute.

Kim, T. (2002). *Factors and Characteristics of Women's Economic Participation*. Seoul: KWDI.

Lee, Y. (1992), Jeogbohwasahoewa yeoseongnodong, (Information Society and women labour; in Korean). *Yeoseonghak Nonjp* 9, Seoul: Ehwa Institute of Research for Korean Women.

Oh, S. W. and Sung, M. (2004). *Bingon yeoseong gajangui salm* (*Life of Poor Women Household head*; in Korean). Seoul: Hwau.

Rosaldo, M. Z. (1974). Women, Culture and Society: A Theoretical Overview. In *Women, Culture and Society*. ed. by Rosaldo and Lamphere. Stanford: Stanford University Press.

Shin, M., et al. (2004). *Sahoejeok baeje-ui gwanjeomeseo bon bingoncheung siltaeyeongu* (*Studies on Poverty Group from the Perspective of Social Exclusion*; in Korean). Research Report for National Commission for Human Rights.

Yi, E. K. (2003). 'Home is a Place to Rest': Constructing the Meaning of Work, Family and Gender in the Korean Middle Class. In *Korean Anthropology: Contemporary Korean Culture in Flux*. ed. by Korean National Commission for UNESCO, Seoul: Hollym.

IV
Family and
Gender

Chapter eight

Imagining the South Korean Family beyond Patriarchy[1]

Lee, Jae Kyung (Ewha Womans University)

1. Introduction

In the past few decades, the South Korean patriarchal family has undergone some major changes, especially with the decline in multi-generational families, the predomination of the nuclear family, and the diffusion of the Western ideals of romantic love and marriage. Furthermore, recent socio-demographic figures have shown more dramatic transformation in the family life than before. Among others, the low fertility rate, the increase in dual-earner family, the growth of interracial marriage and the abolition of legal bases for the traditional Confucian patriarchal family[2] are notable instances.

---

1 Portions of this chapter are reprinted from Lee (2007), "Han-guk gajok beonhwa-ui teukseong-gwa jangjeom," Yang, et al., *Policy and Practice on Family Welfare*.
2 As the revised bill for the Civil Law, whose gist is the abolition of the *hoju-je* or family

Recent changes in the Korean family have led to the conservative discourses on the "family in crisis." Those who lament the "family in crisis" lump an array of serious problems together, as well as changes that are not necessarily problems at all, such as divorce, single parents, childless couples, working mothers, interracial marriages, and the rising age of marriage. Framing the issue in terms of "family in crisis" leads to an overemphasis on personal and moral failures as the source of family and social problems. This also draws attention away from such sources of family change as economic and demographic factors. The "crisis" we are actually concerned about is the "crisis in the traditional patriarchal family[3]." (Kim 2005; Lee 2004a)

Socioeconomic changes in a national and global context seem to have brought the current family change into motion: first, the shift into a "post-industrial" information and service economy has drawn women into workplace; second, a demographic transformation has not only created mass longevity but reshaped the individual and family life course; third, the expansion of consumerism and/or commercialization has transformed everyday life in a global capitalist economy; fourth, a growing sense of individuality and subjectivity concerning self-fulfillment and self-development has led to change in the private life; and, thus, the global capitalist

---

headship system, passed in the National Assembly in March 2005 and became effective in January 2008, the legal basis for the patriarchal family has ended in South Korea.

3 Patriarchal familism dominated family life in traditional Korean society. The ideology of patriarchal familism is characterized by constructs of the primogeniture stem family, authority of the patriarch (rather, husband, eldest son), patrilineal succession, paternal kinship, subordination of women, and division of labor by gender.

economy and post-modern culture has affected the transformation of family life (Beck and Beck-Gernsheim 1999; Skolnick 2000). Those who acclaim "family in change" see the present state as the decline of the patriarchal family and its embedded gender structure. For instance, the younger generation would likely have different perceptions of sexuality, love, dating, marriage and motherhood than older generations. Since modernization, the traditional Korean family structure and values have been steadily weakened over the decades. Traditional family values are still thought to be a safeguard for preserving our identity from Western influences. However, recent socio-demographic changes indicate otherwise. The abolition of the *hoju-je*, the decease of multi-generational households,[4] and the rise in interracial marriages seem to jeopardize traditional patrilineal family. On the other hand, the low fertility rate,[5] a decrease in marriage rates, and an increase in the female economic participation rate can be indications of postmodern shifts in the South Korean family. Moreover, these changes signify that modern gender relations and intimate life are in trouble.

This paper discusses how the patriarchal family has declined and raises issues in the dispute: instability of gender structure; troubled intimate life; suspicious union between modern intimacy

---

4 The proportion of households with three generations or more has declined, whereas proportions of one-generation and single person households are on the rise. The proportion of three-generation households has more than halved from 17 % in 1980 to 6.9 % in 2005, while proportions of one-generation and single person households escalated from 13.1 % to 36.2 % in the same period.
5 In 2009, South Korea ranks among the countries with the lowest fertility rate, 1.15 children per woman at a childbearing age.

and patriarchal familism. Through such discussions, this study also shows that conflict and confrontation between genders is ultimately a mere "change," not a "crisis," that unavoidably can take place in the process of transforming the gender order.

2. Instablity and Conflicts in Gender Order

For the past few decades, expectations of Korean women to participate in economic activity have steadily increased, and the economic activity of married women has also risen gradually. But modern domesticity still requires women to bear the primary responsibility of household work in the family. Women have continuously argued for the need of sharing household labor between couples, but the modern gender structure that passes the responsibility of caring labor to women and the gender division in the family based on this structure has changed slowly. Despite women's more active participation in social activity and the change in their expectation to have a different lifestyle, the family is still dominated by the patriarchal tradition. It is observed that in this reality, the gender conflict in the family has been aggravated. Also, the changes in women, including an increase in their desire for equality and employment, bring about the instability of the gender structure.

1) Blurring of Gender Division of Labor: Working Moms, Working Wives

The household income structure has shifted from the traditional one of having one breadwinner per family, usually male, to the double-income structure. Women's labor-force participation rate has risen from 42.8 % in 1980 to 50.0 % in the year 2008. The composition of the female labor force in the 1960s and 1970s, which was represented by young, unmarried women, has transformed to one that is made up of older, married women. The participation rate of married women, which was 40 % in the year 1980, substantially increased to 49.8 %, and two-income households accounted for 40.1 % in 2006 (KWDI 2009; NSO 2009d). But modern domesticity still requires women to bear the primary responsibility of household work in the family.

Figure 1 Economic Participation Rate: Women aged 15+, 1980, 1990, 2000 and 2010.

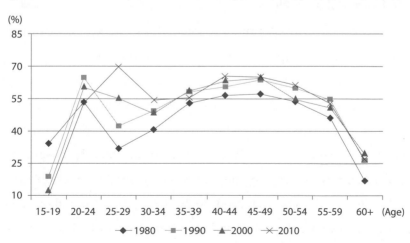

Source: NSO, *Gyeongje hwaldong ingu yeonbo*, downloaded at http://kostat.go.kr

Working wives have continuously demanded that their husbands share in the household labor, but the family is still dominated by the patriarchal order.

The recent phenomena of low fertility and rising divorce rates in South Korea are partly due to conflicts between gender in the family and the labor market. On the other hand, according to a national survey in 2002 (Kim, et al. 2003), unmarried women and men have greater apprehension about the hardship of dual-income couples raising children. When asked about the expectation of difficulties for double-income couples, 49.8 % of the unmarried respondents aged 18-34 answered "the burden of childrearing" and 20.7 % "cannot having enough time with children," resulting in 70.5 % of the respondents citing children as the greatest problem. Moreover, young women tend to stay single until securing their job and career rather than submit to marriage at an early age.

The upward trend of double-income households is also exhibited in the slowly, yet surely, abating M-shaped employment pattern. The female economic participation rate by age group in South Korea still displays the M-shaped employment pattern, but recently this curve has become slightly indistinct (See Figure 1). Except for age group of 60 and over, the age 25-29 group shows the lowest employment in 1980 and 1990, while the age 30-34 group marked the lowest rate in 2000 and 2010. This illustrates that the proportion of women who leave the labor market for marriage, childbirth, and childrearing has decreased, and, at the same time, they have postponed leaving the labor market as late as possible. The findings of various social surveys carried out recently report that many women have the opinion that they will give priority to their work over the family.[6] Women's conflict concerning the balance between work and family has deepened and there is a tendency of shifting toward choosing their work instead of the family.

2) Changing Attitudes and Persisting Patriarchal Practices

According to a survey conducted by Korea Gallop in January 2005, people's attitude on the gender division of labor has been changing noticeably. In response to the statement that "a male adult in the family should take authority to keep order in the family," 51.6 % of 1,500 men and women agreed, an 18.1 % decrease from 69.7 % of the survey results in 1984. Meanwhile, in response to the question of whether "there should be a distinction between the work of husbands and wives," 39.4 % of respondents answered in the affirmative, a decrease of as much as 33.5 % compared to 20 years ago (*The JoongAng Ilbo*, June 8, 2005).

Although the attitude on gender division of labor in a household became flexible, such an attitude has not been carried out very well in practice. A survey on household chores found that women, regardless of their working status, were predominantly

---

6 According to *Sahoe josa bogoseo* (2009), South Koreans showed positive attitudes on women's employment. Eighty point eight percent of men and 86.6 % of women responded that 'it is better for women to have jobs than to devote themselves to the family alone.' Only 4.0 % and 5.9 % of the women responded respectively that the proper period for maintaining their jobs was "until before their marriage" and "until before the childbirth of their first baby," which shows they wish to continue working without being hampered by marriage and childbirth.

Figure 2 Attitude on Household Chores by Gender, 2009

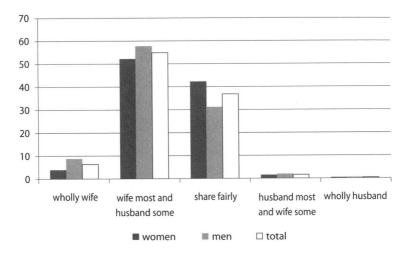

Figure 3 Actual Responsibility for Household Chores by Wives' Employment Status: Responses from Wives, 2009

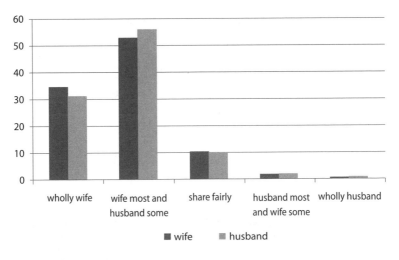

responsible for household duties, which may ignite conflicts between genders. In Figure 2 and Figure 3, we can find the gap between one's attitude and practice. While more than 37.5 % of the respondents replied that household chores should be allocated equally in the attitude survey only 10 % actually put such belief into action.

South Korean wives largely take charge of household work regardless of their employment status. In the case of working mothers, they try to ease the burden of childrearing by utilizing the extended family network or the market. This trend is more dominant in middle class women with a higher educational background and professional job. On the other hand, working mothers who are employed in such low-income jobs as service work or production work do not have many options other than daycare centers (Lee, et al. 2006). In both cases, however, neither women's job duties nor childcare responsibilities are guaranteed completely. The articulation of progressive attitudes and patriarchal practices around family life often causes marital conflicts. Women have a high expectation for share housework and child care, while men are unwilling to participate equal division of labor.

In spite of the more prevalent economic activities of women and subsequent changes expected in the lifestyle of women, men are slow to take part in family responsibilities as men's low participation rate in household chores indicates. The gap between expectation and reality is causing gender conflicts in society and families, which leads to the attenuation of the care provision role in the family.

3) Conflicts in Gender Role and Identity

Today the economic arrow points at the women; it is women who are being drawn into wage work and women who are undergoing changes in their way of life. What is remarkable among the changes that have taken place as women enter the labor market is the change in their identity. It is shown that as women's participation in the labor market has gradually increased, they begin to place more positive value on their career pursuit and professional success in the workplace. The fact that working women identify themselves as workers rather than as wives and mothers shows, in part, that the gender structure has become unstable (Hochschild 2001; Lee and Jang 2004; Lee 2004).

Wives often perceive their husbands' participation in household work as an indicator of equality or view it as the barometer of consideration or love for them (Lee 2003). Therefore, if their husbands do not share the household work, the wives may show a strong resistance and aggravate the conflict between the couple. In other words, the tension between the "faster-changing women" and the "slower-changing men" has now appeared as a cause for conflict between the couples, going beyond the conflict in roles arising from the dual burden of working women juggling work and family.

On the other hand, wife's demand of men to play a greater role in the family and equal relations has threatened men's authority and power. In this process, men have often experienced an "identity crisis." In modern society, their identity as a worker and head of the family was an essential element of masculinity. While growing up to be a man, he internalized his "masculinity" as the husband and father who supports and disciplines the family. But the recent social and economic changes have made it difficult to maintain such masculinity. In the past few years, men's performance of breadwinner roles and identities thereof has become the resources from which they can enjoy power and authority. However, men tend to perceive the recent situation they face as a challenge and a threat from women or wives and feel emotionally confused and experience marital conflict.

Recently, some signs of reconstruction of work and family relations have been found in Korean society. Among the men who pursued only a successful career at the sacrifice of family life and health, working long hours during the period of rapid economic growth, there has been a gradual change of perception toward thinking that private life in the family is also important.

While family becomes more important in men's lives, pursuing a career and professional success has started to gain greater significance in women's lives, especially as their participation in the labor market gradually increases. On the other hand, the identity given to women in the work place has become no less important than the identity of housewife, wife, and mother among women's multiple identities. This suggests that women themselves have begun to take a more positive attitude to escape from conflicting roles.

Meanwhile, as a growing female workforce joins the labor market, a dilemma has surfaced over how to adjust the demands of the capitalist system, which asks women to live as independent individuals competing with each other rather than caring for others, and the family members who ask them to care for them rather than to live as independent individuals. There is an increasing tendency for women, who could not find a way to adjust to the conflicting demands of work and family, to avoid getting married or delay childbirth even after marriage.

3. Intimate Life in Trouble

Modern marriage and the family system seem to be in trouble in South Korea. Romantic love and marriage, the principle of patriarchal family, is simultaneously at work and phenomenal changes have been taking place, including a drop in the fertility rate, a hike in the divorce rate, booming matchmaking companies, and the emergence of transnational family.

1) Marriage as a Matter of Choice

The crude marriage rate is sliding and the mean age at first marriage is increasing. In 2009, there were 309,800 marriages, 93,200 cases fewer than the 403,000 in 1980. The crude marriage rate dropped considerably from 10.6% in 1980 down to 6.2 % in 2009, the lowest level, and it has continued to stay at lower levels (NSO 2009a). Such a downturn in the marriage rate may be attributed to changes in young people's attitude toward marriage and family.

The increase in divorce rate has become more prominent in

South Korea. The number of divorces has been climbing steadily from 11,600 cases in 1970 to 167,100 cases in 2003. After 2003, however, the divorce rate dropped slightly with 124,000 cases in 2009. By 2003, the crude divorce rate has also risen continuously since the 1970s to 3.5, more than ten times the 0.4 rate in 1970. However, the crude divorce rate fell a little in 2007 to 2.5 (NSO 2009b).

The average age at first marriage has been consistently rising. In 2009 the average ages at first marriage are 28.7 for female and 31.6 for male, while 26.5 for female and 29.3 for male in 2000. In the period of 1980–2005, the proportion of never-married women, aged 25–29, increased by almost 45 percentage points. The rate of never-married men in the same age group increased by over 35 percentage points. In 2005, the proportion of women and men, aged 30–34, who had not married, was respectively 19.0 and 41.3 percentage points (NSO 2009a). These marriage postponement trends, often explained by the women's economic independence and empowerment, diminish women's incentive to marry and depress the nuptiality level.

The marriage rate is sliding, the mean age at first marriage is increasing and the number of remarriages is on the rise. Both men and women experienced a considerable hike in remarriages. The proportions of remarriages among total number of marriages are, for men 8.9 % in 1981 and 17.5 % in 2008 and 8.6 % in 1981 and 19.2 % in 2008 for women (NSO 2009a). These trends indicate that the traditional gendered marriage norms, which are the right age for marriage, taboos for women's remarriage, marital unions between older men and younger women and/or ever-married men and never married women, have been weakened. Together with the escalation of the divorce rate, the upsurge in the number of remarriages demonstrates that nuptiality patterns have become more diverse than in the past.

On the other hand, attitudes on marriage differ among generations. The older the people are, they more they tend to regard marriage as a necessity and the younger people are they more they consider it a matter of choice. Living together before marriage or cohabitation has become more acceptable for the younger generation as well (Kim 2005). Table 1 demonstrates that the percentage increases, among older respondents who believe

Table 1 Attitude on Marriage by Age Group, 2009

	must marry	better to marry	doesn't matter whether married or not	better not to marry	must not marry	don't know well
Women	18.8	40.3	35.6	3.4	0.6	1.3
15-19	15.1	42.0	36.8	3.0	0.7	2.4
20-29	16.9	42.4	35.5	2.6	0.6	2.0
30-39	12.1	42.4	41.0	3.1	0.5	0.9
40-49	16.4	43.6	34.9	3.7	0.4	1.0
50-59	26.2	45.9	24.0	2.6	0.3	1.0
60+	41.0	41.6	14.3	1.7	0.5	0.9
Men	24.6	45.9	25.7	2.2	0.4	1.2
15-19	15.1	42.0	36.8	3.0	0.7	2.4
20-29	16.9	42.4	35.5	2.6	0.6	2.0
30-39	12.1	42.4	41.0	3.1	0.5	0.9
40-49	16.4	43.6	34.9	3.7	0.4	1.0
50-59	26.2	45.9	24.0	2.6	0.3	1.0
60+	41.0	41.6	14.3	1.7	0.5	0.9

Source: NSO, *Social Statistics Survey*, downloaded at http://kostat.go.kr

marriage is a must, while the proportion of younger respondents who replied that it is a choice grew larger as the age went down. Their attitude on marriage also exhibited a gender difference. More men than women replied that marriage is a necessity or that it is better to get married, and more women tended to regard marriage as an option. On the other hand, women and young people tend to be more tolerant toward divorce than men and older generations.

2) Love Marriage Goes to the Market

In modern society "emotion," "love," "affection," "intimacy," and "care" are not understood as either materialistic or as work. Rather they are perceived as social roles attached to natural femininity and are separated from the economic realm. This modern myth has been challenged by the increase of the marriage industry, emotional/service work, and care industry. In the postmodern era, individual desires for love and intimacy and her/his economical needs are combined or negotiated (Lee 2009). An analysis on "love" and "economy," not only separated from each other but also controversial, is essential for understanding "intimacy" and transitions of South Korean families in the post modern era. However, the evaluation criteria for commercial trade in "love" and "intimacy" has not been developed yet. Whereas a certain trade is inevitable or essential, others may threaten intimate relationships between people.

There are currently more than 1,500 matchmaking agencies in South Korea. Marriage businesses are booming, matching couples for young men and women in the middle and upper middle classes, finding partners for remarriage, and importing foreign brides for bachelors in rural areas. Young people, who are against traditionally arranged marriages and seem to believe in romantic love and marriage, go to the market to meet/marry the ideal men or women. Seeking to build more accurate databases, matchmaking agencies are competitively adopting scientific management. Membership documents for setting up a database include specific details about an individual and his or her family. Candidates are asked to answer numerous questions concerning their financial, educational and family status, appearance, and job, all of which show the marketability of a person. By demanding such details, agencies can screen out people lacking solid backgrounds from membership. The agencies have made their customers see themselves as products, which have inevitably made the competition for better partners fiercer (*Korea Times*, June 29, 2005).

Other major customers of matchmaking companies are bachelors from rural areas. In 2009, marriages with foreign spouses consist of 10.8 % of all marriages total. Among the total number of foreign spouses, women accounted for more than 75.5 %. International or interracial marriages have been a striking and one of the most visible phenomena in rural Korea. In 2009, more than 38.2 % of grooms in rural area were married import brides, mostly Southeast Asians (NSO 2009a). The percentage is 3.5 times higher than the national average.

International marriage is hardly a topic anymore in South Korea, but reports about unhappy brides and/or couples are increasing. Foreign brides often became victims of international matchmaking schemes. The most common of them end in frequent and early divorces, caused mostly by the husband's violence, language barriers, and culture gaps. But "import brides" are increasing. This phenomenon causes an inquiry into the marriage norm in South Korea. Why do Korean men, who believe in the traditional family and pure paternal descent, solve the bride shortage through interracial marriage and have children of mixed blood.

3) Care Crisis (which is caused by instability of gender structure in the family)

Family transitions in South Korea have implied foreseeing conflicts between genders. At present, adverse outcomes of such conflicts appear inevitable. However, it is expected that cultural and institutional efforts to mediate these conflicts will be made. The most serious family issue involves children and the elderly, who are totally dependent on the care provided by the family. Care-giving work is unequally allocated between men and women, employers and employees, and the state and individuals. Such unfair distribution of care leads to diminishing care-giving roles and fewer recipients, which is affecting the currently dismal fertility rate and elderly problems.

One of the key factors brought on by the "care crisis" is conflicts and practices around gender division of labor in the family. For the last few decades, the economic participation of

Korean women has steadily been elevated, and married women are becoming increasingly more involved in economic activities. However, modern domesticity imposes the domestic responsibility on women first. Women have continuously called for equal sharing of household chores and childrearing responsibilities between husband and wife, but the actual pace of change in gender role division in family is quite slow.

Another key factor of the "care crisis" is that society is institutionally unable to support the changes in families or households. In South Korean society, there has been a long-held belief that the responsibility of caring lays first on the family. Moreover, women are identified as the caretaker, a preconception that may appear to guarantee women's maternity needs but is, in reality, much more complex than it appears. The myth of having separate public and private lives covers up the infringement on women's desire to have children and to work and delays the establishment of a social care system.

4. Suspicious Union beween Modern Intimacy and Patri-archal Familism

Modern marriage and the family system seem to be in trouble in South Korea. The modern concept of romantic love and intimacy, principles of the patriarchal family, is simultaneously at work. Phenomenal changes have been taking place, such as a drop in the fertility rate, a hike in the divorce rate, an increase in the international marriage rate, a boom in matchmaking companies, and the emergence of a transnational family.

1) Bride Import Families: I never thought of my wife as a foreigner

The "importation" of brides from abroad represents one aspect of the dilemma facing South Korean families. Until now, husbands' violence, language barriers, and culture gaps have been the main subject for scholars and policy makers. Besides these "social problems," traditional familism and intimacy have made a suspicious alliance. What does the marriage institution signify to the Korean man that marries a younger foreign bride who cannot hold a simple conversation with him? How is one to explain the experience of these women who use immigration and marriage to achieve their own personal goals?

Korean men who believe in the traditional family and pure paternal descent, solve the bride shortage through interracial marriage, despite nationalism that has long been a part of the Korean culture. In August of 2007, I had the opportunity to visit Vietnam with a group of imported brides and their families as a homecoming project. Vietnamese women, who had married a Korean, had not visited their own families since they were married, and so they brought their husbands and young children with them on this trip. After three days, in which each family was given the chance to visit the respective wife's family, an event was scheduled so that couples could speak of their experience. They were told to write personal letters to each other and read them out loud, and this turned out to be a very moving experience. Husbands thanked their wives for marrying them and bearing them beautiful children, asked them to take good care of their mother-in-law, and also encouraged them to learn the Korean language as quickly as possible. Some husbands were more enthusiastic in expressing their love and intimacy to their wives, and among them there was one man who, on the verge of tears, expressed his love and emotional intimacy by saying that he has never thought of his wife as a foreigner. Another man in his late forties carried his five-year-old son on his back all the time. So I asked if his son was old enough to walk by himself. The man replied that his son is heir to his paternal family line, so he shouldn't get hurt. These stories inspired reflection on familism and intimacy in twenty-first century South Korea.

Foreign brides, meanwhile, seem to have a different agenda of their own. While some do look forward to moving overseas to marry a man from a more developed country and live a relatively more comfortable life, the more practical motive they have is to either strategically place themselves in a situation so as to financially help their own families and/or find a job in an advanced country and fulfill their desire to actively participate in the labor market. However, we should not limit the brides' motivation for marrying foreign men to economical endeavors. Rather, we need to ask what kind of life they are aspiring to live through their choice for a marriage that takes them overseas. In other words, simply branding these foreign brides as victims of international matchmaking schemes and/or in need of the policy programs that emphasize assimilation to the Korean society is ignoring their agency and their gendered experience of overseas marriage and cannot be thought of as sufficient (Kim, et al. 2003; Constable 2005; Lee 2009).

2) Globalizing Family Strategies Question Intimacy: Gireogi Family

As the emphasis on globalization rose in the 1990s, more and more people began to send their children abroad for their studies, which eventually brought about an increase in a new kind of family trend among the middle class, called *Gireogi* family. The *gireogi* family describes a pattern in which the father remains in Korea, while the mother and their school-aged children move to English-speaking countries for the sake of the children's education (Cho 2005). They are separated, often for years, and see each other one or two months a year at the most or, in some cases, only one or two weeks. Most of them are considered a middle-class family who believes in upward mobility through education and nuclear family values, such as emotional closeness and individual happiness rather than patriarchal duties and hierarchies. What does it mean to be a family to people who only experience each other's presence briefly? How can intimacy and a sense of trust between a husband and a wife be maintained when they are separated for the sake of their child and when they must share a relationship in which the main focus lies solely on the child? How can a family's stability be built upon a foundation where the relationship between husband and wife is so unstable?

There is a paradox in the maintenance of these families. The children's achievement and success go with an increase in emotional insecurity between couples, as well as between fathers and children. Some lonely wives insist that she and her husband still love each other, even though they do not make love for months or for years. On the other hand, some lonely fathers claim that their relationship with their children can be sustained or sometimes strengthened through the Internet (Lee, et al. 2006). This exemplifies how instrumental familism works together with modern intimacy.

5. Concluding Remarks

This paper discusses the characteristics of the South Korean family in the context of the postmodern transformation patriarchal family. As demonstrates in previous studies, changes in the family following industrialization have to do with a weakening of the principle of the patrilineal family and a new emphasis being placed on the concept of the conjugal nuclear family. A union of both aspects, traditional and modern, is reflected in the Korean family. This is accompanied by a decrease in the number of children, great importance being placed on children's education, and increase in the number of working wives, a rise in household income due to national economic growth, and an increasing awareness of the values of individualism and equality (Lee 2003). The South Korean family in the postmodern era, has been reconstituted and demonstrates instability of gender structure, transformations of intimate life, and commercialization of family life. A patriarchal family has been changing. Awareness of paternal bloodlines has weakened, and the modern structure of gender division of labor has been changing too. The patriarchal family that placed the primary importance on the succession of the family has been under threat from the low birth rate and increasing remarriages. Because of job insecurity in the global capitalist economy, the status of the male breadwinner has been challenged. But our perception of or institutional prescriptions for these changes in the family seem to have failed to create an alternative way of managing intimate lives. As nationwide interest in family problems has grown recently, various prescriptions have been suggested. They have tried to solve the "crisis situation" within the traditional family norm rather than paying attention to changes in the family structure and intimate life.[7] Socioeconomic changes in the post-modern era require restructuring the modern nuclear family and the gender order. It is likely to be very difficult for discourse on family diversification or equality to resolve the conflict between genders and offer a new way of family life, unless the concept of the traditional patriarchal family is destroyed.

References

Beck, U., and Beck-Gernsheim, E. (1999). *The Normal Chaos of Love*. Blackwell Publishers.

---

7 The legislation of "The Basic Act on Healthy Family" can be seen as a tendency of neo-familism that attempts to adhere to the frame of the traditional family.

Cho, Uhn. (2005). The Encroachment of Globalization into Intimate Life: The Flexible Korean Family in 'Economic Crisis.' *Korean Journal* 45(3): 8-35.

Constable, N. (2005). *Cross-border Marriages: Gender and Mobility in Transnational Asia*. Philadelphia: University of Pennsylvania Press.

Hochschild, A. R. (2001). *The Time Bind: when work becomes home and home becomes work*. New York: Henry Holt and Company.

Kim, H.Y. (2005). Gajok uisikui sedaejeok teukseong (The Generational Characteristics of Family Consciousness; in Korean). *Gajokgwa munhwa (Family and Culture)* 17(1): 115-146.

Kim, S. K., Choi, M. J., Lee, Y. J., Park, J. H., Sun, W. D., Cho, A. J., Kim, Y. K., and Kang, O. H.(2003). *Jeochulsan daebi ingujeongchaek gaebal mit beomjeongbu chujinchege surip yeon-gu (A Study on the Development of Population Policy in Preparation for Low Fertility Rates and the Establishment of Government-wide Measures*; in Korean). Korean Institute of Health and Social Affairs.

Korean Women's Development Institute. (2009). *Seong inji tong-gye (Statistical Yearbook on Women*; in Korean).

Lee, H. K. (2004). Gukgagan nodong ijuwa gukje gyeolhon gajeongui munje (International Work Migration and the Problem of Interracial Marriage Family; in Korean). *Gajokgwa munhwa (Family and Culture)*. Report of Annual Assembly Seminar, Korean Family Association.

Lee. J. K. (2003). *Gajogui ireumeuro (In the Name of the Family*; in Korean). Seoul: Alternative Culture.

Lee. J. K. (2004). Han-guk gajogeun wigiinga?: 'Geongang gajok' damrone daehan bipan (Is the Korean Family in Crisis?: Feminist Critics on 'Family Strength' Discourse; in Korean). *Journal of Korean Women's Studies* 20(1): 229-244.

Lee, J. K. (2007). "Han-guk gajok byeonhwa-ui teukseong-gwa jaengjeom." Yang, et al. *Gajokbokjiui jeongchaekgwa silcheon (Policy and Practice on Family Welfare*; in Korean). Gongdongche.

Lee, J. K. (2009). Love and Economy in Cross-border Marriages in South Korea. *Women's Studies Review* 26(1): 183-206.

Lee, J. K., Cho, Y. M., Lee, Euna, and Yoo, J. M. (2005). Yureobui jeochulsan gwallyeon jeongchaege daehan yeoseongjuuijeok bunseok (Feminist

Approach to Low Fertility and Family Policies in Europe; in Korean). *Han-guk yeoseonghak (Journal of Korean Women's Studies)* 21(3): 133-166.

Lee, J. K. and Jang, M. H. (2004). Goyong jogeoni ilgwa gajoge daehan taedoe michineun yeonghyang (Changing Workplace Implication for the Work-Family Interface; in Korean). *Gyeongjewa sahoe (Economy and Society)* 64: 172-206.

Lee, J. K., Kim, H. Y., Ma, K. H., Lee, Y. S., Cho, Y. M., Hahm, I. H., and Hwang, J. M. (2004). *Han-guk gajogui hyeonsilgwa byeonhwa (Changes and Current Situation of Korean Families*; in Korean). Seoul: Han-guksahoehakhoe: Ministry of Gender Equality, Korea.

Lee, J. K., Lee, Euna, and Cho, J. E. (2006). Negotiating Work and Family Life in South Korea: Class Differences among Working Women. *Journal of Korean Women's Studies* 22(2): 41-79.

National Statistics Office (2009). *Gyeongje hwaldong ingu yeonbo (Economically Active Population Yearbook*; in Korean).

National Statistics Office (2009a) *Honin tong-gye (Statistical Report on Marriage*; in Korean).

National Statistics Office (2009b). *Ihon tong-gye (Statistical Report on Divorce*; in Korean).

National Statistics Office (2009c). *Tong-gye-ro bon yeoseong-ui sarm (Statistical Report on Women's Lives*; in Korean)

National Statistics Office (2009d). *Sahoe josa bogoseo (Social Statistics Survey*; in Korean).

Skolnick, A. S. and Skolnick, J. H. (2000). *Family in Transition*. Boston: Pearson.

Korea Times internet webpage http://www.koreatimes.co.kr
Chosun Ilbo Internet webpage http://www.chosun.com
JoongAng Ilbo Internet webpage http://www.joins.com
National Statistics Office KOSIS http://kosis.nso.go.kr

Chapter nine

Love, Sexuality, and Marriage

Sohn, Seong Young (Dongduk Women's University)

1. Expansion of Love in the Korean Society

Sociologist Arlie Hochschild defines love as a "cultural ideology" emphasizing the ways in which socio-cultural dimensions of societies shape how one experiences the feelings of love. Similarly, peer groups tend to pressure individuals to experience love in a certain way and place love high on the list of priorities. In contemporary Korea, love as a "cultural ideology" is expanding, and this is pressuring individuals to feel as if they "won't be able to live a meaningful life without love." Overall, cultures that dramatize and glamorize love are ubiquitous. The ideology of love can be found among peer groups, popular culture, and even advertisements.

1) Mass media Triggering Heterosexual Dating

Romantic encounters and emotional and physical attractions

between the opposite sexes are a common theme in children's storybooks and animations. Many of us grew up reading or listening to stories that depicted stereotypical love relationships between boys and girls or men and women who embody traditional notions of love and masculinity and femininity. For example, the classic Korean fairytale *Kongjwi Patjwi* and western classics, such as *Snow White*, *Sleeping Beauty*, and *The Little Mermaid*, all have storylines that revolve around a prince who appears out of nowhere and saves the troubled heroine and, then, they immediately fall in love. These stories romanticize love between the brave and masculine boy or man (usually a prince) and the beautiful and innocent girl or woman (usually a princess).

These clichés nonetheless lead individuals to internalize the idealized images of heterosexual love and make them believe that they will magically fall in love one day at first sight. They also reinforce the notion that only heterosexual love is normal and romantic, while treating all other types of love as falling into the realm of abnormality. In addition, these stories usually conclude with the protagonists' marriage, implicitly leading one to believe the two will "live happily ever after" without undergoing any further difficulties in their relationship. Scenarios of love like these, or close versions of these, continue to appear today in numerous TV shows, films, soap operas, and plays. The prevalence of these stories, featuring the traditional female role, reinforces the sexist stereotype. Therefore, the common character of women, who will actually try to use their sexualities as a means of acquiring higher status positions and meet prince-like men, is defined as the "Cinderella Complex."

These popular images of love also reflect common cultural notions that are based on an unequal distribution of power between the sexes. Typically they show economically privileged men's preference to be in relationships with women who will be emotionally dependent upon them. Through various channels, mass media has glamorized love, objectified the women's body and sexuality, and encouraged sex through commodifying it. Relationships between male and female protagonists also tend to separate the stereotypical roles of male domination and female subservience. These results support Firestone's observation that love relationships tend to reinforce the subservient status of third world women by blocking routes to empowerment (Firestone 1979).

Love triangles are also a common theme in many Korean movies and dramas. A common portrayal is two men who compete against each other in order to gain the attention of an attractive and kindhearted female, while a fourth malicious female character intervenes to disrupt the relationship between the main protagonists. These themes of love appear so often on television some say shows that do not portray these stereotypical love relations will not sell.

Another increasingly popular type of show on television is matchmaking programs. In *Introducing Star's Friend*, celebrities introduce their friends to other celebrities or individuals. *Dazzling Blind Date* sets up a female or male with five other individuals of the opposite sex on a bus traveling around town, while the person chooses the most attractive participate as his/her date. *The Single Guy Dates* provides guys, who have never dated, an opportunity to date beautiful women. In these matchmaking programs, men plan for memorable dates with the women, and women choose men who provided the most impressive date. Viewers watch the programs and desire their boyfriends to also look for romantic places to take them, or dream of a date like the one they see on television. A few programs set up dates between unknown female college students and male celebrities and let the female viewers believe they will also get a chance to date someone famous someday. These programs commercialize dating in the pursuit of higher ratings. Competition among programs to draw more attention from viewers leads to more commercialization of sexuality and dramatizing of dating relationships.

2) Commoditization and Materialistic Practices of Love

The love ideology is triggered by mass media for primarily commercial purposes. Through mass media, the formula and content of love, techniques for courtship, methods of meeting partners, and other love-related cultural norms and messages are delivered.

Similar exploitations of the love ideology can be seen in commercial products and advertisements as well. In the past, these yearnings for love appeared in adolescence around puberty; however, now, even children below the age of ten fantasize about love and dating. Chocolate and card companies are busy producing products for Valentine's Day (February 14th) and White Day (March 14th), and cookie companies produced *Pepero-day* (November 11th) in order to sell more products. Couples place importance on celebrating their 100-day and 200-day anniversaries, making couple rings and photo stickers, and the sort. Recently, an advertisement by a fast food chain featured a couple taking a "love-shot" (feeding each other drinks and burgers). Although many people tend to see these advertisements as exaggerating dating behaviors, nonetheless, these images spread a couple-centric image that the fast food company wants to promote. The same company carries "couple set menus" that include two of the same burgers, which quickly became a popular item.

Cell phone companies also feature couples in their advertise-ments and stress the importance of cell phone communication between couples. Popular phrases in cell phone advertisements that reflect this idea are numerous, such as *"I can go anywhere for you," "You don't know women,"* and *"Sleep tight, Dream about me."* Popular "couple phone plans" include 1,000 or 2,000 minutes of free talk between couples. Cell phone companies also provide exclusive membership benefits through membership programs that can be used for getting discounts at their retail partners' restaurants, stores, concert, or accessing member lounges located throughout large cities. Banks advertise couples' checking accounts. One insurance company even has a commercial in which a boyfriend purchases a life insurance for his girlfriend who is joining the military. Budgeting together or having a joint checking account carries a meaning of sharing and unity between couples. Commercial advertisements have increasingly taken advantage of these kinds of feelings among couples as well.

The cultural meaning of love has also taken a materialistic

direction. Proposing or revealing feelings of love on television are becoming more and more materialistic. For example, boyfriends have hired party planners to decorate rooms with numerous flowers, candles, or balloons to impress their girlfriends. They often purchase an expensive ring and other materialistic goods. Some even go as far as to rent expensive limos with wine bars and large screens inside to confess their love. Increasingly, even the methods they use to reveal their feelings seem to follow a set of rules that are regarded as important.

However, the television programs, advertisements, and excessive materialism do not accurately depict reality. First of all, the expensive facilities that the couples use on these television shows are not realistic at all, but merely a show put together by corporate owners willing to invest money in order to advertise their products. Most of these romanticized dates are, in reality, financially out of reach for most young people. Second, television programs and advertisements are producing impossible fantasies that have led people to believe in fateful encounters and love at first sight. One advertisement that became popular among young people featured a woman in a subway saying, "I'm getting off at this station," and a guy answering, "I missed my stop two stops ago." Although many know that this kind of fateful encounter is not realistic, these cultural messages spread an unrealistic ideology of love that can lead people to secretly believe the unlikely encounter can happen to them.

2. Sexual Norms of the Unmarried

Change in the ways in which love has been practiced in the Korean society has also had an effect on the sexual norms and gender roles of the unmarried population. Dating is becoming more frequent and more widespread among young people, and the age at which adolescents start dating is becoming lower than ever. A survey of college students by S. D. Choi in 1975 found 51.9 % of the male respondents and 82.9 % of the female respondents started dating only after entering college. In contrast, a 1989 survey of college students by J. H. Song showed approximately 59.6 % of males and females had already experienced heterosexual dating in high-school or earlier. Similarly, in 1975, approximately half of female college students reported they had not had any dating experience at all. However, in a survey conducted from 1990 to 2000, the number of females without dating experience varied between 0.9 % and 32.4 %, showing a huge drop since the 1970s (Hahm 2001). These survey results lead us to conclude that dating is becoming a more common and widespread practice among Korean college students.

Simultaneously, a parallel change in young people's attitude toward premarital sex has occurred. An increasing number of people think premarital sex is acceptable, if the sex is practiced among two people "who love each other." Some justify premarital sex by saying "It is okay if the couple promised to marry in the future." In surveys conducted in 1985 and 1989 by the National Bureau of Statistics, 68.8 % and 81.1 % of female respondents, respectively, responded that it is important to keep one's virginity before marriage. In surveys conducted in 1995 and 1998, these numbers dropped to 47.5 % and 24.2 %, respectively. On the other hand, the percentage of respondents who agreed premarital sex is acceptable, if the couple loves each other or if there is an agreement to marry between the two, doubled (Hahm 2001). In a 2009 survey, it was found that slightly more females than males place some importance on virginity. However, since less than 20 % of males and females believe that virginity is important, one can see how sexual norms and behaviors have changed considerably over the last few decades.

Furthermore, there is a considerable gender gap on whether or not it is problematic to have sex without any feelings of love. Only 30 % of males felt having casual sex without emotion was problematic, whereas 60 % of female respondents felt that sex without love was problematic. This implies many women have premarital sex only when there are implicit assumptions that the relationship will lead to marriage. In a survey administered in 2009, it was discovered that approximately two-thirds of single men and half of single women have had pre-marital sexual experiences (Lee, et al. 2009).

As these statistics show, there has been an increase in sexual activity among unmarried couples. However, a large number of couples still do not practice safe sex or use contraception. The problematic and still primitive sex education culture in Korea is partially responsible for this tendency. Responding to a question that asked whether or not they had sex without using contraception at least once in the past year, 35.1 % of the male respondents, aged 19-24, and 67.2 %, aged 25-30 answered yes, while only 34.9 % of the female respondents, aged 19-24, 43.2 %, aged 25-30, answered yes. The fact that so many couples are having premarital sex without using contraception can be problematic in that it can lead to an increase in the number of unintended pregnancies and involuntary single mothers, especially since the Korean dating culture is characterized by unequal relationships where males tend to dominate in decision-making processes. Furthermore, there is a lack of open communication regarding sexual issues among men and women in Korea.

Another issue related to the spread of the love ideology and the increase in sexual activities among unmarried males and females pertains to the tendency of couples to conform to traditional gender roles when dating and in relationships. Research suggests that, although both males and females tend to care about their appearance, take showers, do their hair, and wear nice clothes before dates, female college students tend to be affected more psychologically about the date (Park 2000). Females tend to talk about their date more often to friends and family and daydream and get distracted more often by thoughts of the date. This is due to the gendered social construction of dating ideology in ways that make it more socially meaningful to females than males. While dating, females attend to the experience of love in a lot more sensitive way. Females are also socialized to take the role of the care-provider and be more understanding toward their partners within the relationship. For men, work and dating do not tend to disrupt each other, but many females, on the other hand, tend to sacrifice their personal desires and ambitions to act as "desirable" girlfriends (Kwok, et al. 1998). While females work on their "desirability" as girlfriends, males tend to plan the date and conversation topics and even browse the Internet to find the newest jokes and gossip to bring to the date. Men continue to have the role of making reservations at restaurants and buying the movie and concert tickets. Typically, males become the planner and provider within the relationship, whereas women tend to receive and follow their partners' plans and opinions. Males also tend to pay all or the majority of the dating expenses, to arrive earlier at the dating location, to open doors for females, and to assume their role is to "protect" the females. Most females are primarily concerned about conforming to what their boyfriends want rather than taking the lead in the relationship (Park 2000). Therefore, when it comes to dating, the stereotypes do reflect some degree of reality: Men tend to lead, and women follow.

There is also a tendency among males to prefer females who graduated from college with lower prestige levels than their alma mater and who are less intelligent, less successful professionally, and earn less money. In the very least, the male prefers a female younger than him. Although there has been an overall rise in the status of women in Korean society, it is true that younger men increasingly date older women and some women date men regardless of their economic status. However, men with high prestige jobs still tend to avoid the so-called "gold misses" for younger women. These trends still point to the unequal power relationships between the sexes. Because males think they have a superior position relative to their partners, they tend to choose women who meet their patriarchal expectations.

Although tremendous changes have occurred in gender roles in the public sphere, Korean couples' private dating lives are still ridden with patriarchal relationships and traditional role expectations. These culturally gendered roles, where males make the marriage proposals, ask girls out for dates, initiate sexual activities, are expected and still taken for granted. On the other hand, females are expected to not act too assertive or opinionated. As a result, the male-dominated patriarchal love culture, sexual relationship, and dating norms are still affecting Koreans.

3. Selecting Marriage Partners and Parental Intervention

Unlike in the past, when parents played a huge role in selecting their children's marriage partner, the willingness and desire of couples to be involved in the marriage process is becoming a more and more important criterion in Korea. This can be referred to as the "revolution of intimacy" (Whyte 1990) in that individuals have leverage in choosing their marriage partners. However, traditional tendencies still thrive and complicate the picture in that parental approval and support is still needed for most couples, unlike in the West, and marriage is still regarded as a union of two families.

1) Increasing Preference of a "Love Marriage"

Traditional social expectations that linked dating directly to marriage seem to be diminishing. Now people can date without necessarily considering the possibility of marriage. This tends to be truer for people who are still in their teens or early twenties. When young people do not feel the pressure to marry, they tend to date for the experience alone that dating provides, but they tend to date as part of a "spouse-seeking" process as they reach the marriageable ages.

As dating becomes more common in Korean society, more people are beginning to prefer "love marriages" rather than traditionally arranged marriages. According to research conducted by the National Bureau of Statistics from 1981 to 1989, the percentage of couples who married through some form of matchmaking decreased from 58.4 % to 39.4 %, while marriage for love increased from 36.3 % to 54.7 % over the same period. In addition, according to a 2001 study, more people met their spouses through non-family-related social settings, such as school or the workplace, rather than through their familial networks. For example, 37.8 % met their spouses through friends or colleagues from work or school and 22.6 % through other personal sources, whereas only 33.4 % reported meeting their spouses through parents, relatives, or siblings. On the other hand, only 2.3 % of the respondents reported using professional matchmaking services (Lee, et al. 2001). These reports show that love marriage is steadily increasing in the Korean society, but familial networks are still important sources for meeting partners as well.

In addition to the changes toward marriage, the selection criteria for choosing a partner are changing as well. Traditional factors, such as family background or assets, are becoming less important, while personal factors, such as alma mater, economic stability, and professional abilities are becoming more important criteria when selecting partners. When the question about criteria was asked of college students, many responded that love was the most important factor. In 1980, on average, personality, mental maturity, and health were more important than love, whereas, in 2000, personality, love, appearance, family background, and professional abilities were the most important factors (Hahm 2001). Overall, the importance of love at the time of spouse selection is increasing.

Romantic and emotional factors such as love and affection coexist as important criteria along with more utilitarian and practical factors such as professional ability and financial stability in the marriage market. Traditional factors still matter but along with emotional factors or other factors that can affect them, such as appearance. Although many prefer a love marriage, rather than seeking unconditional love, many look for the right combination of practicality and love. Many females also look for spouses who will respect and support their future career plans. There is a significant gender gap in the factors that affect the selection of spouses. Females typically consider a good family background and professional ability as important, while males consider appearance, love, and reliability as more important factors (Park 2003). Recently, many males have begun to prefer a woman with a career and, especially, a woman with a stable career, such as a pharmacist or school teacher. Furthermore, male professionals tend to prefer young females with careers to "gold misses," who tend to be older (Jeon 2007).

2) Consistent Parental Intervention

During the Joseon Dynasty, people tended to marry partners who were selected by their parents. In those days, people often married partners they had never met. This does not seem to be the case in Korea today.

The influence of parents in selecting a spouse for children is indeed weakening. Fewer and fewer parents want to make the "final decision" for their children when it comes to marriage. As Table 1 shows, in 1958, 11.5 % of respondents said they completely respected their parents' opinion when it came to spouse selection, but, in 1992, virtually none said they would give their parents the right to make that choice for them. Furthermore, respondents who said they would make the final decisions without considering their parents' opinion increased from 49.1 % to 93.1 %.

Obviously, parents' influence is decreasing, but traditional Korean attitudes are still prevalent as is evidenced by the need to seek parent's approval when it comes to selecting a marriage partner. There are cases, however, where parents actively ask relatives or friends about eligible marriage candidates for their sons/daughters or they actively oppose the marriage partner when asked for their approval. There are not many cases where two people reach the final decision to marry and then notify their parents about the decision. This is because marriage is not perceived as an individual affair but as an affair between two families. It is not

Table 1 Changes in Partner Selection

Decision Method	HJ Lee (1958)	Choi (1972)	DW Lee (1981)	Lim (1992)
Follow parent's opinion	11.5	3.6	0.7	-
Parents decide and seek agreement	35.9	43.6	37.8	6.7
Respondents decide and seek parent's approval	35.2	40.0	38.5	88.0
Respondents decide	13.9	10.9	21.1	5.1
Non response	3.5	1.8	1.8	-
Total	100.0	100.0	100.0	100.0

Note: Recited from Hahm (2001), p. 18.

necessary for the parents to like the partner their child selects, but, if the parents believe the partner does not fit the status of the family or is somewhat different from their ideal daughter/son-in-law, it will often lead to disapproval and conflict. There is still a widespread notion that children should obey their parents' opinion, which is uncomfortably blended with the more Western notion that individual love and choices are more important.

As a result, spouse selection does not depend only on the more ideal factors of attraction and love but also the more realistic factors, such as the persons' background, parents' assets, education level, religion, or region of origin. In Korea, romantic love tends to be blended with social norms and traditional values.

3) Appearance of Matchmaking Companies

The first professional matchmaking company was the Korea Altman

System, which was founded in 1984, and was followed by Ecorus in 1986. When these companies first appeared, people did not use the contemporary Korean term *Gyeolhonjeongbo hoesa*, which directly translates into "Marriage Information Company," but referred to these companies in an antiquated term that meant "Matchmaking Business Using Computers"(*The JoongAng Ilbo*, January 11, 1991). In the latter part of the next decade, larger companies, such as Sunwoo, entered the marriage market. By 2000, there were at least 10 large corporations and over 100 small matchmaking companies in full operation. Altogether these companies have over 60,000 members (Korea Consumer Protection Center 2000). By 2005, the total number of matchmaking companies was estimated at 900, showing a rapid increase from the past. Among these 900 companies, 20 % handled only domestic matchmaking, 41 % dealt in international matchmaking, and 39 % handled both international and domestic matchmaking (Han, et al. 2006).

Looking at the individual preferences of members sharply reflect the transaction patterns in the marriage market. Marriages through matchmaking companies can be categorized as a "love of convenience" in that they focus on maximizing their personal interests by using the services, although love and intimacy are still important. Through the services of these companies, members try to look for the most ideal spouse with "realistic intentions" as well as fulfill their desire for love. Using Illouz's (2007) terminology, we can categorize this culture where emotive and economic discourses and practices are mutually constitutive as 'emotional capitalism.' Males tend to seek female partners who are pretty, domestic, willing to give them a child, and provide emotional care to them and their family, while females look for males who can provide economic and physical protection. These desires reflect how often economic motives are mixed with the logic of intimacy as a goal of marriage.

Commoditization of love in Korean society is not only being accelerated through matchmaking companies but also through the increase in marriage migration. Marriage migration is a complex phenomenon, where issues of gender, race, and class intersect. The economic transactional dimension of love is even more obvious when considering how patriarchal power relationships between the sexes are shaped through the commercial marriage market. Also the gender dichotomy in how females prioritize males' assets and professional rank, and males prioritize females' age merely reflects the typical dating and romantic love script (Lee 2009). Commoditization of love emotion affects the gender hierarchy and relationship within families as well.

4. Sexuality of the Married

An overflow of discussions on love and sexuality has marked the 2000s in Korea. There has been a deluge of discourses on love and sex. However, little is ever said about the sexuality of married people. Love and sexuality of the unmarried or newly married couples are frequently discussed, but nobody seems to discuss issues of sexuality in regard to couples married for years. What would account for this seeming disparity? It might be that in the Korean society where Confucian beliefs still dictate behavior and values, many believe it is not very proper to openly discuss the relationship issues of married couples. Confucian teachings emphasize fulfilling one's role within the relationship as husband or wife, instead of allowing individuals to claim the importance of their own love emotions or sexual desires. In addition, many even believe it is meaningless to discuss sexually-related issues when the daily interactions among married people are, essentially, repetitive and routine and without novelty after so many years together.

Still, the sexual relationship of married couples is becoming a more important factor than in the past. After all, marriages are formed around love and sex, and there is little justification for not discussing the issues of sexuality in marriage. Attitudes towards divorce, which was once unthinkable, are changing as well and such fact point to the growing importance of individual desire and emotions within married relationships. The rapidly increasing divorce rate of Korea (Ministry of Health and Welfare 2003) speaks to the fact that Koreans no longer necessarily equate marriage to "loving together ever after."

Therefore, it is important to uncover the way in which the sexuality of married couples is constructed as social, cultural, and historical byproducts. Although married people have increasingly higher expectations regarding marriage and sexual relationships, individuals no longer see marriage as a duty but feel that, if they no longer have affection towards their partner, they have the right to divorce the partner. Of course, decisions regarding divorce still affect children in Korea more than children in the west, where divorce has a less of a stigma. Therefore, the once traditional pattern, in which the children's welfare and happiness was the main priority in families, is definitely going through some changes.

One study which analyzed the contents of popular women's magazines demonstrates that the number of articles that deal with the sex and love of married couples have increased over time as well as diversified and become richer in content (Jung 1992). Up until the 1970s, most articles emphasized the traditionally idealized roles of women as desirable wives and mothers. However, in the 1980s, as the number of articles that dealt with sex among married couples increased, a clear double standard emerged. Many articles took the sexual desire of husbands for granted and naturalized it, publishing articles on topics like ways to prevent husbands from having affairs or how to react to a husband's elicit love. In the 1990s, many articles started emphasizing how wives should start taking a more active stance on sex, since many males are fond of women who listen to their own desires. In this analysis, the apparent change in how the wife's role was re-conceptualized over time is evident: in the 1980s, the main role of wives was to understand their husbands' sexual desire, while, in the 1990s, it became important for wives to become sexually attractive themselves. The perception that the main role of married women is to reproduce has dwindled, but married women are still portrayed as instruments to satisfying their husbands' sexual desire. Korean society does acknowledge the existence of the sexual desires of married women, but they prefer to have these desires expressed passively in order to conform to their husband's expectations.

The gendered discourses on the sexuality of married men and women, as well as the double standards that lead to the dichotomous scheme, sharply divides the sphere of "dating" and "marriage." Routine everyday marriage relationships leave sex largely invisible within them, whereas dating relationships allow for both males and females to consent or reject their sexual relationships more freely. Dating relationships tends to be less restrictive and freer compared to marriages that constrain individuals and centralize love and sex as the core purposes.

The sexual norms operate oppressively on women's sexuality. The double standard has led to the husband's forcible demand for sex and domination over his wife in the sexual relationship. Moreover, husbands tend to believe they can have extramarital relationships, regardless of the degree of intimacy with their wives, and they feel free to talk openly about their extramarital affairs with others (Chang 1999). Different sexual experiences and norms between husbands and wives can often lead to a conflict of interests in regard to their expectation towards their partners within marriage. These dynamics have led some radicals to argue that married individuals should stop viewing sex within the boundaries of marriage as the only legitimate act of sex and try liberating themselves from the oppressive norms and expectations of marriage (Kim 1997). As seen in the title of one popular book, *Let's Marry after Living Together*, the advantage of cohabitation as an alternative to the contradictory aspects of marital system is highlighted. If the majority of cohabitating couples saw cohabitation as a pre-step to marriage in the past, today couples do not necessarily intend to marry their live-in partners.

Current studies argue there is a large variation in how married couples lead their sexual lives (Lee 2006), suggesting the recent changes in the sexual relationships of married couples. Although a patriarchal culture is still prevalent in Korea, many more couples have made an effort to improve their relationships. Even though it might be premature to argue that females' sexual autonomy has been growing within marriage, surely marital experiences are becoming more diverse and a movement toward gender equity within marriage exists.

Therefore, it is time to start discussing women's sexual autonomy actively. The focus should be on five specific aspects. First, conventional attitudes that regard sex primarily as an instrument for reproduction need to be changed. Second, with an increasing number of women involved in their own careers, less emphasis should be placed on romanticized yet exclusive love relations and a woman's place is in the home. Third, the double standard that allows men sexual freedom but emphasizes women's chastity should be eradicated. Fourth, the demeaning and violent attitudes of men who regard their wives as their sexual possession should not be emphatically rejected. Fifth, the contradiction in logic that justifies men's extramarital relationships as natural but stigmatizes women's extramarital affairs should be realized.

5. Diastrophism of Intimacy Surrounding Love, Sexuality, and Marriage

The importance of love is growing in South Korea's society. Many even act as if love is the most important goal in life. Mass media is largely responsible for this phenomenon by distributing distorted images of love through soap operas and films. Advertisements have also affected our images of ideal love and have shaped our body images and perceptions of beauty, womanhood, and love. Women tend to view love as being more important in their lives than men. Research on college students clearly shows a gender gap in dating attitudes. While female students tend to spend more time choosing clothes and primping for dates, male students tend to take responsibility in planning dates. There is also a tendency for male students to provide most of the dating expenditures, revealing the static acceptance of traditional gender roles, in which males have power and superiority over females as well as care and provide for them.

The patriarchal ideology of gender division is also reflected in married couples' relationships. Soap operas feature extramarital affairs much more often than love between married couples. In these shows, the wife's sexuality is regarded as an instrument to satisfy her husband's sexual desire. In addition, parenting and household work are performed primarily by women. Although, today, it is popular to emphasize the rising status of women in Korea, a strong patriarchal culture still remains.

However, the sexuality of married couples is emerging as an

important issue these days, especially for those in their honeymoon stage. More discussions on ways to improve a love relationship and reduce conflicts between marital couples are needed. In addition, more changes in intimacy are expected in regards to love, sexuality, and marriage due to the increase in women's educational attainments, labor force participation, independent living styles, and divorce rate. Historical changes in the patterns of sexual relationships and love as well as the meanings given to them (Illouz 1997) have become salient. These changes are concurrent to other social changes in the Korean society, such as the growth of the consumer market. The numbers of women who postpone or reject marriage and/or childbearing and choose cohabitation or homosexual relationships are also increasing. The increase in the number of women and men who desire to live independently from the traditional constraints of marriage, heterosexism, or parent-child relationships demonstrates how an individual's choices for intimacy are diversifying.

As Gagnon (1990) mentioned, the common "scripts of sexuality" and "scripts of love" reflect well the dominant and normative perceptions of love, sexuality, and marriage in Korea. The ideology of romantic love, gender norm, marriage system, and so forth operate on the basis of gender inequality perpetuated by the patriarchal Korean culture. Structural inequality is salient in such a gendered notion of sexuality. Korean women have started to challenge the structural inequality inherent in the Korean family and, as the main victims of the system, became cognizant about these problems much earlier than men.

Women should be guaranteed their sexual autonomy. Both women and men should share the rights and responsibilities related to sexuality and try to develop equal relationships based on mutual respect. By discussing better ways to communicate and to respect each other's decisions and lifestyles with prospective partners, young couples will be better equipped for dating or marriage. Without acknowledging women's need for sexual autonomy, it is difficult to expect pure companionship between husband and wife. The current attitude of Koreans in only allowing wives' sexual expressiveness to the extent that they can satisfy their husbands' sexual desire demonstrates that traditional gender norms are still present. To improve the quality of marital relationships, Korean husbands and wives need to mutually recognize and respect the sexual rights and needs of their spouses.

References

Chang, P. H. (2000). *Yeoseong, mom, seong (Women, Body, and Sexuality*; in Korean). Seoul: Ddohanaui munhwa (Another Culture).

Choi, S. D. (1975). Han-guk namnyeo daehaksaengui deiteusiltae gwanhan josayeon-gu (A Research on Korean Male and Female College Students' Dating; in Korean). *Han-guk munhwa yeon-guwon Nonchong* 25: 131-159.

Hahm, I. H. (2001). Baeuja seontaek yangsigui byeonhwa: Chinmilseong-ui hyeokmyeong? (Changes in Spouse Selection Pattern: Revolution of Intimacy?; in Korean). *Gajokgwa munhwa (Family and Culture)* 13(2): 3-28.

Han, G. S. and Seol, D. H. (2006). *Gyeolhon jung-gye eopche siltaejosa mit gwalli bang-an yeon-gu (Research on Marriage Arranging Company and Management System; in Korean).* Ministry of Health and Welfare.

Jeon, S. A. (2007). Hyeonjangeseo bon gyeolhon munhwaui byeonhwa (Changes in Marriage Culture; in Korean). *Jendeo Libyu (Gender Review)* 5: 33-38.

Jung, E. H. (1992). Oneului seongmunhwawa bubuui seong (Today's Culture of Sexuality and Sex and Husband-Wife; in Korean), *Han-gukgajogui bubugwangye (Married Couple's Relationship in Korean Family; in Korean)*, Institute of Society and Culture.

Kim, J. M. (1997). Seks maind (*Sex Mind*; in Korean). Seoul: Hwangkeumgaji.

Korean Consumer Protection Center (2000). *Gyeolhon sangdam eopche unyeong mit iyong siltae josa (Management and Use of Marriage Counseling Company; in Korean).*

Kwok, S. K., Kim, H. M., Sohn, S. Y., Lee, S. H., and Joo, E. H. (1998). Ilsang-ui yeoseonghak (*Gender Study of Everyday Life*; in Korean). Seoul: Parkyoungsa.

Lee, D. W., et al. (2001). *Hangugui gajok munhwa (A Report on Family Study; in Korean).* Seoul: KBS, Korean Family Studies Association.

Lee, J. K. (2009). Saranggwa kyeongjeui gwangyereul tonghae bon ijugyeolhon (Love and Economy in Cross-border Marriages in South Korea; in Korean). *Yeoseonghaknonjip (Women's Studies Review)* 26(1): 183-206.

Lee, M. J., Byun, H. S., and Kim, E. J. (2009). Cheongnyeoncheung seksyueolli-tiwa chinmilhan gwangyeeseoui seongpongnyeok yeon-gu (*Sexuality of Adolescents and Sexual Violence in the Intimate Relationship*; in Korean). Korean Women's Development Institute.

Lee, S. E. (2006). Han-guk gihon namnyeoui sexualitywa chinmilseongui gaenyeomhwa (A Research on Sexuality and the Re-construction of Intimacy within Married Couples; in Korean). *Gajokgwa munhwa (Family and Culture)* 18(2): 1-36.

Ministry of Health and Welfare (2003). Bokjiwa gyeongjeui seonsunwhan gwangye yeon-gu (A Study of Cyclic Relationship between Welfare and Economy; in Korean).

National Bureau of Statistics, Korea, 1981, 1985, 1989.

Park, M. J. (2000). Han-guk daehaksaengdeului deiteugwajeong-e natanan namnyeoui chai (Gender Difference in the Dating Process among Korean College Students; in Korean). *Gajokgwa munhwa (Family and Culture)* 12(1): 53-66.

Park, M. J. (2003). Honinui uimieseoui namnyeo chai: Daehaksaengeul jungsimeuro (Gender Difference in the Meaning of Marriage; in Korean). *Gajokgwa munhwa (Family and Culture)* 15(2): 3-32.

Song, J. H. (1989). *Daehaksaengdeului iseonggyojesiltae mit gyeolhongwane gwanhan yeon-gu (Dating Pattern and Marital Value of College Students in Daejeon*; in Korean). Master's Thesis, Ewha Woman's University, Seoul.

Firestone, S. (1970). *The Dialectic of Sex: The Case for Feminist Revolution.* N.Y.: William Morrow.

Gagnon, J. H. (1990). The Implicit and Explicit Use of the Scripting Perspective in Sex Research. *Annual Review of Sex Research* 1: 1-43.

Illouz, E. (2007). *Cold Intimacies: The Making of Emotional Capitalism.* Polity Press.

Whyte, K. (1990). *Dating, Mating, and Marriage.* New York: Aldine de Gruyter.

Chapter ten

Women's Work and Kin Relationships since the 1960s

Kim, Hye-Kyung (Chonbuk National University)

1. Introduction

In the modern era, the changes in the family were characteristically driven by birth of the new gender structure in which men worked outside the home and women played the role of the emotional center in the family. However, since the late twentieth century, the family has radically changed when women as well as men participate in paid work outside the home. This indicates that the changes in the family are closely related to the changes at work. In the 1990s, it became the norm for married women with young children to be economically active. Consequently, conflicts between family and work have increased, and efforts to ease the conflicts, by introducing family-friendly policies, have also been made in various ways. In 1994, for instance, the European Union established a network to conduct substantial research on how people balance work and family (Drew, Emerk, Mahon 1998). In Korea, too, one of the most pressing issues, regarding women and family policies over the past decade, is the work-family balance. With record-low birth rate of 1.17 as of 2002, the issue of work-family balance has received considerable attention from policy makers who see the family-friendly policy as a key to lifting the nation's birth rates.

The obstacle to raising the birth rate has been assumed to be the environment which lacks in the family-friendly institutions in Korea. But, moreover, we should pay a special attention to the fact that rather than blaming profit-seeking corporations or the government's limited social policies, the ongoing inequities of gender relations within families, which allow men to escape domestic labor and child care activities, have created too big a burden for married women to bear a child or develop the career. Despite its considerable importance, the gender question has not been raised sufficiently in studies of work-family balance. In order to understand work-family conflicts, we need to analyze how the gender relationships are in gear into work-family conjuction, and in addition, the kinship structures are interlockingly adapted to it. Unlike many Western societies, in which the market and/or the state has been the major player for facilitating work-family balance, in the contemporary post-modern Korean society, the family or the ideology of familism remains the fundamental organizing principle of work-family interface.

By examining the life histories of working women from the 1960s of the early industrialization period to the present era of neoliberalization, this chapter explores how women workers have held their jobs in the absence of family-friendly policies, how the kinship system has adapted to the labor market in the process, and how the generational and gender relations combine with each other to create a work-family structure peculiar to Korea.

2. Perspectives on the Work-Family Relations

1) The Social Organization of Labor: Articulation of Work and Family

Historically, the articulation of work and family has been related to the distribution of the social organization of labor in a society (Glucksman 1995). The paid work outside the home and the unpaid work inside the home, as well as work in social relationships and care in personal relationships, have been interrelated in the distributional system of labor in a society. Historically the male provider work system allocated women's labor to the care at home like in USA during the first half of twentieth century. Who plays the major role of care giver/ wage earner differs greatly according to each country's cultural and historical context and policy trajectory. "Theoretically," the state or the capital is to be the major care giver for dual earner households (as seen in Type Ⅲ of Table 1), while, in the Southern European countries, it is the family that provides most of the care-giving services (Del Boca 1998).

However, with the growing neo-liberal market system, where Fordism, usually based on the male single earner household model,

Table 1 The Social Organization of Labor with Gender Arrangement

Type I : Male Breadwinner	Type II : Partial Transformation of Male Breadwinner	Type III : Dual Earner / Socialization of Care			Type IV : Gender Equity
Male Breadwinner Female Carer	Dual Earner/ Female Part-time Worker	Dual Earner/ State Carer	Dual Earner/ Marketized Carer		Dual Earner/ Dual Carer
Western Countries Under Fordism at the First Half of twentieth century	England, Netherlands, Germany	Finland	France	USA, England	Ideal type

Source: Crompton (1999), p. 205; Pfau-Effinger (1999).

withers and job insecurity deepens, the family is taking a bigger role in care-giving. Sometimes it takes a form of "extreme capitalism" in which "shift parenting," a way of parenting where multiple adult family members have "flexible" working hours and take turns to perform caring work at home, becomes prevalent (Crompton 2006).

2) Industrialization and Family Changes: Aspects of Kin Relationship

The existing research on the effects of industrialization on the family focuses mainly on the functional fitness of the nuclear family form to industrialization. For example, there are arguments industrialization has broken traditional three-generation families into nuclear families, or industrialization has led to massive human migration to urban areas and, consequently, to disintegration of the traditional kinship system (Parsons and Bales 1955; Goode 1963).

But there are other arguments too. According to the findings of Hareven (1993), based on research of the one-hundred-year-long history (1838-1936) of a textile factory in Manchester, England, kinship ties and networks were persistently working rather than withering. Major family events of 'family time' such as marriage and childbirth, were organized around the 'industrial time' of employment and migration to the industrial place. This shows the inseparable relationship between the history of labor and family history.

Since the 1960s, the relationship between work and family in the Korean industrialization process was also characteristically family-based, making the factory system and the kinship network of the workers interdependent. The workers, especially girls, usually remitted the money from their small wages to their poor rural families and often went home when they were unemployed or injured (Kim 2002). Rural families also sent foodstuff to their children working with low wage in urban factories during 70's and 80's. Since the 1990s, the post-industrialization era, this kind of extended family network is still in effect. Married children maintain kinship ties with their parents, adding the matrilineal relationship to the existing patrilineal one (Cho 1997). So, in consideration of the strong familialism of Korea, some family sociologists insist that Korean families cannot be said to have changed into a nuclear family structure, although the statistics of the family forms may show that they have (Chang 1993). Some researchers emphasize that the priority of the patrilineal extended family, where the eldest son is supposed to be the center, still remains strong despite the demographic and morphological nuclearization of the family (Ahn 1991). The nuclearization of the family is also said to be a multi-level constitution that involves not only the morphological level but also the material and emotional levels (Chang 1992: 50).

3) Gender Relations and Balancing Work and Family

Has women's participation in the labor market improved their status? According to Tilly and Scott (1987), well-known Western historians who explored the connection between the labor history of women and their family lives, women's participation in the labor market did not improve their positions in society nor in their families. They argue women's participation in the labor market was a part of their family responsibilities and appreciated only as a "family strategy."

What changes has the women's dual role in the family, as paid worker and family care-giver, brought to their spousal relationships then? Some academics argue that, unlike in the 1970s, women workers in the 1990s have demanded that their husbands share in the family responsibilities equally, which shows that the issue of family responsibilities has started to cause spousal conflicts (Rubin 1994: 94-96). Men as well as women experienced big changes. A new masculinity, a nurturing and involved type of masculinity was found not so uncommon in the 1990s, which was unthinkable in the 1970s (Gerson 1993). In Korea, however, family responsibilities have not been considered as a major cause of spousal conflicts. According to a survey of 732 working wives in 2007, only 12.5 % said they shared family responsibilities equally with their husbands. What is interesting is that 33.5 % of the 732 wives, who did not share the responsibilities equally, still perceived the sharing as equitable (Lee and Kim 2008).

A few researchers in the West have recently pointed out that, due to the hardships in the rapidly changing family life, some women showed work-oriented attitude over family. For these women, they argue, workplace paradoxically seems more restful than home, where marital instability and care-giving work never cease (Hochschild 1997). Wives in dual-income families experience a tremendous lack of time for balancing work and family and tend to regard their worker-friendly workplace as a resting place, where their personal efforts are recognized and appreciated more. There are some researchers who disagree with this argument, asserting that what women workers really want is a balance of work and family not an escape from them (Jacobs and Gerson 2004: 157-59). A part of their criticism focuses on the class differences among working women, pointing out that the family responsibilities, which white professional women may call "drudgery," can actually be more "liberating" work for working class women whose labor conditions at work are often worse than "drudgery" (Williams 2000).

3. Research Methods and Subjects

This study is a qualitative analysis of 23 life history narratives of women in South Korea who worked "representative" jobs for women in certain chronological points of time since the 1960s. The "representative" jobs were chosen by using the mid-level classifications of occupations[1] from the data of the 1965, 1985, and 2000 census. This time period was divided into three sub-periods. The first period is from the early 1960s through the mid-1970s, which saw the beginning of rapid industrialization by the developmental state under the regime of President Park Chung-Hee. The second period covers the late 1970s through the early 1990s when the growth of heavy industry and the service sector attracted not only more young women but also married women into labor market. The third period is from the mid-1990s to early 2000s, a neoliberalization period of job instability that destabilized the norm of the "male-breadwinner."

Since the focus of this investigation was how women manage the full time jobs while rearing children, women who worked outside the home during the early years of child care for five or more of years in each period were chosen for this study. Furthermore, for consistency, the women interviewed had work experiences in metropolises, including Seoul. Interviews were conducted for a three-month period between March and May in 2006.

---

1 Except for agricultural jobs (58.9 %), the typical jobs for women in the 1960s included sales, textile, domestic service, cooking, tailoring, livestock industry, daily labor, clerical work, food industry, hair-dressing, education, and mechanics in the order of percentages (sample survey of the 1965 census). In the 1980s, although over 40 % of women workers were still in the agricultural industry, the numbers of women working as clerical workers were increasing fast. The percentages of women workers by type of work are: 33 % in agriculture, 7.9 % in agricultural management, 6.9 % in sales, 6.5 % in bookkeeping, 6.4 % in self-employed retail/wholesale business, 4.4 % in garment/needlework, 3.9 % in cooking and waiting, 3.2 % in education, 3.1 % in clerical work, 2.9 % in self-employed lodging business, 2.1 % in textile (1985 census). In the 1990s, the percentage of professional or semi-professional women workers in education increased notably. And professions in industries, such as culture, art and broadcasting, became among the top 15 women-concentrated occupations (2000 census).

In order to understand the historical change of working experiences of women an oral history approach is more useful, because the women's work tends to be complicated crossing over the boundary between the work place and family along the family cycle. The total work experience of women tends to be unrecognized or omitted when a study focuses only on written materials. Narratives provide key material for studying women at home. But we also pay attention to the particular story lines of the narrator women looking back the past. According to scholars of qualitative research, the life history is a story of a history laden with the norms of an age, and at the same time a story of a personal life. It values the particular perspectives of the storyteller and the plots through which the speaker understands and interprets the world and her life (Denzin 1989; McAdams 1993).

4. The Change of Kinship Formation Strategies for Work-Family Balance in Historical Stages

The major goal of this research was to examine the history of kinship dynamics as the main family strategy for balancing work and child care. The research subjects were women who are or were employed full-time. The results revealed that the majority of them had extended or modified-extended families[2] rather than

---

2 Unlike Parsons and Goode, who predicted the weakening of kin relationships or isolation of the nuclear family in modern industrial societies, Sussman and Litwak suggested the

nuclear families. But one form of family was not dominant during a particular period of time. Moreover each form of family was not one uniform structure but changed along the family cycles. So, in order to analyze the peculiar characteristics of one period, "representative families," which retained relatively consistent family forms throughout the whole family cycle in each period, were selected.

1) Period I (the early 1960s to the mid-1970s): An Inseparable Relationship between Work and Family and the "Patrilineal" Extended Family

The industrialization project and the related social mobilization process named "the New Village Movement"[3] in the 1960s and 1970s became a major driving force for compelling married women in rural areas to enter the agricultural workforce. Often living in circumstances of absolute poverty, women's agricultural work was indispensible not only for the survival of their own families but for the reproduction of society in general. Until the mid-1970s, 48 % of the women employed were agricultural workers, and 21 % of the families were extended families (1975). Accordingly, the majority of the women interviewed from Period I were chosen from former agricultural workers, and the rest were a sales woman, a domestic

---

argument of "the modified extended family," pointing out that contacts and exchanges of help between relatives were sustained.

3 "The New Village Movement(sae-ma-eul un-dong)" was initiated by the government from the year of 1971 for the purpose of stabilizing the regime by economic, social, and mental mobilization, resulting the hegemonic control of president Park's political power.

maid, and a "family-planning agent," a brand-new job at that time for lowering the fertility rate.

Out of the seven interviewees, three had patrilineal extended families which were patrilineal, and another three had nuclear families. Only one had a modified extended family, with much contacts and exchange of help though not living together in the parents' house, which became more common in the following periods. Regarding the three cases of the women with nuclear families in Period I, they chose to take in work at home, so they could take care of their young children while working (hairdresser,

Table 2 Characteristic of Cases in Period I

No. (Age)	Occupation	Occupation of Husband	Birth Year · Marriage Year(Age)	No. of Children	Family Form · Kin Relationship
I -1 (68)	Hairdresser	Cosmetics Sales, etc.	1939 1961 (23)	2 sons	Nuclear
I -2 (54)	Domestic maid	Coffee shop chef. Died in 1988	1952 1981 (30)	1 son	Nuclear → Single mother since the age of 37
I -3 (59)	Farmer	Farmer	1947 1959 (23)	1 daughter & 2 sons	(Patrilineal) Extended
I -4 (66)	Family planning agent	Teacher	1936 1962 (27)	1 daughter & 2 sons	Nuclear
I -5 (54)	Draper sales	Public employee	1952 1978 (27)	2 sons	(Patrilineal) Extended
I -6 (62)	Farmer	Farmer	1944 1965 (22)	2 daughters & 2 sons	(Patrilineal) Modified extended
I -7 (69)	Farmer	Farmer	1937 1958 (22)	2 daughters & 2 sons	(Patrilineal) Extended

case 1; domestic maid, case 2). Many also used diverse community or kinship networks like neighbors, care-giving from older daughters who themselves need care, or low-paid domestic maids often called as relatives.

A representative case among the patrilineal extended families from this period is an interviewee who was a farmer (age 59) and had lived with her parents-in-law and seven siblings-in-law in a rural area. The woman's narrative consists of her experiences with an extended family, poverty, labor, recognition as the eldest daughter-in-law by her in-laws, the education of her children, and the eventual sense of success in her life. Since the extended family took part in rearing her children, work-family conflicts were not cited in her narration as a central problem for her.

> I was born in a big, poor peasant family. I was the eldest daughter. Even when I was an elementary school student, I had to cook barley for my little siblings and take care of my sick grandmother. I even had to clean up her excrement. At the age of 14, I went to Seoul to make money, worked as a sewer for 10 years, and returned home to get married. My husband was the eldest of the seven siblings, and his family was very poor, too. That meant a lot of work for me both at home and at field. I had three children. When I gave birth to my daughter, I wanted her rather to die. I was even thinking to put her into 'silkworm excrements.' I thought that because I couldn't raise her while doing so much work. I ran away to Seoul several times, but my husband found me and dragged me back home.... I worked on the rice field, vended vegetables at the market, worked as a domestic help. I

worked really hard and saved as much money as possible. Thus, I eventually built family fortunes. All my children went to college. One of them studied abroad and became successful enough to be even on TV. I helped seven siblings-in-law to get married and even took care of their marital problems. Now my siblings-in-law thank me a lot, saying "You did a really good job." "You really worked a lot for us." (Period I, Case 3, farmer)

She strongly emphasized the compensation she has received, such as the family recognition of her status as the eldest daughter-in-law. This may be a self-justification of her life in the extended family system to which she successfully adapted herself. This may also show the limited number of survival strategies women could employ when there were very few other alternatives but to adapt to the system.

Women in an extended family had comparatively fewer conflicts over childrearing because many in the family, especially the parents-in-law could lend a helping hand for it. At the same time the strong relationship between the parents-in-law and the husbands hindered in focusing the attention on couple relatioinship. So, the women did not enjoy affectionate relationships with their husbands, which the interviewees remembered very regretfully. For example, the draper sales woman (age 54) had to leave her children with her parents-in-law and three sisters-in-law while she worked at the market, as the economic need of the extended family required her to work outside the home. However, she did not want to live with the patrilineal extended family. Although her husband was the third son in his family, his parents wanted to live with him, which was not common at that time. Therefore, she had no choice but to live with her parents-in-law. She said, "I didn't like living with so many people... I wanted a small, cozy family." She had several serious arguments with her husband about this, but some of the arguments ended with his use of violence. She was sorry that she could not raise her children by herself and that she could not cook for her husband. Now, she said, "I envy those young couples these days and the way they live." At the same time, she strongly identifies with her work. She said, "I worked really hard. I've earned this decent life, you know." This sense of pride and identification with work was not uncommon especially among those who worked during Periods I and II when few women had the successful career.

2) Period Ⅱ (the mid-1970s to the early 1990s): Separation between Work and Family and Various Forms of "Conjunction"

This period between the mid-1970s to the early 1990s was marked by the outward migration of people from rural villages to urban cities, and the employment rate of women in non-agricultural sectors skyrocketed. The employment rates of married women and the rates of dual-earner households were also increasing. The rates of family-member employees, a typical form of employment in agriculture, decreased from 47.9 % in 1975 to 21.1 % in 1995, coinciding with the increase in employment outside home. In the late 1980s, the employment of married women increased significantly, especially in the manufacturing industries. During the same period, the proportion of extended families decreased from 21 % to 10 % (1995 census). This section focuses on the cases of eight interviewees who had worked as factory workers, services and sales workers, or professionals which were the representative jobs at those times according to census.

Unlike Period I, where work and family were barely inseparable from one another, and consequently showed the stability of the family form, Period II began to see the changing living arrangement of family as a strategy for balancing work and childcare along the family cycle, as more. women became employed outside the home while living in nuclear family forms. Of the eight cases four were moving back and forth between a "modified" extended family and a nuclear family for child care along the family cycle. It means that they chose the more flexible family forms for balancing the care needs of children and the privacy needs of couple. Moreover all of whom once had an experience of the matrilineal relationships in their work lives, which reflected the enhancement of the women's status.

Among the eight interviewees, two, the stenographer and the insurance sales person, were selected as the representative cases, because their family forms were consistent and their occupations reflected the increasing number of women working as professional and sales workers. The stenographer (case 6, age 46) lived with her widowed mother, who took complete responsibility for raising her grandchildren. The matrilineal extended family is evidence of the changing social conditions at the time. With the declaration of the "International Women's Year" in 1975 by the United Nations, the

Table 3 Characteristic of Cases in Period Ⅱ

No. (Age)	Occupation	Occupation of Husband	Birth Year · Marriage Year (Age)	No. of Children	Family Form · Kin Relationship
Ⅱ-1 (58)	Insurance sales	Milk sales, but Pastor now	1948 1975 (28)	1 daughter & 1 son	Nuclear
Ⅱ-2 (51)	Factory worker	Factory worker, daily laborer. Died in 1991. (Subject 37)	1955 1979 (25)	2 daughters & 1 son	Nuclear → Single mother since the age of 37
Ⅱ-3 (57)	Factory worker	Factory worker	1949 1970 (22, co-habitation)	2 daughters & 1 son	(Matrilineal) Modified extended → Nuclear
Ⅱ-4 (70)	Poultry sales	Daily laborer. Died in 1985(subject 50)	1936 1955 (20)	3 sons	Nuclear → Single mother since the age of 50
Ⅱ-5 (51)	Bank clerk	White-collar employee	1955 1981 (27)	2 daughters & 1 son	(Bilineal) Modified extended
Ⅱ-6 (46)	Stenographer	Self-employed	1960 1983 (24)	2 daughters	(Matrilineal) Extended
Ⅱ-7 (45)	Newspaper reporter	Actor	1961 1989 (29)	1 daughter	(Matrilineal) Modified extended
Ⅱ-8 (51)	Nursing officer	Soldier	1955 1979 (30)	2 sons	(Matrilineal) Modified extended → (Patrilineal) extended → Nuclear

women's movement for gender equality and democratization of society became active in Korea, and, beginning in the 1980s, more women than ever began to go to college. The stenographer grew up with a lot of support and encouragement from her parents and was able to successfully balance work-family due to the help from her mother and her stable and substantial income. This type of matrilineal extended family functioned as both help for childrearing and for elderly support who had no income.

Although the matrilineal extended family eased some conflicts and ameliorated the balance between work and family, it also led to the husband assuming less of the family responsibilities. The woman said she felt "an emptiness in the relationship with her husband." She also said she "worked her ass off" until her mid-40s, and she feels sorry now that she was never able to enjoy a "juicy family life."

In the meantime, the insurance sales worker (case 1, age 58), one of the interviewees who represented a nuclear family of the same period, existed like a "superwoman," performing "the work of 10 men," both rearing children and caring for a husband and having a job outside the home without any help from other family members. Her flexible working hours of insurance salesperson made it possible for her to keep a balance between work and family. It was not unusual at that time for neighbors to help each other with childrearing.

On the other hand, the factory workers, who used to live far away from their rural extended family, began to have a lot of difficulties balancing work and family. One woman, who had been a factory worker (age 57), still remembers the anxiety she felt leaving her children alone at home while she worked the midnight shift. Usually lower-class married women, living in cities, showed a fluctuating employment history throughout their life cycle. When their children were very young, they worked in the informal sector (such as a self-employed, small-shop owner, or a home worker) and, after their children were grown, they worked in the formal sector.

One of the interviewees had to quit her job, because she did not have support from her relatives, the only resource that allowed a woman to balance work and family at that time. She (case 5, age 51) was a bank teller in the early 1980s. After giving birth to her first child, she stayed at home for a year before returning to work. She tried various strategies to keep a balance between work and family. For example, her mother-in-law raised her first child, and her mother raised the second child. When she got pregnant with her third child, after the efforts to widen the interval between children, her mother-in-law got Alzheimer's disease. She had no choice but to quit her job. Meanwhile, the issue of work-family balance is also a class issue. The professional woman (case 7, age 45), who was a reporter, had an autistic child, but she was able to keep her job thanks in large part to help from all her birth family members.

3) Period Ⅲ (mid-1990s to the present): Separation between Work and Family and the Increase of "Modified" Extended Family with Matrilineality

During this period, public daycare policies and family-friendly corporate policies began to be established. The proportion of women wage workers increased from 59 % in 1995 to 67 % in 2005. Education and a positive view of women's social participation were not the only factors that led to the increase of women's employment. The growing job instability among men, precipitated by the neo-liberal globalization, and resulting financial hardships on the family also explain the increase in the employment of women. The women interviewed for Period III include not only highly-paid professional woman of the global age, such as researchers, IT specialists, and business managers, but also many low-paid irregular workers, such as house-call tutors, broadcast writers, and telemarketers.

The women who had raised children in the 1990s had more stories regarding work-family conflicts than women in previous periods. To maintain a balance between work and family, they employed various strategies, crossing borders between the extended

Table 4 Characteristic of Cases in Period Ⅲ

No. (Age)	Occupation	Occupation of Husband	Birth Year · Marriage Year(Age)	No. of Children	Family Form · Kin Relationship
Ⅲ-1 (32)	Broadcast writer	Broadcast PD	1975 2002(28)	2 sons	(Matrilineal) Modified extended
Ⅲ-2 (36)	House-call tutor	White-collar employee	1971 1999(29)	1 daughter & 1 son	(Patrilineal) Modified extended
Ⅲ-3 (38)	Corporate manager	White-collar employee (same company as the interviewee's)	1969 1998(30)	2 sons	(Matrilineal) Modified extended
Ⅲ-4 (39)	Researcher	Researcher at a financial company	1968 1998(32)	1 daughter	(Matrilineal) extended → Currently matrilineal modified extended
Ⅲ-5 (41)	Doctor	Doctor	1966 1991(26)	1 daughter & 1 son	(Patrilineal) Extended → Single mother (divorced a year ago)
Ⅲ-6 (38)	Telemarketer	Self-employed	1969 1995(27)	1 daughter & 1 son	(Matrilineal) Modified extended
Ⅲ-7 (37)	Manager at IT company	White-collar employee	1970 2002(33)	2 daughters	(Matrilineal) Modified extended
Ⅲ-8 (30)	Preschool teacher (welfare center)	Business	1977 2004(28)	1 daughter	Nuclear

family and the nuclear family. At the time of the interview, it was believed that each of the eight interviewees had a nuclear family. However, in reality, each family was actually a "modified" extended family in that it kept the extraordinarily strong relationships with the other extended family members not living together, which had the matrilineality of the women's birth family (five out of the eight cases).

Among the six interviewees of the modified extended family five have experienced the matrilineality, moving near their birth families after having child. Among them the broadcast writer (case 1, age 32) was chosen as the representative narrative considering the job characteristics of the Period III. Although her work required intense concentration and commitment, she rejected the fixed extended family form for help. Instead, she moved next door to her parents' house, so she could be close if she needed help. Nonetheless, after the birth of her second child, she started to worry about the situation.

> I moved next door to my parents.' But my mother is not in good shape, so one of my cousins helps her take care of my kids. One of my colleagues recommended I hire a live-in nanny. But I don't feel comfortable with the idea of living with a stranger. I'm looking for a nanny who lives nearby, so she doesn't need to sleep in my house. Broadcast writing is a tough job. It has crazy working hours and requires tremendous commitment. I considered leaving my job right after I gave birth to my second baby, but we are going to need a lot of money in the future. You have to make as much money as possible when you can (Period,

III, Case 1, broadcast writer).

As this interview indicates, there are tremendous challenges and tough dilemmas for professional women who are now raising young children while, at the same time, are holding a demanding job that requires a high level of commitment. Nevertheless, these women do not seem to have work-centered identities. Rather, they strive to balance work and family, trying to keep both healthy and sound. For the majority of non-professional women, however, childbirth is the main reason for leaving their job. The telemarketer (case 6, age 38) went to a commercial high school, so she could get a job more quickly and make money for her little brother. After graduating from high school, she got a clerical job at an insurance company. She worked there for nine years until she had a miscarriage, when she quit the job to become a full-time housewife. However, the 1997 economic crisis began shortly thereafter, and her husband's job became unstable. She went back to her former employer and started working as an irregular telemarketer this time. Although her mother took care of her children, she paid her 500,000 won per month (USD 450). Unfortunately, after working there four years, she got sick with an occupational disease at ear and throat and retired. Another irregular worker (house-call tutor, case 2, age 36) experienced a similar situation.

> I worked as a kindergarten teacher, since I graduated from college in 1994. Then I got pregnant and had to leave the job. In those days, once you got pregnant, you had to leave. After then,

I worked as a part-time kindergarten teacher from time to time for about 10 years, but quit them, too, because the pay was not good at all. After giving birth to my second child in 2004, I started working as a house-call tutor. The pay was good. The initial pay was 1,500,000 won a month (USD 1,350), and my mother-in-law said she would take care of my children. She lives near my place. I still work, and pay my mother-in-law 550,000 won a month for her work for my children. But now I'm pregnant with the third baby, and the job is getting tougher. I'm thinking to leave the job soon (Period III, Case 2, house-call tutor).

Most of the interviewees had a formal nuclear family. However, after the working kin relationships are considered, in reality, most of the women operated with the help of a modified extended family.

5. Discussion on the Meaning of the Emerging Modified Extended Family: Intersection of the Generational and Gender Relationships

The woman of this story maintained the life of work-family and tried to secure power and identity, employing diverse strategies. Each woman often controlled her fertility (including abortion). Each woman managed to move back and forth between work and home either by working at home in order to take care of young children, or by taking a job outside home. Each woman also took advantage of the community and kinship networks, to get it all done. Among these, the use of kinship networks proved to be the most effective resource, especially due to the lack of public or corporate support for working women with children. In this part, I will disscuss the meaning of those phenomena in respect of the charateristically bendable relationship between generations compared to the stubbonly unbending relationship between gender in Korean society.

1) (In-Family) Gender Relationships: "Unbending Gender"[4]

Did the women's employment and contribution to the family economy change gender roles and relationships in family? No. Listening to the fierce stories like war of their lives, struggling to balance work and family, a crucial question arose: "Where were their husbands?" Evidently, even today, husbands rarely participate in the caring work for their families, regardless of whether it is a nuclear or extended family.

Out of the 23 women, only two (the domestic maid from Period I, case 2, and the factory worker from Period Ⅱ, case 2) reported that their husbands had actively participated in childrearing and housework. However, the husbands of these two women passed away a long time ago, which could have softened the women's opinion, making them more lenient and subjective toward their late husbands. There

---

4 The term "unbending gender" is from Williams (2000). I intentionally use the similar term "bendable generation" in the next section to emphasize the relative flexibility, in contrast to the solidity of gender relationships.

was also one woman (the manager from Period Ⅲ, case 3) who said that, since she gave birth to twins, her mother helped her to take care of the children during daytime and her husband took turns with her during nighttime, which seemed the inevitable choice to them. And another interviewee (the broadcast writer from Period Ⅲ, case 1) said her husband participated actively in housework, more than likely because he had lived in a Western country.

Except for these four women, the husbands of the remaining 19 women were more like shadows in the family, especially regarding childrearing and housework. Moreover, as the "matrilineal" modified extended family became more prevalent, the husbands' participation at home lessened even more. For example, the husband of the stenographer from Period Ⅱ case 6, who had a matrilineal modified extended family, was hardly at home and almost completely absent from childrearing activities.

Surprisingly, not many of the women expressed discontent with their husbands during the interviews. Even the notion of "sharing housework equally" must have seemed a very foreign idea to the women from the old time of Period I. In meantime, one woman from Period Ⅱ, who was strongly critical of her conservative husband, commented, "Nevertheless, women should yield to their husbands in order to stay in marriage." The stenographer (Period Ⅱ, case 6) said she was very progressive when she was young and even asked her fiancé not to expect her to be a conventional type of wife and daughter-in-law after marriage. However, she did not criticize her husband for his passive role in the family either.

Nor did the women with higher education levels from Period

III show much discontent toward their husbands' lack of involvement in housework. For example, the house-call tutor (Period III, case 2) said she was grateful to her husband for being committed to his job, although he was not very committed to housework. The IT specialist (Period III, Case 7) said, "He wanted to do housework, but was simply too busy to do it. It's hard to come home after having such a long day and start running house chores, isn't it? It's pretty understandable." She too had an exhausting work life as a high-tech specialist, but she did housework anyway. She said, "I was exhausted, too. But I took care of the children, because I loved them so much." After struggling to juggle work and family, she finally transferred from a program developer to the less hectic work of a manager.

Although the women in this study were lenient and generous toward gender inequality within the family, the women were very critical of gender inequality in their workplace. The professional women from Period III were the most critical of gender discriminatory practices in their companies, such as promoting men before women (the manager, case 3) and requiring only women to wear uniforms (the IT specialist, case 7). Such progressive attitudes by women in the public sphere contradict the gender inequities in the family. The next section explores the generational relationships adapted for childcare to the unbending gender structure, which seems to mitigate the potential for conflict caused by the contradictions of gender relationships in the family.

2) "Unbending Gender" Combined with a "Bendable Generation"

Faced with firm, gendered relationships in the family, married women workers who especially had a professional jobs requiring high commitment have chosen to rely on generation relationships with their relatives and to adopt modified extended families rather than to challenge the existing gender order in the family. The generation relationships tend to be the matrilineal relationships with the woman's parental family. The woman's parental family provided reliable help and support for raising her children.

The foundings from the analysis of the narratives of the subjects could be discussed in detail as follows according to the distinctive periods.

First, Period I, during early industrialization, is characterized by inseparableness between work and family and the existence of the patrilineal extended family, which led to relatively few conflicts between work and family. However, women had to fulfill several roles — as daughters-in-law and agricultural laborers. They had to be submissive rather than resistant to the burdens imposed on them by the patrilineal family system. Although one woman (Period I, Case 3) tried to resist and "escape" from the family twice during the early stage of her marriage, it was a futile effort. After she changed her mind and decided to accept her role as the first daughter-in-law, she ultimately, increased the family's wealth, successfully managed the marriages of her brothers-in-law, and finally got settled down in the patrilineal family.

Like this woman's story, the major focus of the stories told by other agricultural women from this period was also about their daily lives in patrilineal in-law families. They tended to emphasize how much their fathers-in-law loved them, perhaps, because recognition from their in-law family members helped them to survive the patrilineal extended family.

Secondly, during Period Ⅱ, the late 1970s through the early 1990s, a lot of changes took place in the patrilineal extended family. Discourses on gender equality were broadly disseminated by the media, and the values of the nuclear family which were bolstered up by the love marriage became highly desirable. In fact, extended families decreased from 21 % in 1975 to 10 % in 1995. However, the gender-role division in the new nuclear family didn't change that much. In spite of working full-time outside the home, married women workers still bore the burden of duties at home including sole responsibility for childrearing. Husbands participated very little, even in childrearing. During this period, families that were formally nuclear but relationally extended were introduced, probably in response to the unbending gender divisions in the nuclear family and, thus, the need for help. However, these were matrilineal, not patrilineal, extended families.

Finally, the matrilineal modified extended family has strengthened in period Ⅲ (mid-1990s to early 2000s). Although several laws have been enacted to improve the balance between work and family, such as the "the Equal Employment Opportunity Law," the long working hours and intense working conditions in Korea have forced women to rely heavily on family-dependant strategies. After her one-year maternity leave, the IT specialist (Period III, case

7) for example, moved next door to her parents' house, so her parents could take care of her two children while she was at work. Because of the high level of job commitment required at work, professional women tend to lean toward more matrilineal family-dependent strategies than do non-professional women workers. Women irregular workers have also had to rely on their parents in order to work. The extended kinship networks should be flexible for the nuclear family to withdraw from them when women flixible workers lose jobs and have to go back home as a fulltime housewife.

However, the spread of the matrilineal modified extended family did not bring entirely positive or satisfactory results. The husband's position remained static in the newly restructured extended family order with childrearing at its center. As a result, women were unable to effectively communicate with their husbands. A few men often had conflicts with their mothers-in-law, whose role in the family became more important than before. The highly educated women from Period Ⅲ were unwilling to sacrifice their careers; however, at the same time, they held themselves to a high standard of motherhood. Not surprisingly, they often suffered psychological distress from their immense workloads.

3) Conclusion

In conclusion we can make some brief comparisons to similar cases in other countries and discuss some theoretical implications.

First, as some scholars have pointed out, industrialization has, in some ways, strengthened traditional kin relationships (Hareven

1993), and the concept of the nuclear family cannot be defined by only residence-based family forms of census data (Chang 1993). The results of this study support that statement. But, it is the modified form in two respects like the lineality of matrifocality and moving between the nuclear family and the extended kinship system along the family cycle for childrearing as strategies to balance work and family.

Second, informal networks for balancing work and family in Korea are much more dependent on parents than other personal networks, such as siblings and friends, than other countries, such as the United States (Hansen 2005). This is probably because the tradition of the stem family structure still works more importantly than the collateral family line (Choi 1982). Moreover, lineality tends to follow the matrilineal line, reflecting women's increasing decision making power and responsibility at the same time.

Third, woman's role both as workers and careers, are widely accepted today, while men as nurturers are not, even though men's traditional patriarchal attitudes have weakened to some extent. Although this study found a very few cases of husbands shared childcare responsibilities, the statistics still reveal the unbending gender division in childcare. According to a recent survey on dual income families, the wife spends 2.7 hours on housework, while the husband spends 38 minutes, only 18.3 % of the housework hours (Lee and Kim 2008). The emergence of nurturing and participatory trends at home found in men, beginning in the 1990s' in the United States (Gerson 1993), seems quite different from their Korean counterpart.

What is intriguing is the fact that women in this study showed contradictory attitudes toward the gender norm at home and workplace. The cases that had held professional jobs since the 1990s seemed resentful of their workplaces, resisting the practices of sexual inequality, while showing very permissive attitudes toward their husband's minimal contribution to care work at home. They were able to be permissive, because they had helping hands from their kinship networks. So, essentially, the kinship network could be told as a cushion to mitigate gender conflicts.

Finally, since 2001, family-friendly policies have expanded to include parental leave. Women workers now get three months of maternity leave with full salary, and workers of both sexes can take parental leave for one year with a small portion of their salary. Unfortunately, half of the women from Period III in this study were irregular workers, and they were not for eligible for these benefits. Generally speaking the 2/3 of women workers are said to be the irregular workers in Korea. Therefore, in spite of the growing family-friendly governmental policies since the later part of the 1990s, kinship networks have become a more important factor in righting the balance between work and family.

References

Ahn, H. Y. (1991). Han-guk gajok-ui hyeongtae bullyu-wa haekgajokhwa-ui uimi (The Typification of Family Form and the Meaning of Nuclearization of the Family in Korea; in Korean). *Han-gugui sahoe-wa yeoksa (Society and History in Korea)*. Seoul: Iljisa.

Beck, Ul. and E. Beck-Gernsheim (1995). *Normal Chaos of Love*. Blackwell Pub., trans into Korean, Seoul: Saemulgyeol chulpansa, 1999.

Chang, H. S. (1993). Han-guk sahoe-neun haekgajok-hwa-hago-inneun-ga?" (Are the Korean Families on the Way to the Nuclear Family?; in Korean), *Sahoe-wa Yeoksa (Society and History)* 39: 42-80.

Choi, J. S. (1982). *Han-guk gajok jedosa yeon-gu (Study on the History of Korean Family*; in Korean). Seoul: Iljisa.

Cho, J. M. (1997). Han-guk sahoe chinjok gwan-gye-ui yang-gye-hwa gyeong-hyang-e daehan yeon-gu (The Study of the Bilateralization of Korean Kin Relationship; in Korean). *Han-guk yeoseong-hak (Korean Journal of Women's Studies)* 13(1): 87-114.

Crompton, R. (1999). Discussion and Conclusions. In *Restructuring Gender Relations and Employment: The Decline of the Male Breadwinner*, ed. R. Crompton. Oxford: Oxford University Press.

Crompton, R. (2006). *Employment and the Family: The Reconciliation of Work and Family Life in Contemporary Societies*. New York: Cambridge University Press.

Del Boca, D. (1998). Labor Policies, Economic Flexibility, and Women's Work: Italian Experience. In *Women, Work, and the Family in Europe*, ed. E. Drew, R. Emerek, and E. Mahon. London: Routeledge.

Denzin, N. (1989). *Interpretive Biography*. Sage.

Gerson, K. (1993). *No Man's Land: Men's Changing Commitments to Family and Work*. New York: Basic Book.

Giddens, A. (1992). *Transformation of Intimacy*. Diane Pub Com. trans into Korean, Seoul: Saemulgyeol chulpansa, 1996.

Glucksman, M. A. (1995). Why 'Work'?: Gender and the Total Social Organization of Labor. *Gender, Work, and Organization* 2(2): 63-75.

Goode, W. (1963). *World Revolution and Family Patterns*. NY: Macmillan; Free Press.

Hansen, K. (2005). *Not-So-Nuclear Families*. New Brunswick, NJ: Rutgers University Press.

Hareven, T. (1993). *Family Time and Industrial Time*. University Press of America.

Hareven, T. and A. Plakans, eds. (1987). *Family History at the Crossroads: A Journal of Family History Reader*. Princeton: Princeton University Press.

Hochschild, A. R. (1997). *The Time Bind: When Work Becomes Home and Home*

Becomes Work. New York: Henry Holt and Company.

Jacobs, J. and K. Gerson (2004). *The Time Divide: Work, Family, and Gender Inequality*. Cambridge, MA: Harvard University Press.

Kim, H. K. (2002). Gajok/nodong-ui galdeung gujo-wa gajok yeondae jeollyageul jungshimeuro bon han-guk gajogui byeonhwawa yeoseong (Recent Familial Changes and Women in Korea: Work-Family Conflicts and Familial Solidarity). *Gajok-gwa Munhwa* 14(2): 31-52.

Kim, S. Y. (2000). Dong-asia-ui jabonjuui baljeon-gwa gajok (Capitalist Development and the Family in East Asia: The Cases of Korea and Japan). Ph. D. Dissertation, Korea University, Seoul.

Lee, J. K., et al. (2005). *1960-70 nyeondae nodongjaui saeng-hwalsegyewa jeong-che-seong (The Life Worlds and Identities of Workers from 1960s to 1970s of Korea.* Seoul: Han Wool Academy.

Lee, S. M. and Kim, H. K. (2008). Bubugan gasa-nodong bundam-e daehan gong-pyeong-seong injiui yeong-hyang yoin yeon-gu (Exploring the Working Wives' Perceptions of Equity on the Unequal Gender Division of Domestic Work; in Korean). *Gajok-gwa Munhwa (Family and Culture)* 20(1): 1-25.

McAdams, D. P. (1993). *The Stories We Live by: Personal Myths and the Making of the Self*. New York: The Guilford Press.

Parsons, T. and R. F. Bales (1955). *Family, Socialization and Interaction Process*. Glencoe, Ill: Free Press.

Pfau-Effinger, B. (1999). The Modernization of Family and Motherhood in Western Europe. In *Restructuring Gender Relations and Employment: The Decline of the Male Breadwinner*, ed. R. Crompton. Oxford: Oxford University Press.

Rubin, L. (1994). *Families on the Fault Line*. New York: Harper Paperbacks.

Tilly, L. and J. W. Scott (1987). *Women, Work, and Family*. New York: Routledge.

Williams, J. (2000). *Unbending Gender: Why Family and Work Conflict and What to Do about It*. Oxford: Oxford University Press.

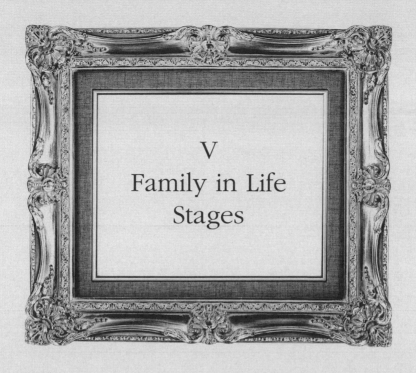

V
Family in Life
Stages

Chapter 11

The Early Years of Marriage

Chapter 12

Korean Families in Mid-Life: Over-Emphasis on Children's Education

Chapter 13

Korean Family Relationships in Later Life

Chapter eleven

The Early Years of Marriage

Chung, Hyunsook (Sangmyung University)

Since the late twentieth century in Korea there have been tremendous shifts in attitudes toward marriage from the tradition of arranged marriage to a more liberal view where the partners should have a leading role in the decisions of whether, who, and when to marry. There have also been decreases in the marriage and fertility rates. However, marriage is still treated as the norm or the prerequisite for human development as an adult in Korea. Hence cohabitation is treated as a somewhat deviant behavior, because marriage has always been the norm. This trend is well represented by the data from the Korean Statistical Information Service (2005), which showed that about 97 % of women had been married at least once in their lifetime.

Being married is different from dating or living together. Many researchers from abroad have confirmed that marriage is a developmental process that involves change, adjustment, and growth. In many societies, marriage is also treated as a process of emotional, legal, and economic independence for adult children from their parents. But in Korea, the newly married tend to be dependent on their parents, especially in terms of housing costs as well as costs of a marriage ceremony. Specifically, in 2008, 9 % of Korean offspring responded that the "parent should support entirely" and 82.3 % said the "parents should offer some support" for their children's marriage expenses (Statistics Korea 2009a). It is also very natural for children in Korea to want their parents' assistance immediately after their birth. During the postpartum period, they expect to receive aid from their parents. This pattern is more pervasive in highly educated groups (Rhee & Cho 1992). Thus, the variables for the adjustment of newly-wed couples are a little bit different from their Western counterparts. In this chapter, demographic issues and research that have dealt with variables related to the adjustment of the early years of marriage will be reviewed. Also, parenting issues and challenges for the early years of marriage will be addressed.

1. Demographic Issues in the Early Years of Marriage

Demographic issues related to the marriage life and couple's relationships during the early years of marriages have affected the changing patterns of marriages and divorces. Especially, a decrease in the marriage rates, an increase in the age of marriage and international marriage, and a high divorce rate during the early years of marriage have had a great impact on the couple's life as well as policy makers in Korea.

1) Decrease in the Marriage Rates and Increase in the Age of Marriage

The number of marriages was 327.7 thousand cases in 2008 (see Table 1) and the crude marriage rates, the number of marriages per 1,000 persons stood at 6.6 in 2008, down 1.4 from 1998. The average age of the first marriage for males and females continued an upward trend in 2008, recording 31.4 years and 28.3 years, respectively. Since the late 1980s, high school attendance has become nearly universal for both men and women, thus, it is assumed that this pattern will continue for a relatively longer period of time.

As seen in Table 2, the marriage rate of males, aged 30 to 34, recorded 54.5 cases per 1,000 persons, marking the highest figure. The marriage rate of females, aged 25 to 29, recorded 79.0 cases per 1,000 persons, marking the highest figure. In 2008, the average age of the first marriage for males was 31.4; and, in 1998, the average age of the first marriage for females was 28.3 years, which marked

Table 1 Crude marriage rates and change rate from 2007 to 2008

	2008 (thousand cases)			Change from the previous year (thousand cases)			Change rate from the previous year (%)		
	Total	First marriage	Re-marriage	Total	First marriage	Re-marriage	Total	First marriage	Re-marriage
Males	327.7	270.2	57.2	-15.8	-15.2	0.1	-4.6	-5.3	0.1
Females	327.7	264.5	62.8	-15.8	-16.3	0.9	-4.6	-5.8	1.4

Source: Statistis Korea (2009), Marriage Statistics in 2008.

Table 2 Age Specific Marriage Rates in 2008

	Males				Females			
	20-24	25-29	30-34	35-39	20-24	25-29	30-34	35-39
Age-specific marriage rate in 2008	6.6	51.8	54.5	19.7	24.1	79.0	35.4	11.3

Age-specific marriage rates refer to the number of marriages per 1,000 people.
Source: Statistics Korea (2009b), Marriage Statistics in 2008.

an increase from 28.8 for males and 26.0 for females.

The percentage of international marriages increased during the last decade (see Table 3) and was higher in rural areas than in urban areas. The marriages of Korean males who were engaged in agriculture, forestry and fisheries amounted to 6.5 thousand cases in 2008. Out of these males, 38.3 percent (2.5 thousand cases) married foreign females. Of the Korean males engaged in agriculture, forestry and fisheries, 1,290 married Vietnamese, occupying the

Table3 Marriage Cases with Foreigners (cases, %)

years	2000	2001	2002	2003	2004	2005	2006	2007	2008
marriage cases	332,090	318,407	304,877	302,503	308,598	314,304	330,634	343,559	327,715
marriage w/ foreigners	11,605	14,523	15,202	24,776	34,640	42,356	38,759	37,560	36,204
ratio	3.5	4.6	5.0	8.2	11.2	13.5	11.7	10.9	11.0
Marriage of Korean male w/ foreign female	6,945	9,684	10,698	18,751	25,105	30,719	29,665	28,580	28,163
Marriage of Korean female w/ foreign male	4,660	4,839	4,504	6,025	9,535	11,637	9,094	8,980	8,041

Source: Statistics Korea (2009b), Marriage Statistics in 2008.

highest share of marriages to foreigners. This figure was followed by the Chinese.

Because of increase in international marriages, international families became highlighted topics in Korean society, as well as in the area of family policies, as was the relationship between the decrease in the marriage rate and the increase in the age of first marriage to the low birth rate in Korea. In recent years, these were the most widely researched topics, because the birth rates are highly related to the age at the first marriage. The crude birth rate stood at 9.4 persons in 2008, down from 13.6 persons in 1998. The total fertility rate, which is the number of births that a woman would have if they experienced the current age specific birth rates throughout their childbearing years, marked 1.19 in 2008, which decreased by 0.26 from 1.45 in 1998. The number of live births for mothers aged 35 and over marked an increase, while mothers aged less than 35 marked a decrease (Statistics Korea 2009c). Thus, because of the continued increase in the educational level of the women and labor force participation, it is assumed that this kind of pattern will last for a longer period of time.

2) High Divorce Rates during the Early Years of Marriage

Even though the number of divorces and the crude divorce rate showed a downward tendency since 2004 in Korea, the total number of divorces amounted to 116.5 thousand cases (couples) in 2008. The crude divorce rate, which is the number of divorces per 1,000 persons, marked 2.4 cases in 2008, down 0.1 cases from the

Table 4 Number of Divorces and Crude Divorce Rates

	1998	1999	2000	2001	2002	2003	2004	2005	2006	2007	2008
Number of divorces (thousand)	116.3	117.4	119.5	134.6	144.9	166.6	138.9	128.0	124.5	124.1	116.5
Change (thousand)	25.1	1.2	2.0	15.2	10.3	21.7	-27.7	-10.9	-3.5	-0.5	-7.5
Change rate (%)	27.6	1.0	1.7	12.7	7.7	15.0	-16.6	-7.8	-2.7	-0.4	-6.1
Crude divorce rate*	2.5	2.5	2.5	2.8	3.0	3.4	2.9	2.6	2.5	2.5	2.4

* It refers to the number of divorces per 1,000 persons.
Source: Statistics Korea (2009d), Divorce Statistics in 2008.

previous year (Statistics Korea 2009d). Divorced couples who had lived together less than 5 years stood at 28.4 percent, the largest share. This figure showed a steady increase from 2003, because divorces between Koreans and foreign spouses increased.

Because of the high divorce rates and the international trend for the health family movement, in 2005 the **Framework Act on Healthy Family** was enacted in Korea. Based on this framework, in 2005, a three month divorce deliberation period for the couples with children and a one month divorce deliberation period for childless couples have been introduced. It is assumed that the decrease in the number of divorces was partly the result of this policy. Also, special attention has been paid to marriage preparation education in academia as well as in fields that deal with marriage. Beginning at the end of twentieth century, many programs were developed and implemented in diverse settings.

2. Crossing the Threshold: Attitude toward Marriage

Even though marriage is treated as a very natural process of human development, there are not many studies dealing with the early years of marriage in Korea. However, there is a consensus about the developmental tasks during the early years of marriage in Korea, i.e. the adjustment between couple and becoming the parents. Because of this kind of marriage culture, in 2007, households composed of "married couple with child(ren)" amounted to 6,889 thousand, occupying 42.0 percent. This figure was followed by "one-person" households (3,298 thousand, 20.1 percent), "married couple without child(ren)" households (2,391 thousand, 14.6 percent), "mother with child(ren)" households (1,120 thousand, 6.8 percent), and "married couple with child(ren)" and "one parent" households (575 thousand, 3.5 percent) (Statistics Korea 2007). Also, according to World Values Survey data in 2000 (www.worldvaluessurvey.org), a majority of Koreans think marriage is not an outdated institution, although males prefer marriage more than women, and this kind of tendency tends to increase as they get older. Interestingly, only 22 % of single and 57 % of divorcees think marriage is an outdated institution. The number of remarriages after divorce comprised about 55.4 %, and this figure is increasing (Korea Legal AID Center for Family Relations 2003). The increment of remarriage rates after divorce implies that marital status is still very important among adults in Korea.

According to Chung (2004), couples' attitudes toward a happy marriage are different, based on marital status and length of marriage. As seen in table 6, unmarried people thought "love" is the

Table5 Korean's Attitude toward Marriage by Demographic Characteristics

Marriage is the outdated institution		No (%)	Yes (%)	Total (n)
Sex	Male	88.2	11.8	604
	Female	80.5	19.5	595
Age	15-29	76.0	24.0	313
	30-49	86.1	13.9	619
	Over 50	90.3	9.7	267
Marital status	Married	87.6	12.4	823
	Cohabitation	57.1	42.9	7
	Divorce	42.9	57.1	14
	Separation	83.3	16.7	6
	Separation by death	88.9	11.1	27
	Single	78.3	21.7	322
Social class	Upper	82.7	17.3	463
	Middle	85.7	14.3	680
	Low	82.1	17.9	56

Source: 2001 World Value Survey (www.worldvaluessurveys.org) data

single most important factor for a happy marriage, while "mutual trust" for newly married couples and "mutual trust" and "economic stability" for the middle age couples were important.

Table 6 Rankings of Factors for Happy Marriage among Three Groups

Factors of happy marriage	Unmarried persons	Newly married couple	Middle aged couples
Love	1	2	4
Mutual trust	2	1	1
Economic stability	3	3	1
Respect to partner	4	4	4
Patience & understanding	5	5	3
Religiosity	6	7	5
Expression of affection	7	6	–
Same hobby			–
Sexual satisfaction	8	8	8
Similar philosophy for life			6
Equality			11
Children		9	7
Respect for each other's individuality	9	11	–
Mutual sexual satisfaction		12	12
Respect to each other		10	8
Faithfulness			8
Time together	10	13	13
Attraction of partner			8
Mutual decision making			7
Openness & honesty	11	14	11
No conflict with in-laws	12	15	3
Good listener	13	16	13

Source: H. Chung (2004), p. 95.

3. Factors Related to Adjustment During Early Years of Marriage

The most important developmental task during the early years of marriage is the emotional, economical, and psychological adjustment between couples and their relatives. The overall pattern of marital satisfaction showed a U-curve when data were analyzed with length of marriage, birth cohort, and marriage cohort. Also husbands and wives perception of their marital satisfaction differed during their entire life span, with wives becoming more dissatisfied over time (Chung 1996). The overall score of marital satisfaction is relatively high among Korean couples (see Table 7), but the score decreased as the length of marriage increased. Even in the happy group with no intent to divorce, their ambivalence, and affectionate expressions tended to decrease negatively over time. However, the amount of change was not as large as that of the unhappy group (Kim & Kim 2005). Based on this result, Kim and Kim (2005) concluded this kind of pattern is probably a normative and a natural consequence of the transition from the first year of marriage to a more mature relationship.

The perception of marital satisfaction among Korean couples differed by sex, according to the sub dimensions of Korean Marital Satisfaction Scale (Chung 2001) (see Figure 1). Korean couples showed

Table 7 Marital Satisfaction among Couples (number, %)

N (%)	1 (Very unsatisfied)	2	3	4	5 (Very satisfied)	Don't know/ No response
Total 3,922 (100.0)	44 (1.1)	205 (5.2)	1461 (37.2)	1935 (49.3)	272 (6.9)	5 (0.1)
Husbands 1,961 (100.0)	13 (0.7)	82 (4.2)	699 (35.6)	1017 (51.9)	149 (7.6)	1 (0.1)
Wives 1,961 (100.0)	31 (1.6)	123 (6.3)	762 (38.9)	918 (46.8)	123 (6.3)	4 (0.2)

Source: Korea Women's Development Institute (2005), *Current Status of Korean Families*.

high marital satisfaction especially when their partner performed their personal role very well as a worker, and husbands tended to have high marital satisfaction when they perceived their wife was a good care partner, carrying out their parenting roles as well as household chores well. On the other hand, wives showed high marital satisfaction when they thought their husband showed care and respect to their wives. There are statistical differences between husbands and wives in the sub dimensions of negative communication, parenting role, household chores role, respect to partner, and cohesion score. In this chapter, factors related to the adjustment during the early years of marriage will be reviewed. There are several variables related to the adjustment of newly married.

Figure 1 Mean Marital Satisfaction Score of Korean Marital Satisfaction Sub Scales

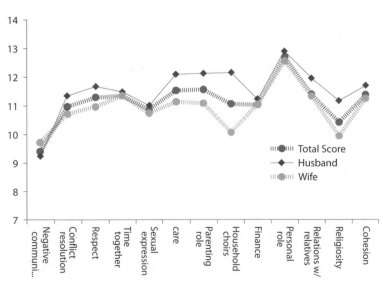

Source: H. Chung (2001), p. 17.

1) Demographic Characteristics between Couples

One of the distinct marriage patterns in Korea is the educational assortative mating. According to Park and Smits (2005), educational assortative mating in Korea has three major dimensions: (1) educational similarity (the tendency of people to marry within their own educational group), (2) uniform association (the tendency of people who marry outside their educational group to marry a partner with a closely related educational level), and (3) gender asymmetry (the tendency of husbands to have a higher educational level than their wives). Uniform association and educational similarity among people with tertiary education (both absolute and relative) were found to increase significantly over the period. This indicates that, in the last decades of the twentieth century, the boundary between the educational elite and the rest of Korean society has become stronger. One reason for this may be the increase in the preference among Korean males for a highly educated spouse, who can help their children in the competitive Korean educational system. Many studies confirm that the educational level had a positive relationship to couples' marital satisfaction.

2) Individual Characteristics

Many Koreans point out personality as the most important factor when they are considering a marriage partner. Ironically, in 2008, 47.8 % cited "disharmony in character" as a reasons of divorce, followed by "economic problems" at 14.2 % (Statistics Korea 2009d).

Another frequently mentioned reason of conflict during a new marriage was the personality factor (Lee & Jeon 2001)

3) Attitude toward Marriage

Attitude toward the marriage is also related to marital adjustment. According to Ha and Chung (2000), the degree of irrational belief among wives was higher than their husbands, and wives' marital satisfaction was lower than their husbands.' Furthermore, the degree of irrational belief of both husbands and wives was negatively correlated with marital satisfaction respectively.

4) Balance between Work & Families

Because of social prejudices concerning working mothers, it is necessary to maintain a balance between work and family during the early period of marriage. In Korea, the participation of young unmarried women in the labor force is as high as that of their male counterparts, but, even among college graduates, participation by married women is remarkably low. Are married women at a disadvantage in the labor market vis-à-vis single women? In Korea marriage and childbearing form two very big hurdles for women's continuing labor force participation and career development. Without access to low-cost public childcare services, it is very difficult for married women to continue to participate in the labor market after child birth (Kim, et al. 2003). The lack of public childcare services decreases the opportunity cost of married women to participate in the labor force (Lee, Jang & Sarkar 2008). Thus, many Korean women tend to quit their job after marriage.

It is not expected, however, that all new mothers will have the same experience. According to the Double ABCX model, an event or a transition that creates family hardship could occur with other stressors simultaneously. A mother's work outside the family may cause much more stress on the couple after they have their first child (Leonard 1993). Even though the number of employed mothers has increased rapidly, the belief that the mother's place is at home with their children still remains strong (Kim 1990). According to Lewis (1991), employed mothers are thus doubly stigmatized by social definitions that cast them as deviant both as mothers and as employees. Moreover, research on employed mothers has reported that most of their stress is related to the lack of day care for their children (Spitz 1988). Therefore, it is expected that the balance between work and families is very important criteria for the newly-wed couples' marital satisfaction.

5) Family of Origin

Relations with family-of-origin had an impact on the adjustment of newly-wed couples. According to Lim, Park and Kim (2008), the group with a stable attachment to their parents showed a smoother adjustment in their relationships with their spouses after marriage. Positive relations with parents also have a positive impact on newly-wed couples' marital adjustment (Chung 2004). Chung (2004) also

Table 8 Result of Regression Analysis for Marital Satisfaction of the Newly-wed

Dependent variables	B	β
Length of marriage	-.13	-.06
Sex (male=1)	.09	.02
Family earnings	-.00	-.08
Number of children	-.20	-.06
Educational level	.08	.05
Job (yes=1)	-.31	-.03
Premarital education (yes=1)	.72	.12
Conflict resolution	-.37	-.43*
Relations with their Parents	.21	.31*
Subcategories of marriage preparation		
Work & economic issues	-.01	-.03
Child & in law relations	.05	.14
Communication	-.01	-.03
Understanding partner	-.02	-.02
Quality of premarital relations	.27	.30*
Understanding oneself	-.08	-.09
Maturity	-.05	-.10
intercept	8.10	
R^2	.57*	

$* p<.05 ** p<.01 *** p<.001$
Source: Chung (2004), p. 97.

pointed out conflict resolution, relations with their own parents, and premarital relationship quality had a positive relationship with their marital satisfaction during the newly-wed stage (see Table 8). Also, psychological independence before marriage and less anxiety with their parents after marriage positively related to their marital intimacy during the newly-wed stage (Nam & Han 2003).

4. Parenthood: Choices & Challenges

It is widely recognized in Korean society that becoming a parent is a very natural process for an adult in the life span development process. But perceptions toward the value of children have been changed from the instrumental to the emotional value. Lim, Choi and Oh (2008) analyzed data between 1970 and 2000 among a matched sample of 110 adolescents, mothers, and their grandmothers on their value of children. By analysis, the preference for boys has declined, and the value of children has shifted from instrumental value to emotional and social values. In this chapter, variables related to the transition to parenthood and parenting role will be reviewed.

1) The Challenge of Parenthood: Variables Related to the Transition to Parenthood

Becoming a parent is a very important developmental task for Korean couples. Koreans expect the birth of a child to be a natural life event that comes within one or two years after marriage. In traditional Korean society, the status of the daughter-in-law in her husband's family increases substantially when she bears a child. Indeed, the quality of the parent-child relationship is still considered to be a more essential part of family life than the marital relationship for marital happiness. For the Korean family, which puts more emphasis on the "blood-related" relationship of the parent-child tie, the birth of a child is an opportunity for couples to affirm their oneness in body and spirit.

Many studies have focused on the impact of the birth of a child on his/her parents. Married women's employment status and family income play an important role in their decisions on childbirth (Lee, 2002). It has been reported that the marital satisfaction of couples in Korea declines after the birth of a child. For wives the transition to parenthood has an especially negative effect on postpartum marital adjustment (Koh & Ok 1993). But with a positive perception of motherhood and familial assistance from extended kin networks, the entry of a child may not negatively influence marital satisfaction of Korean couples (Lee & Keith 1999). Also, marital satisfaction, participation of birth planning education, and kinship's emotional support were important criteria for men's perceived costs about the transition to parenthood (Song & Han 1994). It was also reported that the processes of transition to motherhood for employed mothers were more difficult than those of non-employed mothers due to the lack of a social support system (Lee 2002). Therefore, unemployed married women tend to have more children than employed married women in Korea (Ryoo & Piao 2009). According to Kim (2007), women, 39 years old and younger, with a job tend to have fewer children and find an endogenous problem between child birth and labor force participation as well. Although the education level of married women has positive effect for giving a birth, it has a negative impact on the number of children.

Family of origin is also a very important factor in the process of transition to parenthood. According to Synn (1993), mothers who lived in traditional family settings received more support from their families and were more likely to use their mothers as sources of information on childcare, such as to observe the traditional customs related to childbirth, than mothers in nuclear family. In spite of living in nuclear family setting, the nuclear family mothers maintained close contact with their families of origin. Their husbands were more involved in childcare, and the mothers were more likely to use books and peers as sources of knowledge about childcare. They were more self-reliant and less depressed than the traditional family mothers. However, the transition to parenthood was also influenced by the mothers' lack of information about pregnancy and child care, by the lack of previous experience in childcare, and by the quality of the support mothers receive. Also, preventive educational programs, designed to provide information and modeling of childrearing practices for new mothers had a positive impact on the process of transition.

The variables explaining the father's satisfaction in transition to parenthood were found to be the perceived spousal support and the gender of child. Fathers who perceived higher spousal support, a younger child, and married for a longer period of time reported higher marital satisfaction (Lim 2004).

2) Parenting: Variables Related to the Parenting Role

More traditional people tend to believe that to marry for love and to have a child is a very natural process of life as well as a gift from God. However, few people today continue to hold this perception of marriage and parent-child relations. Diverse variables were reported to be related to the parenting attitude and parenting behavior.

Among the factors related to parenting is a rise in the age of childbirth and educational levels of childbearing mothers, as well as the high rates of labor force participation by mothers.

Usually, the wives' level of involvement in child care was higher than the husbands (Koh 1998). Also, the traditional attitude on gender roles limits the level of involvement in child care by the husband. For husbands, the age and degree of job importance of the wife has some effect on their level of involvement. For wives, however, their perceptions of support services for infant care, as well as gender roles, affected their level of involvement in infant care. It would seem gender role attitudes are the most influential and common factor for a couples' participation in child care in Korean society.

References

Chung, H. (1996). Dosibubuui Gyeolhon manjokdo byeonhwa paeteon (Developmental pattern of marital satisfaction; in Korean). *Han-guk gajeong gwalli hakhoeji (Journal of Korea Home Management Association)* 14(2): 51-60.

Chung, H. (2001). Han-gukhyeong gyeolhon manjokdo cheokdo gaebal yeongu (A study of development of the Korean-Marital Satisfaction Scale; in Korean). *Daehan gajeong hakhoeji (Journal of the Korea Home Economics Association)* 39(12): 205-224.

Chung, H. (2004). Gyeolhon jeon gyoyuk peu-ro-geu-raem (A basic study for developing "The marriage preparation program"; in Korean). *Han-guk gajeong gwalli hakhoeji (Journal of Korea Home Management Association)* 22(1): 91-101.

Ha, S. H. & Chung, H. J. (2000). Sinhon-gi bubuui bihamnijeok sinnyeomgwa gyeolhon manjokdoui gwangye (Relationship of irrational belief and marital satisfaction of newly married couples; in Korean). *Han-guk seanghwal-gwahakhoeji (Korean Journal of Human Ecology)* 3(2): 27-38.

Hong, S. M. (2005). Bumo jeonigi namseongui abeojidoeme daehan geungjeong-jeok, bujeongjeok jigakgwa abeoji yeokhal suhaeng (Positive/Negative Perception about Fathering and Father's Role Performance among Men in Transition to Parenthood; in Korean). Master's Thesis, Yonsei University, Seoul.

Kim, H. (2007). Urinara gaguui ja-nyeosu gyeoljeong yoine gwanhan caunteu mohyeong bunseok mit gyeongjejeok hamui (The economic and social implication of count regression models for married women's completed fertility in Korea; in Korean). *Han-guk-in-guhak (Korean Journal of Population Studies)* 30(3): 107-135.

Kim, H. B., Choi, J. S., & Oh D. H. (2008). Yeoseongui chulsanyul gyeoljeong yoin-gwa chulsanjanglyeojeongchaegui banghyang (Determining factors of age specific fertility rate and policy direction for enhancing birth rate; in Korean). *Jiyeok-yeon-gu (Journal of the KRSA)* 24(1): 23-37.

Kim, S. Y. & Kim, Y. H. (2005). Jisokjeokin gyeongje seongjang-eul wihan yeoseong iljari changchul bangan (Couple relationship factors predicting marital satisfaction and divorce intention over time; in Korean). *Daehan-gajeonghakhoeji (Journal of the Korean Home Economics Association)* 43(9): 41-57.

Kim, T. H., Kim, J. S., Chang, M. S., & Kim, N. J. (2003). *Jisokjeogin gyeongje seongjang-eul wihan yeoseong iljari changchul bang-an (Policies for female job creation for sustainable economic growth*; in Korean). Korean: Korea Women Development Institute.

Koh, S. J. (1998). Involvement on infant care after transition to parenthood and associated variables in dual earner families. *Journal of family relations* 2(1): 115-139.

Koh, S. J. & Ok, S. W. (1993). Bumogiroui jeonie gwanhan yeon-gu 2: Bumogiroui jeonie ttareun bubu gyeolhonjeogeungui byeonhwa (Transition to parenthood II: Couples' Dyadic Adjustment Change Across the Transition to Parenthood; in Korean). *Daehan-gajeonghakhoeji (Journal of the Korean Home Economics Association)* 31(3): 127-141.

Korea Legal AID Center for Family Relations (2003). *Jaehon (Remarriage*; in Korean). Seoul.

Korea Women's Development Institute (2005). *Current Status of Korean Families.*

Seoul.

Kwon, Y. E. & Kim, U. C. (2004). Ja-nyeogachiwa chulsanyul (Value of children and fertility; in Korean). *Adong-gyoyuk (The Korean Society for Child Education)* 13(1): 211-226.

Lee, B. S., Jang, S., & Sarkar, J. (2008). Women's Labor Force Participation and Marriage: The Case of Korea. *Journal of Asian Economics* 19: 138-154.

Lee, I. K. (2002). Bumojeonigi eo-meoniui eoryeoum gwallyeon byeonin (Related Variables with Mother's Difficulties during the Transition to Parenthood; in Korean). Master's Thesis, Yonsei University, Seoul.

Lee, S. C. & Keith, P. M. (1999). The Transition to Motherhood of Korean Women. *Journal of Comparative Family Studies* 30(3): 453-470.

Lee, S. M. & Jeon, G. Y. (2001). Gyeolhon chogi nampyeon-gwa a-nae-ui bubugaldeunggwa galdeungdaecheobangsigi gyeolhonmanjokdoe michi-neun yeong-hyang (The Effects of Marital Conflict and Conflict-Coping Method on Couple's Marital Satisfaction in Early Stage of Marital Life; in Korean). *Han-guk gajeong gwalli hakhoeji (Journal of Korean Home Management Association)* 19(5): 203-220.

Lee, S. S., Choi, H. J., Oh, Y. H., Suh, M. H., Park, S. K., & Doh, S. R. (2009). *2009 Jeon-guk gyeolhon mit chulsan dong-hyangjosa (2009 national survey on dynamics of marriage and fertility; in Korean)*. Han-gukbogeonsahoe-yeon-guwon (Korea Institute for Health and Social Affairs).

Lee, S. Y. (2008). Chulsanuijie yeong-hyang-eul michi-neun yoin yeon-gu (An Analysis of the Effect on Childbirth Will of Married Women; in Korean). *Han-guk gajokjawon gyeong-yeong hakhoeji (Korean Family Resource Management Association)* 12(2): 15-30.

Leonard, V. W (1993). Stress and Coping in the Transition to Parenthood of First Time Mothers with Career Commitments: An Interpretive Study. Dissertation Abstract International 54-08.

Lewis, S. (1991). Dual-Career Families in the UK: An update. Woman in Management Review 6(4).

Lim, K. A. (2004). Bumojeonigi namseong-ui jeongseo pyohyeonseong-gwa buinui jiwon mit yeokhal manjokdo (The Relations of Emotional Expressiveness and Spousal Support with Role Satisfaction among Men in Transition to Parenthood; in Korean). Master's Thesis, Yonsei University,

Seoul.

Lim, Y. J., Park, J. Y., & Kim Y. H. (2008). Wongajok bumowaui aechak mit simnijeok dongnipsim jigakgwa sinhongi gyeolhonjeogeung-gwaui gwan-gye-e gwanhan yeon-gu (The Study Effect to Attachment to Family-of-Origin and Psychological Separation on Newly-Wedded Marital Adjustment; in Korean). *Han-guk gajeong gwanri hakheoji (Journal of Korean Home Management Association)* 26(5): 143-154.

Nam, S. H. & Han, S. Y. (2003). Sinhongi bubuui bumorobuteoui simnijeok dongnipgwa gyeolhon hu chinmilgame michi-neun won-gajogui yeong-hyang (The Influence of Family of Origin on Wedded Couples' Psychological Independence from Parents and Marital Intimacy; in Korean). *Han-guk simnihakhoeji imsang (Korean Journal of Clinical Psychology)* 22(3): 505-523.

Park, H. & Smits, J. (2005). Educational Assortative Mating in South Korea: Trends 1930—1998. *Research in Social Stratification and Mobility* 23: 103-127.

Rhee, K. C. & Cho, E. J. (1992). Dosi sinhon-gi-gagyeui gyeolhonbiyonggwa sinhonjugeo jageume daehan yeon-gu (A Study on the Marriage Costs and First Housing Costs of Urban Establishing Families; in Korean). *Han-guk gajeong gwallihakhoe (Journal of Korean Home Management Association)* 10(1): 95-113.

Ryoo, K. C. & Piao, Y. H. (2009). Yeoseong-ui chulsanyul byeonhwawa chulsan-gan-gyeok yeong-hyangyoin (The Change in the Fertility Rates and the Determinants of Birth Interval of Korean Women; in Korean). *Han-guk in-guhak (Korean Journal of Population Studies)* 32(1): 1-23.

Song, J. E. & Han, G. H. (1994). Namseong-ui bumogiroui jeonie daehan bosang — daega jigagui yuhyeong (Typology of Men's Perceived Costs and Benefits about the Transition to Parenthood; in Korean). *Daehan-gajeonghakhoeji (Journal of the Korean Home Economics Association)* 32(4): 73-83.

Spitze, G(1988). Women's Employment and Family Relations: A Review. *Journal of Marriage and the family* 50: 585-618.

Statistics Korea (2007). Household projections from 2005 to 2030.

Statistics Korea (2009a). 2008 Social Survey.

Statistics Korea (2009b). Marriage Statistics in 2008.

Statistics Korea (2009c). Birth Statistics in 2008.

Statistics Korea (2009d). Divorce Statistics in 2008.

Synn, B. P. (1993). The Transition to Parenthood: A Descriptive Study of First-time Mothers in Nuclear and Traditional Families in Korea. Electronic Doctoral Dissertations for UMass Amherst.

Chapter twelve

Korean Families in Mid-Life: Over-Emphasis on Children's Education

Chin, Meejung (Seoul National University)

1. Introduction

In his famous article on social and human capital, Coleman (1988) discusses how Asian immigrant families accumulate social capital by devoting their resources to maximize the human capital of children. To illustrate Asian immigrant parents' educational aspirations for their children, Coleman offers an anecdote of Asian parents buying two copies of a textbook, one for the child and the other for the mother so she can help her child with school work (Coleman 1988: S110). Like Coleman's immigrant Asian families, Korean families devote a majority of their resources to maximize the human capital of their children. Korean parents invest significant time and money to create an optimal environment and opportunities for their children's education. Aside from school education, Koreans spent 21.6 trillion won (approximately USD 18 billion) on supplemental education programs in 2008, which was equivalent to 2.8 % of Korea's GDP. These funds paid for additional private education for their children, who were already attending public elementary, middle, and/or high schools (KNSO 2009d). If we include the cost of early childhood education and education for college students, the expenditure becomes much larger.

Due to the high educational aspirations for and investment in the children of Korean parents, it is not surprising to find high rates of educational enrollment and achievement. In 2008, 99.7 % of middle school graduates chose to attend high school, and 83.8 % of high school graduates entered college (Korean Educational Development Institute 2009). Korean children's academic achievement is also high on international standards. Among high school students from the 40 Organisation for Economic Cooperation and Development (OECD) countries, Korean students ranked first in reading and math in the 2006 OECD Programme for International Student Assessment (PISA) (Kim, et al. 2009).[1]

The education of children provides a key to understanding Korean families, especially families in mid-life. The education of children influences a household's expenditure pattern, parents' retirement plan, employment status of the mother, living arrangements, parent-child relationships, and even marital relation-

---

1 The Programme for International Student Assessment (PISA) is an internationally standardized assessment that was jointly developed by participating economies and administered to 15-year-olds in school. Tests are typically administered to between 4,500 and 10,000 students in each country. For more information, check http://www.pisa.oecd.org

ships. Although the education of children influences Korean families across the life span, its impact seems greater among families in mid-life. Thus, in this chapter, I focus on how the education of children influences Korean families in mid-life and, particularly, in the areas of parent-child relationships and marital relationships.

My argument in this chapter is based on multiple national statistics, primarily from a National Social Survey, Private Education Survey, Marriage Statistics, and Divorce Statistics conducted by the Korean National Statistics Office (KNSO) and from a nationally representative data set from the Korean Longitudinal Study of Women and Family (KLOWF), which surveyed 9,997 Korean women, aged 20 to 65. The data from KLOWF is particularly useful for this paper, because it contains information on household expenditures, marital history, work history, marital quality, generational exchanges, child-rearing, and many other aspects of family life.

2. Middle Age as a Developmental Stage

Middle age is a developmental term which refers to a period between young adulthood and old age. In general, middle-aged individuals have achieved the possible highest position in their careers and consequently earn higher incomes compared to those from other age groups. With respect to the family life during this period, couples have moved beyond the early marital adjustment stage and have reached some level of reconciliation between work and child-rearing. They enjoy a more stable life with relatively secure relationships. At the same time, many development theorists describe middle age as a turning point in life, because people experience significant changes in physical and psychological conditions. They also tend to experience a change in their perspective of time, and begin to think about the limited time remaining in their lifetime.

Middle age is also called the sandwich generation, because adults are expected to provide support for both the younger and older generations. From a family development perspective, a mid-life family is in the throngs of preparing children for adulthood. Children in adolescence or in young adulthood are expected to achieve psychological and physical independence from their parents, so families launch their children out into world and become empty nesters. At the same time, families during this period often need to support both sets of elderly parents. Although some of the care is now rendered to public and private institutions, families still have the main responsibility of caring for their elderly family members. Korean families in mid-life share many of these general characteristics of middle age. However, there are also unique characteristics in Korean mid-life families. In the next section, I discuss the uniqueness of Korean families by providing an example of cohort differences in family characteristics.

There is no single age criterion of middle age. Some argue that it ranges from 35 to 64, which is the most generous age range, while others refer to people in their 40s and 50s. If middle age is restricted to 40s and 50s, then they are the 1950–1970 birth cohorts. This is quite a wide age range, so it might be difficult to find common characteristics in the family lives. Suppose a family follows a marriage and birth trajectory of an average Korean woman in this age range. Using the KLOWF data set, this study compares the age at first marriage, the number of children, the age of the first child, and the age of the youngest child across five different birth cohort groups from 1950 to 1970 in five year increments. Incorporating this approach, a fairly significant difference in demographic profiles was found. As seen in Table 1, the 1950 birth cohort married at age 23.56, but the 1970 birth cohort married at age 26.94. The first marriage of the latter cohort was delayed about 3.4 years compared to the earlier cohort. The number of children was also different. The number of children was 2.96 for the 1950 birth cohort and 2.08 for the 1970 birth cohort. The youngest cohort had one child fewer than the oldest cohort. The age of the first child was 35.41 for the oldest cohort and 11.89 for the youngest cohort. The first child of the 1950 cohort was highly likely to be married and have left his or her parent's home, but the first child of the 1970 cohort was

Table 1 Comparisons of Family Demographic Profiles: 1950-1970 Birth Cohorts

Age	40	45	50	55	60
Birth Cohort	1970	1965	1960	1955	1950
Age at (1st) marriage	26.94	26.58	24.62	24.32	23.56
Number of children	2.08 (.04)	2.08 (.04)	2.13 (.05)	2.55 (.07)	2.96 (.08)
Age of the first child	11.89 (.21)	17.49 (.24)	24.04 (.30)	29.87 (.29)	35.41 (.26)
Age of the youngest child	8.57 (.21)	13.97 (.26)	20.69 (.33)	26.04 (.26)	30.20 (.28)
Age difference between children	3.46 (.17)	3.53 (.21)	3.36 (.22)	3.83 (.20)	5.21 (.24)

Source: Korean Longitudinal Survey of Women and Family (2007)

more likely to still be a middle school student. These demographic profiles imply that, although both of the cohorts are in their middle age, their family life and relationships are likely to differ on many important aspects. Thus, if we want to reduce the degree of heterogeneity among middle aged families, we need to focus on women between the ages of 40 and 55 from the KLOWF data. The average age for first marriage in Korea was 31.4 for men and 28.3 for women in 2008 (KNSO 2009c), so families in this age range are more likely to have unmarried children in the household. Since the age of the youngest child was 26.04 for the 1955 birth cohort, women from this cohort are more likely to have unmarried children. Korean families consider unmarried children dependents regardless of their age, because they believe that the independence of children begins with marriage and setting up an independent household. For these reasons, mid-life families in this study are defined as families who are still are responsible for their unmarried children.

Just a word of caution: while middle age is described as a development stage, some characteristics of contemporary mid-life families may be related to their cohort characteristics. This age period encompasses the baby-boom generation in Korea, who were born between 1955, after the Korean War, and 1963. During this period, there were over one million births every year as compared to only 466 thousand births in 2009. Similar to the US baby-boomers, mid-life families of Korean baby-boomers have a different social context compared to previous or later generations. They have a large cohort size, have benefited from post-Korean War economic prosperity, and have enjoyed an enhanced standard of living.

However, the quality of life in old age may not be as prosperous as the one they enjoyed when they were younger because of the recent demographic and economic changes in Korea. The population growth rate of Korea has declined due to a drastically declining birth rate. The total fertility rate dropped from 4.53 in 1970 to 1.19 in 2008 (KNSO 2009a). The current growth rate of the economy is also lower than in earlier periods. This means the social costs to support the baby-boom generation continue to increase. Thus, some aspects of mid-life families might stem from a cohort effect rather than a developmental effect. Since it is difficult to differentiate these two types of effects, it requires caution by readers.

3. Social Contexts of Korean Family and Education

Korea has experienced compressed modernization in a far shorter time than Western countries. Koreans experienced within only four or five decades what had been experienced by Westerners over two or three centuries (Chang 1999). For example, in the KLOWF sample, a far smaller number of people grew up in rural areas with only 54 % of the 1970 cohort being born and raised in rural areas as opposed to 78 % of the 1950 cohort. In other words, during those 20 years, the proportion of those who grew up in rural areas dropped by 24 %, although the process of modernization differed across social sectors.

More importantly, the family has been the driving force of the compressed modernization of Korea (Chang 1999; Cho 2004). Families have provided human resources by sacrificing their personal lives for the cause of modern nation-building. Families have been willing to collaborate with the nation and to contribute to Korea's economic growth. Families have believed they could achieve success and economic advancement through the economic expansion of the nation. In contrast, in many Western countries, modernization was achieved through the development of individuality. People attained freedom and autonomy from the influences of kinship and established an individual identity differentiated from a group identity. Korean modernization, however, was based on the ideation of family without individuality.

Familism, which is a pre-modern ideation of placing the family over an individual, was not incompatible with modernization in Korea and has been a unique characteristic of Korean families. Koreans have an ideation that the family has to function as an instrument for its members' social competition for status, wealth, and power (Chang 2009). For example, in the 1960s and 1970s, it was not uncommon for the eldest son to receive more schooling than his siblings. Younger siblings had to work on a farm or in a factory to financially support the eldest son, whose educational achievement was the most secure way for the family to climb the social ladder (Han & Yoon 2000). It was a strategic decision in order for the entire family to survive social competition. If the eldest son received a post-secondary education and obtained a non-agricultural job in a city, the family could assume they would achieve a higher social class. Although this type of social mobility is no longer as viable, many families strongly believe that education is the most important way to obtain better social standing or maintain their current social standing.

Changing social and economic conditions have driven Korean families toward more education. Since the 1997 financial crisis, the growth rate of the Korean economy has slowed. Thus, young adults find themselves in less favorable economic situations than their parents' generations. The increasing difficulty in finding employment has led to greater family investment in education to help the younger generation succeed.

There are some common patterns to invest in children's education. Some families try to invest as early as possible by sending their children to early childhood education programs. Because there are no public early childhood education programs in Korea, it is very common to receive early childhood education through the private institutions. Early childhood education starts by age 3 for most children. Other families invest in private education (extracurricular courses such as math or English) to boost their children's academic performance. Still other families invest in their children's education by sending them abroad. Because these families believe that studying abroad gives their children better educational opportunities and advancement in English competency, they are willing to send their children abroad for high school, middle school, or even as early as elementary school. Most of these children are sent to English-speaking countries like the United States, Canada, Australia, New Zealand, and the Philippines (Yi & Kwon 2009). By sending their children abroad, they also choose to live apart for many years. Some families send their children to private boarding schools by themselves, and other families send the mother abroad as well to take care of the children. When the mother and children go abroad and the father remains in Korea to earn money, they are called "wild goose families." The wild goose family is a typical example of instrumental familism practiced by Koreans (Cho 2004), where a couple sacrifices their family life, especially their marital life, for the education of their children. It is important to understand these social and cultural contexts in order to understand parent-child relationships among Korean families in mid-life.

4. Education of Children and Parent-Child Relationships

The Korean parent-child relationship in mid-life can be best summarized by the terms "over-socialization" and "prolonged dependence." Adolescence is a period when children seek autonomy (Hill & Holmbeck 1986) and when they begin to learn how to achieve physical, psychological, and financial independence from their parents and families. However, Korean adolescents are heavily dependent on their parents because of the heavy daily burden of study and prolonged years of schooling. They are over-socialized by the goal of educational achievement and are characterized by prolonged dependence. Their everyday life is filled with various educational activities and their adolescence is filled with preparation work for educational achievement.

Korean adolescents are well known for the long hours of study. Students, aged 15–24, on average, spend almost six hours on extra-curricular education, which is two hours longer each day than their peers in other countries (Kim, et al. 2009). Using the 1999 and 2004 National Time Use Survey data, Chin (2009) examined how much time Korean students spent on various activities. Table 2 shows the average time 4th to 12th graders spend in school, on extra-curricular education, on self-study, on family time (conversation and meals), and on passive play (for example, TV, computer games). As the table shows, Korean students have traditionally spent long hours on various types of studying (in school, extra-curricular courses, and self study) and the length of time increased even more between 1999 and 2004. For example, elementary school students (4th to 6th grades) spent 6 hours and 20 minutes studying each day in 1999 and 7 hours and 8 minutes in 2004.

Another troubling result of the long hours of study is that Korean adolescent children spend little time with their families. As seen in Table 2, in 1999, elementary students in Korea spent only 51 minutes per day on family meals and conversation and even less (41 minutes) in 2004. These numbers do not suggest, however, that the influence of parents on children is meager in Korea. Regardless of how little time they spend with their children, the level of Korean parents' involvement is high. Rather, their involvement in their children's education takes the form of providing their children with useful information about private educational programs after school and entrance exam preparation for high school and college, planning and managing schedules for their children, and closely monitoring academic performance. Generally, a mother takes on the main responsibility of educating the children and plays multiple roles as an information collector, a time manger, counselor, and

Table 2 Time Spent on Each Activity during Weekdays: 1999 and 2004

	Elementary students 4-6 grades		Middle school students 7-9 grades		High school students 10-12 grades	
	Rate (%)	Time	Rate (%)	Time	Rate (%)	Time
1999						
In school	85.4	4:25	86.5	5:42	85.9	7:20
In extra-curricular education	47.4	0:46	39.5	0:50	21.4	0:25
Self-study	84.5	1:09	78.6	1:17	65.3	1:16
Family time	96.0	0:51	88.9	0:38	76.7	0:28
Passive activity	78.8	0:50	84.4	0:55	88.3	1:00
2004						
In school	99.3	4:54	99.0	6:09	99.0	8:48
In extra-curricular education	75.1	1:26	63.5	1:28	29.3	0:34
Self-study	80.4	0:58	67.5	0:57	52.9	0:52
Family time	93.2	0:41	82.5	0:28	63.0	0:17
Passive activity	86.4	0:50	90.5	1:00	90.6	0:59

Source: Chin (2009).

health care provider. Although there is limited time for parents to spend with children, mothers still have many opportunities to interact with their children between study times.

Because Korean parents are deeply interested in the education of their children, their conversation with children tends to be limited to this topic. According to the KLOWF data, when mothers were asked about their conversation topics with their children, the majority reported that the most common topic was academic performance and school life. They seldom had conversations about friends, family issues, or the children themselves. In addition, when they were asked about their concerns about their children, the most frequent response was academic performance. Almost 80 % of the mothers reported that they were worried about their children's academic performance, regardless of how well the child was doing in school.

From the perspective of adolescent children in Korea, adolescence is a period where they seek to satisfy and fulfill their parents' educational expectations, which is quite different from the typical developmental task of achieving autonomy and self-esteem that existing developmental theories have suggested (Allen, et al. 1994), Instead, in Korea, what concerns adolescents are issues related to studying or career (along with physical appearance). As seen in Table 3, issues that seem relevant during adolescence, such as family, friends, boy/girlfriends, and even money are not the strongest concerns for adolescents in Korea.

Korean students not only study for long hours on a daily basis, but they also attend school for many years. The extended years of education are associated with the high unemployment rate among young adults in Korea. While the unemployment rate is 3.7 % for the entire labor force, it is 8.2 % for those who are between 15 and 29 years old. Because it is more difficult for young adults to find a job, they invest more in education and postpone entering the job market. During their college and graduate education, parents often pay for most or all of the tuition and living costs for their children. According to the 2008 National Social Survey, 61.9 % of college students received all of their tuition and 36.7 % of the students received some of the tuition from their parents. About 20 % of graduate school attendees received all of their tuition from their parents. In that it takes 11 months, on average, to become employed after graduation (KNSO 2009c), the financial burden of parents often continues throughout their children's young adulthood. As long as children depend on their parents financially, they are less likely to achieve autonomy in their life. They must consult their parents regarding their academic and career plans and decisions. Any decisions that do not satisfy their parents' expectations are not likely to be approved. This prolonged adolescence results in an imbalance of power in the relationship between the parents and their children.

Interestingly, parent-child satisfaction develops differently for parents and children in Korea. According to the 2008 National Social Survey, while parents report their satisfaction with their children has decreased over time, children report their satisfaction with their parents has increased over time (KNSO 2009e). In Korea,

Table 3 Concerns of Adolescents and Young Adults

	Appearance	Health	Family	Money	Study	Career	Friends	Date	Other	No concern
15-18	12.2	2.4	4.0	5.0	62.3	6.7	2.4	1.6	0.9	2.5
19-24	13.2	4.3	6.1	5.5	17.8	39.1	2.0	3.9	1.5	6.6

Source: 2008 National Social Survey (KNSO 2009e)

Table 4 Satisfaction of the Parent-Child Relationship

	Children Ages 15-19	Children Ages 20-29	-
With Parents	68.2	70.1	-
	Parents in their 30s	Parents in their 40s	Parents in their 50s
With Children	85.5	75.3	67.2

Source: 2008 National Social Survey (KNSO 2009e)

intense parental involvement may help children advance in their academic performance, but it may also lead to low relational satisfaction because their developmental task of autonomy cannot be fulfilled during the adolescent years. As they age, they become more independent from their parents and feel satisfied. By contrast, parents may become less satisfied and feel isolated when children become more independent and need less parental involvement and supervision.

5. Marital Relationships in Mid-Life Families

Traditionally, Korean families place greater importance on the parent-child relationship, especially the father-son relationship, than on the marital relationship. Although this traditional priority given to the father-son relationship has become weaker, the parent-child relationship is still the most important relationship in Korean families. The marital relationship in Korean families is more instrumental than emotional compared to Western families. In other words, a parental role in Korea is much more salient than a spousal role. Married couples share the goal of giving a better education to their children, and they collaborate to achieve it. They are even willing to sacrifice their marital relationship for this mutual goal. The example of the "wild goose family" shows that the marital relationship can be disregarded for the family goal of educating the children. Wives and husbands in these families live separately for several years and only meet once or twice each year. Their marriage can be characterized by the traditional gender role division, a legitimate absence of a sex life, and a lack of marital intimacy (Kim & Kim 2009).

The tendency to prioritize the parental role over the spousal role can be problematic when the couple's children finally become independent. Many married couples find themselves sharing nothing but their children in their late middle age. They have not developed a shared identity or shared activities as a couple. The only thing they shared during their married life was their children, who have now left home. According to the 2008 National Social Survey in Korea, marital satisfaction decreases with age. The percentage of couples who are somewhat satisfied or very satisfied in their marital relationship was 74.6 % for younger married couples in their 30s, 65.8 % for couples in their 40s, and drops to 58.9 % for couples in their 50s. The low marital satisfaction reflects the strong inclination to the primacy of the parent role. Some parents become involved in their children's lives even after they get married. They actively take part in the process of mate selection and the marital lives of their children (Chin & Ok 1993). Other couples cannot overcome marital problems and choose to divorce, so the divorce rate of middle-age couples is quite high in Korea. About 14 % of all divorces reported in 2008 were couples who had been married for 14-19 years, and 23 % were couples who had been married for 20 or more years. Thirty-seven percent of all divorces are couples in the middle or old ages (KNSO 2009b). Although the divorce rate in Korea is declining, in general, there is still a steady increase in divorce among older couples who have been married 20 years or longer.

Table 5 Divorce Rates by Duration of Marriage

	Number of Divorce (in thousands)	Proportion (percent)
0-4 years	33.1	28.4
5-9 years	21.7	18.6
10-14 years	18.3	15.7
15-19 years	16.5	14.1
20 years and more	26.9	23.1
Total	116.5	100.0

Source: 2008 Divorce Statistics (KNSO 2009b)

Economic burdens also contribute to marital instability for middle-age couples. In general, middle age is a period when adults can enjoy the highest achievement and income in their careers. In Korea, it takes 10.1 years, on average, to save enough money to purchase a family's first house, and it takes 4.7 moves before they settle into their own house (KNSO 2004). People who marry at age 30 probably will not be able to buy their first house until their early 40s. Although they have to pay for a mortgage, they are finally able to settle into a community and do not have to move around in their 40s. Thus, the middle age stage is considered a period of residential and economic stability.

In spite of the relative stability in a family's living situation, employment instability increases for middle-aged people in Korea. The likelihood of early retirement from a primary job becomes higher during this period. Early retirement refers to a voluntary or involuntary retirement from a primary job before the formal retirement age which is 55-58 for the majority of the private and public sector. The phenomenon of early retirement has become common since the large-scale restructuring of public and private sectors following the 1997 financial crisis in Korea. Although the formal unemployment rate for is as low as 2.7 % for men in their 40s and 3.0 % for men in their 50s, the perceived unemployment rate is much higher than the formal rates, because the formal unemployment rate does not include those who are not in the labor force due to long unemployment. Using the 2006 Korean Longitudinal Study of Ageing, which is a nationally representative data set for the middle and old populations, Yoon and Jun (2009) estimated that 8.8 % of men and women, ages 45-55 and 29.4 % of 55-64-year-olds have no job. Using the 2007 wave of the same data set, Chang, Shin, Shin, and Lee (2009) investigated the retrospective work history of middle and old aged people and found that only 40.9 % of the respondents have maintained their primary employment status during their life span. In other words, only 12.1 % have maintained their status as wage earning employees, 8.8 % have maintained their status as self-employed, and 12.8 % have maintained their status as agricultural/fishery workers.

An involuntary job change, particularly in middle age, affects the marital relationship and family life, especially because household expenses are the highest in middle age. Due to increased spending on the children's education, mid-life families have a heavy financial burden. Kim (2007) estimated the proportion of education spending of the total household budget, using the 2005 National Household Expenditure Survey data, and found that education accounted for 22.7 % of the household expenses. The study also found that 64 % of the education expenses were for private education. Eighty three percent of the couples in their 40s and 50s perceived that they had a heavy financial burden because of their education expenses (KNSO 2009e). In order to spend on the education of children, families must reduce their other spending and savings, which may put them at risk after retirement (Lee 2006). Due to the job insecurity and financial burden, middle aged families are likely to have financial problems that, in turn, can negatively affect their marital quality and relational satisfaction (Yoon & Jun 2009).

6. Conclusion

In this chapter, Korean families were examined in mid-life in the context of their children's education. Although this approach has a limitation in explaining family life in detail, it provides a useful perspective. Because Korean parents place an over-emphasis on the education of children, they experience an imbalance in their family relationships and lives. Parent-child relationships center mainly on education. They may lack opportunities to develop a mutual relationship with their children that can be enjoyed without educational achievement. The prolonged dependence of children undermines possibilities to develop an interdependent parent-child relationship and increases the psychological and financial burden and insecurity of parents in middle-age. As families devote their resources to the education of their children, they may experience an erosion of their marital relationship. Married couples often do not prepare for their own relationships after the children leave home, which can jeopardize their happiness and marital satisfaction in later life. Previous studies argue that playing multiple roles can enhance mental health in the middle age (Coleman, et al. 1987; Thoits 1983; Han, et al. 2002), so having multiple social roles as parent, child, spouse, and worker may decrease depression and increase psychological well-being in Korean middle aged couples (Han, et al. 2002). However, if they are engaged only in a parental role, they are less likely to have a healthy life in their later life. While this is a general risk for all middle-aged individuals, it may be more severe for Koreans whose lives are strongly child-centered.

As mentioned earlier, this could be a cohort effect rather than a developmental effect. Contemporary middle-aged Koreans have achieved modernization through their own efforts and have witnessed the importance of education in achieving personal and family success. They have also experienced the power of education in advancing up the social ladder, so they may think that the most important role as parents is to support the education of their children. Thus, given the fast changes in recent Korean economic development, it is possible for the next middle-aged generation to live a different family life in Korea.

Finally, it is important to keep in mind that there could be a wide range of differences according to social class in family life and relationships. Although the majority of Koreans believe in the importance of education regardless of their income or educational level, there are significant differences in the actual investment in children according to social class. The highest family income group spends 8.4 times more on child education than the lowest income group (KEDI 2009). Thus, significant class differences may exist in how the education of children affects family life. Low class families do not have low aspirations for their children's education, but they lack resources to support these aspirations. One of the most significant frustrations of low class mothers is that they cannot invest enough resources in the education of their children (Sung & Chin 2009). Therefore, this description of mid-life families is more likely to be a picture of middle class, middle-aged families rather than low class families.

Parental over-emphasis on the education of children is a common, significant characteristic of Asian families, including Korean families. By understanding the role of education in the compressed process of modernization in Korea, it may not be surprising to appreciate the over-emphasis on the education of children among Korean families. We may better comprehend the characteristics and dynamics of Korean families through the lens of education employed in this chapter.

References

Allen, J. P., Hauser, S. T., Bell, K. L., & O'Connor, T. G. (1994). Longitudinal assessment of autonomy and relatedness in adolescent-family interactions as predictors of adolescent ego-development and self-esteem. *Child Development* 65: 179-194.

Chang, J., Shin, D., Shin, K., & Lee, H. (2009). *Jung-goryeongja geullosaeng-aesa yeon-gu (A study on the work life history of the middle and the old*; in Korean).

Report 2009-02. Seoul: Han-guknodong-yeon-guwon (Korean Labor Institute).

Chang, K. (1999). Compressed modernity and its discontents: South Korean society in transition. *Economy and Society* 28(1): 30-55.

Chang, K. (2009). *Gajok, Saeng-ae, Jeongchigyeongje: Apchukjeok geundaeseong-ui misijeok gicho (Family, life course, and politics: The micro foundation of compressed modernity in Korean)*. Paju: Changbi.

Chin, M. & Ok, S. (1993). Jung-nyeon-gi yeoseong-ui eomeoniyeokhal suhaengbudamgwa simnijeok bokji (Mother-role burden and psychological well-being in mid-life women; in Korean). *Daehan-gajeong-hakhoeji (Journal of Korean Home Economics)* 32 (5): 1-13.

Chin, M. (2009). Sahoejaboneurosseoui Gajok (Family as Social Capital: Its Vulnerability and Possibility; in Korean). Presentation to The Family Forum. The Healthy Family Foundation.

Cho, E. (2004). Segyehwaui choecheomdane seon han-gukui gajok (Korean Families on the Forefront of Globalization; in Korean). *Gyeongjewa sahoe (Economy and Society)* 64: 148-344.

Coleman, J. (1988). Social Capital in the Creation of Human Capital. *The American Journal of Sociology* 94: S95-S120 (Supplement: Organizations and Institutions: Sociological and Economic Approaches to the Analysis of Social Structure).

Coleman, L. M., Antonucchi, T., & Adelman, P. K. (1987). Role Involvement, Gender, Well-being. In *Spouse, Parent, Worker: On Gender and Multiple Roles*, ed. F. J. Crosby. New Haven: Yale University Press.

Han, G., & Yoon, S. (2000). Ddeonan jangnam, Nameun jangnam (Failed parental strategy?: Determinants of the living arrangements among the rural elderly in Korea; in Korean). *Han-guksahoehak (Korean Journal of Sociology)* 34: 649-669.

Han, G., Lee, J., Ok, S., Ryffs, C., & Marks, N. (2002). Jung-nyeon-gi namnyeoui sahoejeok yeokhalgwa jeonsingeongang (Gender, Social Roles, and Mental Health in Mid-Life; in Korean). *Han-guknonyeonhak (Journal of Korea Gerontological Society)* 22 (2): 29-225.

Hill, J.P. & Holmbeck, G. N. (1986). Attachment and autonomy during adolescence. *Annals of Child Development* 3: 145-189.

Kim, K. (2007). Gaguju gyoyuksujun-e ttareun janyeo gyoyukbi jichul-aek-gwa jichulgujo (Householder's Education Level and Education Expenditure for Children; in Korean). *Daehangajeonghakhoeji (Journal of Korean Home Management)* 25(6): 111-120.

Kim, K., Ahn, S., Chang, S., Kim, M., & Choi, D. (2009). *Adong, cheongsonyeonui saenghwalpaeteon gwanhan gukjebigyoyeon-gu (An International Comparison of Life Patterns of Children and Adolescents; in Korean).* Report 11-1351000-000305-01. Han-gukjeongchaek-yeon-guwon (National Youth Policy Institute).

Kim, Y. & Kim, T. (2009). Gaguju gyoyuksujun-e ttareun janyeo gyoyukbi jichul-aek-gwa jichulgujo (A Study of the Families in Long-Term Separation: Marital Relationship of "Wild Geese Families."; in Korean). *Daehanjajeonhakhoeji (Journal of Korean Association of Family Relations)* 14(3): 297-326.

Korean Educational Development Institute (2009). *2008 Education Statistics.* Seoul: KAEDI.

Korean National Statistics Office (2004). *2003 National Social Survey.* Daejeon: KNSO.

Korean National Statistics Office (2007). *2006 National Social Survey.* Daejeon: KNSO.

Korean National Statistics Office (2009a). *2008 National Birth Statistics.* Daejeon: KNSO.

Korean National Statistics Office (2009b). *2008 National divorce statistics.* Daejeon: KNSO.

Korean National Statistics Office (2009c). *2008 National Marriage Statistics.* Daejeon: KNSO.

Korean National Statistics Office (2009d). *2008 National Private Education Survey.* Daejeon: KNSO.

Korean National Statistics Office (2009e). *2008 National Social Survey.* Daejeon: KNSO.

Lee, S. (2006). Dosigagyeui sagyoyukbi budamgwa jichuljeollyak (Household Strategy for Private Educational Expenditure Burden; in Korean). *Han-guksobijahak-yeon-gu (Journal of Consumer Studies)* 17(2): 115-132.

Sung, M. & Chin, M. (2009). Bingon hanbumo yeoseongui bumogwon bojanggwa ilgajok yangnip (Work and Family Balance of Low-Income Single Mothers from the Perspective of Parental Right; in Korean). *Gajokgwa munhwa (Family and Culture)* 21(3): 1-28.

Thoits, P. A. (1983). Multiple Identities and Psychological Well-being: A Reformulation and Test of Social Isolation Hypothesis. *American Sociological Review* 48: 174-187.

Yi, S. & Kwon, M. (2009). Han-gugui jogiyuhak (South Korean Early Study Abroad; in Korean). *Adong-hak-yeon-gu (Korean Journal of Child Studies)* 30(6): 297-308.

Yoon, J. & Jun, H. (2009). Jung-goryeongjaui gyeongjehwaldong sangtaewa jeongsingeongang: Sodeuksujun-gwa gajokgwan-gye manjokdoui maegaehyogwa geomjeung (Economic activity status and mental health among middle and older adults: The mediating effects of income level and satisfaction in family relationship; in Korean). *Han-guk-nonyeonhak (Journal of the Korean Gerontological Society)* 29(2): 743-759.

Korean Family Relationships in Later Life

Sung, Miai (Korea National Open University)

1. Introduction

The purpose of this chapter is to outline demographic issues in later life families and to explain the family relationships in later life. Later life families are receiving more attention as the average life expectancy increases. Generally, since people are living longer than they did in the past, later life is becoming a greater part of life as a whole. In particular, because the Korean family is changing from Neo-Confucianism to individualism, there is a lot of confusion between the traditional hierarchy and modern equality norms. These kinds of ambiguous role expectations are the main source of relational tensions today.

Originally, care of the aged was not a problem in Korean society because the filial piety norm was strongly enforced in the traditional society. Furthermore because maintaining the family was the supreme task of the eldest son, father-son relationships were more important than couple relationships in the traditional Korean family. However, these days, equality and independence are emphasized in family relationships. This traditional situation is changing. Therefore, caring for the elderly has become a social problem in Korea. In addition, because couples aren't having many children, the empty nest period is longer than it was in the past. Therefore, nowadays, the quality of couple relationships is increasingly important in later life.

In this context, this chapter starts with demographic issues and deals with Korean elders' family relationships focusing on adult children and spouses. Relationships with daughters-in-law and sons-in-law are mentioned along with relationships with adult children. Issues of elders' divorce and remarriage are also discussed as part of elderly couple relationships.

2. Demographic Issues in Later Life Families

1) Increased Life Expectancy

Due to improved living standards and medical care, the average life expectancy has increased around the world, and Korea is no exception with a rapidly aging nation. Traditionally, Koreans have honored a person's 60th birthday with a special celebration, called "return to the birth sexagenary cycle" (*hwangap* or *hoegap*). This celebration represents the completion of a life circle, because only the very fortunate few were expected to live to that age in the past. Typical Korean sayings clearly represent this tradition, including "From the 60th birthday one becomes a living ancestor," "The second life begins after the 60th birthday," and "Life after the 60th birthday is not for his (her) own life but for others' lives" (Kim, Park, & Hong 2005: 197). Traditionally, elders over 60 years old did not need to work anymore, so they could just enjoy a comfortable later life and give advice to younger people as "living ancestors."

As Table 1 shows, as recently as the 1960s, the average life expectancy was 51.1 years for men and 53.7 years for women, so celebrating a person's 60th birthday was viewed as a privilege. However, in 2008, just 50 years later, the average life expectancy had increased by almost 26 years to 75.1 years for men and 82.3 years for women. A person's 60th birthday no longer seems to be the completion of a life, as the average life expectancy has continuously increased to 80 years and over.

Koreans' increased life expectancy has significantly changed people's perspectives about later life. In the past, life after 60 was an inactive period, when the elderly had retired from productive work. Disengagement theory, which considers elderly life as the

Table 1 Life Expectancy in Korea

Year	1960	1970	1980	1990	1995	2000	2005	2008	2010	2020	2030	2040	2050
Average	52.4	62.3	66.2	71.7	73.5	75.9	78.6	78.7	79.6	80.7	83.1	84.6	86.0
Male	51.1	59.0	62.3	67.7	69.6	72.1	75.1	75.1	76.1	77.5	79.9	81.4	82.9
Female	53.7	66.1	70.5	75.9	77.4	79.5	81.9	82.3	82.9	84.1	86.3	87.7	89.0

Source: Korea National Statistical Office (2006), *Estimation of Future Population.*

process of disengaging from social and economic activities provides a framework for this period of life. In contrast to just 50 years ago, today most elders do not want to retire, preferring to hold on to an active and energetic life for as long as possible. A popular joke "9988234" reflects that desire: live vitally ("88" is pronounced the same as a word meaning "vitally" in Korean) until the age of 99, be sick 2-3 days, and then die ("4" is pronounced the same as a word meaning "die" in Korean).

2) A Growing Elderly Population

A growing elderly population is a common phenomenon around the world; however, in Korea this change has been much faster and more recent than most industrialized countries. Early industrialized Western countries became aged societies over many years. For example, the population of France aged over 115, 85 years in Sweden, 71 years in the United States, and 47 years in Great Britain (Kim 2007: 11). In contrast, Korea's population is only now rapidly becoming an aged society (see Table 2). Not until 2000 did Korea officially become an aging society with 7.2 % of the population aged 65 and over, and this percentage is estimated to reach 14 % in 2018 and 20 % in 2026. As these predictions suggest, in less than 30 years Korea will have changed from an aging society to a super-aged society.

The rapid increase in the population aged 65 and over raises an important question: Who will care for these elders? In Korea, caring for elders has usually been considered the family's responsibility,

Table 2 Increase in the Elderly Population in Korea (unit: 10,000 people)

Year	1995	2000	2005	2010	2018	2026	2030	2050
Total population	4,509	4,701	4,814	4,887	4,934	4,903	4,863	4,234
Population aged 65 and over	266	339	437	537	705	1,020	1,182	1,617
Proportion (%)	5.9 %	7.2 %	9.1 %	11.0 %	14.3 %	20.8 %	24.3 %	38.2 %

Source: Korea National Statistical Office (2006), *Estimation of Future Population.*

because traditional Korean families functioned as a unit, protecting and caring for all family members. Reflecting these traditional norms, families today are still expected to be the first and major caregivers for elders. This is especially reflected in Korean welfare policies. Korea's "forcible redemption of a maintenance allowance" is a clear example of the government's attitude. Although the government will provide poor elders with a maintenance allowance, this is really only a loan. Therefore, after helping the elder, the government will search for the elders' adult children and force them to repay the allowance, regardless of relationship between the adult children and their elderly parents. For example, adult children are required to repay the allowance advanced to an elderly parent even if they are estranged. This policy often forces elderly parents to depend on their adult children for financial support, regardless of the relationship, and can strain the family relationship even further. Thus, the increased average life expectancy has created an even greater challenge for adult children who have to care for their parents even longer.

3. The Relationship between Elderly Parents and Adult Children

1) Characteristics of the Parent-Adult Child Relationship

In order to understand the new modern conflicts between elderly parents and adult children, it is very important to understand the history, characteristics, and dynamics of the traditional family in Korea. Families in Korea are known for strong family relationships and, particularly, filial piety, a term referring to children's respect and care for their parents. The relationship between elderly parents and adult children is based on blood ties. It cannot be substituted by other relationships and terminates only upon the death of the parents or children. In other words, there are significant internal and external barriers to terminating the familial relationship (Sung & Ok 1997). Furthermore, the relationship dynamics between group members are usually dominated by concepts of reciprocity and fairness (Finch 1989: 162), so unreciprocated or unfair interactions can significantly lower the quality of the relationship between elderly parents and adult children, even though the relationship itself could continue (Johnson 1988). It is important, therefore, to analyze whether or not the modern relationship between elderly parents and adult children is reciprocated and fair. This concept is far more important in Korea, because Koreans tend to blame the children for the insufficient care of elders not the Korean social support system.

2) Family Care Giving in the Past

Filial piety has been emphasized so much that it is accepted as the absolute justified truth and moral obligation, which has been reinforced by religion. This concept has been prevalent in Korean society since its beginning.

(1) Emphasis on Filial Piety

In traditional Korean families, relationships between parents and children could be summarized by filial piety (*hyo*), children's respect and care for their parents. Filial piety has been the primary norm affecting all families' everyday lives. One of the core meanings is that the younger generation cares for the older generation, thus returning the parents' endless love. Parental love was usually expressed as "down-flowing water" (*naerisarang*), which could not be fully rewarded by the children's love, flowing upward.

Every ancient religion in Korea emphasized filial piety. For example, Buddhism, which was the dominant religion until the fourteenth century, explained that filial piety is natural gratitude and the return of the parents' care giving. Filial piety in Buddhism also included respect and affection for all elders, not only the parents. In addition, it assumed fairness in relationships, focusing on the parents' affection for the children. With the development of an agricultural and patriarchal society, the concept of filial piety was transformed into being more unilateral and obligatory.

In the fourteenth century, Buddhism was replaced by Neo-Confucianism, an ideology that instituted the patriarchal system.

Instead of Buddhism's equality, hierarchy became important. The world of Neo-Confucianism was based on "order and obedience" between all hierarchical relationships, including the king and his subjects, father and son, husband and wife, and owner and slave. The concept reinforced the theory that if every member knows his or her duty, then society becomes moral, rational, and well-balanced (Korean History Research Society 1990: 280). Thus, Neo-Confucianism became the basis of Korean social and political life, becoming the guiding principle for how all Koreans should live.

Around the middle of the seventeenth century, the patriarchal lineage system perpetrated by Neo-Confucianism became dominant with a greater emphasis on the relationship between fathers and sons, particularly the eldest son. In patriarchal society, the father was the head of the family and controlled all agricultural production of the household. The father also held ownership of the land, the most valuable resource in an agricultural society. Koh (1983) and Kim (1975) noted that the filial piety of Neo-Confucianism was closely related and necessary to an agricultural society; thus, the relationship between fathers and sons was mutually dependent. A father's sons depended on their father and their fathers' land for their living, and, in turn, the father required their labor and obedience. Although this could be seen as an unreciprocated and unfair relationship, sons were eventually rewarded because they inherited the land after their father died. In this manner, a long-term relationship of trust and commitment was established between father and son (Sung & Ok 1997).

(2) Filial Piety as Behavior Norms

Neo-Confucianism's filial piety was the root of all virtue as well as all behavioral norms and caring for parents was the starting point of every virtue. In addition, respect and love for one's parents had to be performed in actions because filial piety was not only an ideology, it was also practical ethics.

Filial piety was divided into three aspects. Respect and gratitude to parents was the first vital role for children. Not to make parents ashamed of the children was the second aspect. Children had to be very careful to not embarrass their parents, causing them to lose face. The third filial piety aspect was to care for one's parents, providing food, clothing, and housing. In short, filial piety was systematic behavioral norms. To learn how to perform filial piety, ancient books gave examples of impiety. For example, one key theme was laziness, because "lazy" children cannot earn enough money to care for their parents.

The emergence of a patriarchal family culture, combined with filial piety norms, significantly affected relationships between parents and children. Until then, sons had no special privileges over daughters. All children inherited equally from their parents and had equal obligations. The ancestor worship ceremony (*jesa*), one of the most important familial obligations, might have been held by every adult child on a rotation basis (*yunhoe bongsa*) or by dividing ancestors to be worshipped between the children equally (*bunhar bongsa*). Moreover, the ceremony was usually held at a Buddhist temple, not at home, and was organized by monks (Kim, et al. 2005: 249). Thus, the sons' contribution was limited until the emergence of a patriarchal family culture when the son became wholly responsible for the ceremony. Beginning in the middle of the seventeenth century, the roles of sons and daughters became sharply differentiated. A married woman was now regarded as a member of her in-laws family, not her own, so she did not need to fulfill any obligations to her family of origin. There was even a saying, "Married daughters are strangers" (*chulgaoein sasang*) (Kim, et al. 2005: 31).

Nor were all the sons equal either. Only the eldest was responsible for caring for his parents and holding the ancestor worship ceremony. Furthermore, the equal inheritance norm was replaced by an unequal one, giving the eldest son the majority of the property (Kim, et al. 2005: 27-29). With this change, the role of the eldest son's wife, the eldest daughter-in-law, became essential. She was expected to give birth to a son who would continue the patriarchal family line. She also had to care for her parents-in-law, prepare food for the ancestor worship ceremony, and take care of visiting relatives and guests (Kang 2008).

If couples did not have a son, they were expected to adopt a son who would care for them in their later lives. Therefore, the adoption rate grew rapidly from the middle of the seventeenth century. Adopting a child from strangers was unusual, however. Preferably an adoptee was taken from a close paternal relative who had two or more sons, and, as such, adoptions were the paternal family's decision more than the individual couple's decision. The opinion of the soon-to-be adoptive mother was not considered and was often totally ignored, even though she would be the one to take care of the adopted child (Kim, et al. 2005).

Another source of conflict that stemmed from Neo-Confucianism was "differentiation of self." Family therapy pioneer Murray Bowen emphasized the concept of differentiation of self, the ability to separate one's own intellectual and emotional functioning from that of the family (Kerr & Bowen 1988: 101). The eldest son in a traditional Korean family could not differentiate himself, as he had to remain a core member of his natal family. Moreover, the relationship between the eldest son and his wife and their parenting decisions were considered to be the concern of the whole patriarchal family. Relatives and parents believed they had the right to decide every aspect of the son's family life, especially decisions concerning his wife. The mother of the eldest son gained her status only by giving birth to a son who would carry on the family line. This often led to family problems, such as relationship conflicts between the mother and her daughter-in-law.

3) Modern Relationships between Parents and Adult Children

In addition to strong religious influences, Korean families have been greatly changed by historical events, such as Japan's colonial rule (1910-1945), the Korean War (1950-1953), the division of the country into north and south (1945), rapid industrialization and urbanization, political instability toward democratization, and the economic crisis in the 1990s.

The major influence to come out of these major historical events on modern society has been a change in gender equality. The idea of gender equality spread quickly throughout society, which led to a revision of civil laws. For example, equal inheritance was legislated in 1991, and, in 2005, the patriarchal family registry system was abolished (Korea Court 2005). Children now inherit their parents' property equally regardless of gender or birth order. Nor does the eldest son represent the whole natal family or is required to take sole responsibility for care giving. Most importantly, traditional family norms are no longer protected by law.

In spite of the legal changes, reality has changed far more slowly than the law. Research about changes in Korean families in the industrialized period (Sung 2006; Sung 2009; Ok, et al. 2000; Chang 1994; Han & Yun 2004) consistently report that total reconstruction of the traditional patriarchal family system into a system that reflects modern families with equal rights and individual freedom has not yet been totally realized. The changes have been limited to partial transformation and adaption. For example, the scope and function of families or relatives have just diminished rather than been reconstructed (Ok, et al. 2000). Of course, the family structure has been modernized: the nuclear family seems to have replaced the traditional stem (extended) family, but that is just a surface phenomenon.

Korean family norms are now in a state of confusion, since traditional and modern family norms exist side by side. With a lack of common principles, family norms are different for each individual, which causes conflicts and problems between family members (Sung 2006). For example, while the eldest son may think that equal inheritance means equal responsibility in caring for his aging parents, the other brothers and sisters may believe care giving is the eldest son's responsibility despite the changes in inheritance practices. In addition, since the Western idea of living an independent lifestyle is highly valued, dependence between family members tends to be regarded as a burden. These confusing family norms are reflected in a survey conducted by the Korea National Statistical Office (2006), which found the percentage of respondents who thought children must care for their elderly parents dropped from 90.2 % in 1998 down to 63.4 % in 2006. In just eight years, there was a sharp decline in the traditional belief that adult children must care for their elderly parents.

Nor do elderly parents want to depend on their adult children anymore. When the Korea Retiree Association (2008) surveyed 317 people, aged from 20 to 70 in 2008, 79 % of the elders, aged 60 and over, responded that they did not expect their children to provide care giving. In addition, 74 % of these elders thought that they would not ask their adult children for financial support, and 55 % planned to live in nursing homes when they could not take care of themselves.

Despite these rapidly changing attitudes toward elderly parents, the tradition of intimate relationships between elderly parents and adult children still influences Korean elders' perspectives. Numerous researchers have found that elderly parents' life satisfaction is significantly affected by their children's support and the good relationship they have with them (Lee 2005; Jeon 1993). They have also found that elderly parents are lonelier when their relationships with their children are not satisfactory. The parents want to maintain intimate emotional relationships with their children, but live separately, and not depend on them financially or physically (Won 1995; Han & Yoon 2001).

Empirical studies have also shown that elderly parents' physical, economic, and social dependence negatively affects their relationships with their adult children (Park & Um 2007; Choi 1994; Choi & Kim, 1991). Comparing adult children's care giving with the relationship quality in Korea and the United States, Choi (2009) found that Korean adult children care more for elders, but they felt that the quality of the relationship with their elderly parents was much lower than the relationship quality in the United States. Moreover, both elderly parents and children perceived their solidarity as low and their conflict as high (Choi 1994; Choi & Kim 1991).

Another interesting report (*The Dong-A Ilbo*, 2006) is that some adult children take their parents' economic support for granted in Korea and do not think about reciprocity or care giving. Children typically receive the parents' house and other property but ignore the responsibility of care giving for their elderly parents. It is not rare to read news reports about withdrawal of property transfers by elderly parents who are disappointed with their "unfaithful adult children" (Chung & Ok 2008: 117). One survey conducted by the Korea National Statistical Office (2002) found that 88.5 % of respondents believed elders should keep their property until they die, so they would be treated decently by their adult children.

Research about inheritance practices (Lee & Kim 2001; Park & Jung 1999) also found many unequal cases in spite of the equality principle in the revised civil law. In particular, they discovered that sons inherit more than daughters, and eldest sons inherit more than younger brothers. In some cases, daughters are totally excluded from inheritance with the stated reason that it is sufficient to educate their daughters and support them for their weddings. Unequal inheritance is reported to cause considerable conflicts among family members. Elderly parents who transfer property to children unequally often find that it generates stress and fear rather than respect and caring from their children.

Today, Korean elders are often not adequately cared for as was the case in the former traditional society. There is a huge gap between belief and reality with more than half of Koreans believing that caring for elderly parents is the children's responsibility. Nevertheless, elders are fearful about their futures and want to find ways to live independently (*Korea JoongAng Daily*, 2009). If the current trends continue, it will become far more difficult to expect adult children to care for their elderly parents. Analyzing the practice of family care giving in local agricultural villages, Yang (2009) concluded that the intergenerational family support system of a patriarchal society has transformed into an intra-generational family support system and social support system. As a result, poor elders who have few resources to live alone are suffering.

4) The Relationship between Mothers and Daughters-in-law

Conflicts between mothers and their daughters-in-law are an inevitable result of patriarchal systems. Patriarchy means male domination over females by social and cultural institutions (Kim, et al. 2005: 30). In traditional patriarchal families, married women can enhance their status only by giving birth to a son. A common saying is, "The dead without a son will wander around, suffering from hunger and thirst," because they will not be fed in the ancestor worship ceremony, which is held by the son. Mothers and sons maintain the most intimate relationship in these families. Wolf (1972: 33) found the same kind of intimate mother-son relationship in Taiwanese patriarchal families and named it "the uterine family."

After the son marries, the mother perceives the daughter-in-law as a great threat to her relationship with her son, so conflict typically begins (Jung, et al. 2006: 240). If the married son is conscious of filial piety and takes care giving more seriously than his role as a husband and father and if he cannot differentiate himself from his parents to the level his wife expects, then the disappointed wife may have considerable conflict with her parents-in-law, blaming her mother-in-law. However, this conflict between mothers and daughters-in law tends to be less severe in modern families, where the adult children have their own financial resources apart from their parents and the children's obligation for care giving is weaker.

Many researchers have analyzed the characteristics of this conflict between mothers and daughters-in-law (Koo 1999; Bae 1997; Lee 2003), and many of these scholars have offered suggestions to solve these problems and making the relationship more satisfactory (Kim 2008; Park & Lee 2003; Lee 2002; Lee, et al. 1996; Hong, et al. 1996). In addition, Korea has initiated various life education programs for daughters-in-law, such as problem-solving methods or positive thinking training. Another new research area has been the relationship between Korean mothers and foreign daughters-in-law

(Lee 2009; Cho 2009), reflecting the increase in international marriages.

5) The Relationship between Mothers and Sons-in-law

In Korean tradition, a son-in-law was called an "eternal guest." Mothers treated sons-in-law as best as possible, believing their daughters' happiness depended on their husbands, mitigating conflict between the mothers and the sons-in-law. However, this situation has also changed as other family relationships have changed. As more women continue to work after marriage or childbirth, mothers actively participate in child care and housekeeping for their daughters. The social support system for working wives, such as maternity leave or reliable child care centers, are still far behind the demand in Korea. Therefore, mothers commonly sacrifice their time and energy with the hope that their daughters' lives will be different from that of traditional housewives. Their daughters' social success is a matter of great pride and reward for mothers. Daughters, in turn, thank their mothers for the help, but the sons-in-law tend to think that the help is only for their wives and not for themselves. Often, they even feel that their privacy has been violated, so they reluctantly interact with their mothers-in-law, which may cause further problems in their family relationships.

Considering the increasing interaction of modern Korean couples with the wives' families, a scholar (cho 1997) has recently suggested that the traditional patriarchal unilateralism has been replaced by bilateralism. However, the current situation can be more precisely explained as the expansion of the working wives' support system (Sung 2006; Han & Yoon 2004). Working wives ask for help from both their own parents and parents-in-law. As a result, financial and emotional support from all parents is not unusual. One interesting research finding is that husbands' interaction with the parents-in-law was found to be closely related to the level of economic support from the wives' families (Sung 2006).

Mothers' obsession with daughters, the daughters' dependence on their mothers, and sons-in-laws' indifference toward their mothers-in-law seem to be factors that could deteriorate the relationship between mothers and sons-in-law. Further research is needed to determine the degree to which these factors influence family relationships.

4. The Couple Relationship

1) Characteristics of the Relationship

In Korean traditional marriage, according to the concepts of stability and quality of a couple's relationship (Lewis & Spanier 1979: 269), stability has been far more emphasized than the quality of the couple's relationship. Blessings to the newlyweds were "Live until your black hair turns as white as the root of the leek," instead of "Live happily, loving each other." Weddings were a family matter rather than only the joining of two individuals. The purpose of marriage was to give birth to children, especially sons. In their importance for families, the couple's relationship was far below the father-son relationship. Until the beginning of the twentieth century, the majority of marriages ended with the death of one spouse before the last child departed from the home. Now, with the longer average life expectancy and fewer children, the couple's post-parental period has been prolonged. Figure 1 shows that wives who were married before 1974 typically spent only 4.2 years in the post-parental period, whereas those who were married after 1994 spent 14.2 years, almost 10 more years.

In the research of later life satisfaction by Lee and Kim (2002) a couple's relationship quality appears to be a more significant factor compared to individual or family variables. Elders who had a spouse-oriented family network showed higher life satisfaction than those who had a children-oriented network or those who had no family network (Kim & Park 2004). Furthermore, for elders who live

Figure 1 Married Wives' Family Life Cycle (comparison by marriage cohort groups)

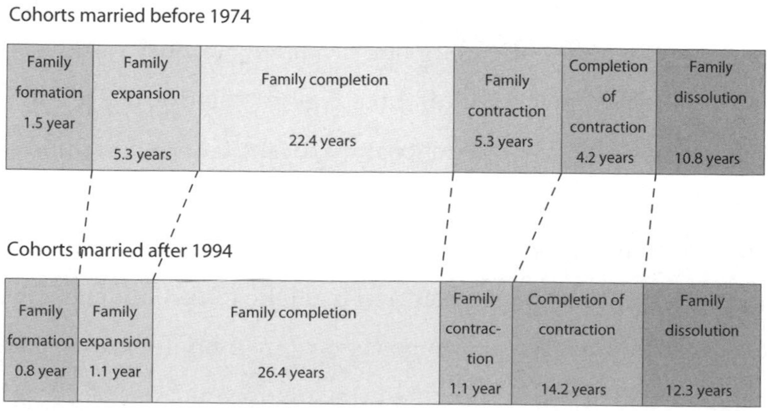

Cohorts married before 1974

Family formation 1.5 year	Family expansion 5.3 years	Family completion 22.4 years	Family contraction 5.3 years	Completion of contraction 4.2 years	Family dissolution 10.8 years

Cohorts married after 1994

Family formation 0.8 year	Family expansion 1.1 year	Family completion 26.4 years	Family contrac-tion 1.1 year	Completion of contraction 14.2 years	Family dissolution 12.3 years

Source: Kim, et al. (2003), *Family Relations Studies.*

with spouses, the couple relationship and self esteem significantly affected their subjective perception of well-being (Lim & Jeon 2004). In contrast, other studies noted the importance of older parents' relationships with their adult children. The frequency of contact with their children positively influenced their ability to adapt to the post-parental period (Kim & Jun 1997). One recent study even found that elders' depression due to cognitive problems could be reduced through a satisfactory relationship with their children (Yoo & Sung 2009).

2) Divorce in Later Life

Recently, the divorce rate among older couples has increased. Elderly wives are choosing to divorce instead of sacrificing their personal happiness for their families (Chung & Yoo 2002: 515). In the past, it was almost impossible for women to initiate divorce. The patriarchal system emphasized women's obedience to men: A woman must obey her father in the early years, obey her husband in marriage, and, finally, obey her son after her husband's death. In contrast, husbands could divorce legitimately for the following seven reasons: His wife did not bear a son; she engaged in improper sexual activities; she did not take care of her parents-in-law; she was jealous; she talked too much; she had an infectious disease; or she stole property. Wives were protected from the forced divorce only in three cases: Those who held three years of memorial services for her parents-in-law; those who helped make a fortune; and those who had no home to go to after being divorced.

Since the beginning of the twentieth century, inequality in marriage slowly decreased through new legislation, and, in 1915, monogamy became the only legal form of marriage. In 1923, divorce by agreement was legislated, giving women the right to initiate divorce, but, in reality, traditional unequal divorce practices were largely maintained. In 1958, the civil law regulated divorce processes by agreement, arbitration, and court judgment. Then, in 1977 and 1989, revision of the civil law introduced the claim for property division and the right to meet children after a divorce (National Archives & Records Services 1991).

With the improved legislation, negative attitudes toward divorce have changed. While divorce was regarded as a problematic, pathological life event in the past, now younger generations show much more accepting attitudes toward divorce, although more than half of the respondents still hold negative attitudes (See Table 3). Females, slightly more than males, think that divorce can be a positive option. Interestingly, there are a relatively high proportion of respondents who say their divorce attitudes are determined "case by case," stating that divorce can be regarded as a way to liberate oneself from an unhappy marriage and an opportunity for self development. This may indicate a greater acceptance that divorce is a positive option in some cases, even if their overall attitude is negative. Interestingly, people between 40-59 years-of-age show a slightly more traditional view, but they still show a somewhat similar attitude, indicating that even among the elderly attitudes about divorce are changing.

Prolonged post-parental period, ironically, appears to be

one of the factors that contributes to conflict and divorce in later life. Elderly couples now spend more years together due to the increased average life expectancy and early retirement. However, unequal rights and obligations in everyday life remain. Husbands do not take care of much of the housework, such as cooking and cleaning, believing it is the wives' duty. In many cases, wives cannot participate in the financial decision making process (Shin & Cho 1999). Communication problems in elderly couples also frequently cause conflicts (Kim & Lee 2001). Numerous studies have revealed that elders' life satisfaction and depression are significantly influenced by personality differences with the spouse and authoritative attitudes of husbands, among other factors (Kim & Lee 2003; Kim, et al. 2006; Sung & Ok 2004; Lee 2005; Lee & Kim 2002).

In a traditional patriarchal society, wives sacrificed their whole lives for their husbands and children in order to secure the marriage. However, according to empirical studies, female elders feel couple stress and marriage instability significantly higher

Table 3 Changing Attitudes toward Divorce (2008) (%)

		Negative	Case by case	Positive	Don't know
Sex	Male	63.8	27.8	5.7	2.6
	Female	53.7	35.8	8.3	2.2
Age (years)	15 ~ 19	39.9	42.4	10.6	7.0
	20 ~ 29	43.3	43.5	10.0	3.2
	30 ~ 39	50.5	40.4	7.1	2.0
	40 ~ 49	58.9	32.5	7.1	1.5
	50 ~ 59	68.9	23.3	6.2	1.5
	over 60	82.9	12.3	3.0	1.8

Source: Korea National Statistical Office (2009), *Korea Society Index*.

than their spouses (Kim & Lee 2003; Kim 1999; Lim & Kim 2002). Today, elderly wives are no longer forced to live a prolonged life with their traditional husbands. They have the opportunity to have a second life (*Ilyosisa* 2009). Thus, in many divorce cases, the women initiated the process. As Table 4 shows, the cases of divorce in later life have sharply increased in Korea. In 1995, divorce cases by couples who had cohabitated for more than 20 years was just 5,571, constituting 8 % of the total divorce rate. By 2000, the divorce rate of elderly couples constituted 14 % with 16,978 cases, and, in 2005, it had risen to 19 % with 23,837 cases. In 2008, the elderly couple divorce rate jumped to 23 % with 26,942 cases, resulting in almost every fifth divorce case being a couple who had lived together for more than 20 years.

In short, the increasing divorce rate in later life can be interpreted as older females hoping for a happier life. As discussed above, a strong couple relationship has much more meaning in later life, because they spend more time together. Children depart

Table 4 Divorce Cases by Duration of Cohabitation

Divorce year / Cohabitation years	Total divorce cases	0~4 years	5~9 years	10~14 years	15~19 years	20 years or more
1995	68,279	22,272 (32.6 %)	17,179 (25.2 %)	14,052 (20.6 %)	8,974 (13.1 %)	5,571 (8.2 %)
2000	119,455	35,047 (29.3 %)	26,643 (22.3 %)	22,360 (18.7 %)	18,342 (15.4 %)	16,978 (14.2 %)
2005	124,524	33,023 (26.5 %)	27,266 (21.9 %)	22,384 (18.0 %)	18,014 (14.5 %)	23,837 (19.1 %)
2008	116,535	33,114 (28.4 %)	21,694 (18.6 %)	18,307 (15.7 %)	16,478 (14.1 %)	26,942 (23.1 %)

Source: Korea National Statistical Office (2009), *Demographic Change Statistics.*

from the home and friends are passing away. Elderly couples are not only husbands and wives but friends and life companions, so it seems necessary to emphasize the importance of their relationship. However, for relationships to work well in the later stage, elderly couples must often learn new skills for inter-relational communication and division of household chores.

3) Remarriage in Later Life

Remarriage in later life has been considered very positive in the Western society as a way to solve older people's loneliness and desire for a fuller life. In Korea, however, there has been less acceptance of remarriage, particularly for older women. Remarriage in later life is often called a "December marriage," which originally meant female elders' marriage. In spite of the traditional stereotypes, remarriage in later life could be an escape from a lonely world as well as restoration of the lost human relationship (Park, 1984). Interaction with a spouse has an important meaning, especially to elders who are often weak physically and mentally. The major reasons given for elders' remarriage are loneliness and the need for companionship (Lee & Choi 1997). In several studies, remarried elders reported that their loneliness problem was solved partly, if not fully, by remarriage, and life became more satisfactory after remarriage (Kim & Han 1996; Park & Bae 2003; Yang 2004; Lim 1997).

There are, however, many barriers to elders' remarriage. Many people in Korea still think that elders' remarriage is inappropriate and believe they (particularly women) should live silently, hiding

Table 5 Remarriage of Elders Aged 65 and Over

	1995	2000	2005	2007
Male	940	1,002	1,573	2,004
Female	172	209	414	610

Source: Korea National Statistical Office (2008), *Demographic Change Statistics.*

behind the curtain. In addition, adult children often oppose their elderly parents' remarriage, worrying about their own relationships with a step parent, or they worry about property transfer problems. Thus, many Korean elders give up the idea of remarriage because of their children's opposition (Yang 2004), and the numbers of remarriage cases among elders remain low (See Table 5). Although the number of cases doubled from 2000 to 2007 for men, female elders remarry far less than their male peers, probably due to the traditional ethical norm of "one husband in one lifetime."

Considering the increased average life expectancy, for the synthesis of studies in this investigation suggest Korean society should abandon the negative or prohibitive attitudes toward the remarriage of older adults, especially the double standard, which restricts elder females but not men from remarriage.

5. Conclusion

Korean families in later life reflect the recent social changes in Korean family relationships. Traditionally, elders were respected and cared for by adult children. Filial piety was emphasized as the central value and behavioral norm in the Korean agricultural patriarchal society. In recent years, however, this situation has dramatically changed. The average life expectancy has increased, which has led to a significant increase in the elderly population. Korea has become industrialized and urbanized, and Western ideas of independence have influenced family relationships. Modern Korean elders no longer want to depend on their adult children. However, older Koreans still cling to the hope of an intimate relationship with their adult children. Koreans also continue to believe adult children should take responsibility for proving care to their elderly parents. In this respect, government approaches to welfare policies have not changed significantly, so caring for elderly parents is still primarily the responsibility of an elder's adult children, which can negatively affect the relationship between the elderly parents and adult children. More importantly, poor elders, without adult children who can afford to take care of them, suffer from lack of care and resources.

Another residual result of the traditional patriarchal system is that conflict between mothers and daughters-in-law remains. To improve the relationship, various counseling and education programs have been provided by family support institutions. Interestingly, however, relationships between mothers and sons-in-law have seen the least conflict in traditional Korean families, but an increase in the employment of married women is beginning to change the former lack of conflict. Daughters now depend on mothers for child care and housework. Mothers help as much as possible, hoping for their daughters' social success, so now sons-in-law often feel uncomfortable or feel that their privacy has been invaded, creating more stress on the family relationships.

Another interesting change in modern families is the older couple's relationship, which has become more important in later life because of the prolonged post-parental period. Unfortunately, for this same reason, many couples divorce in later life. Unreciprocated and unfair marital relationships, based on traditional norms and the sacrifices made by the wife, are especially fragile. Revised divorce laws, a decline in negative attitudes toward divorce, and an increase in life expectancy have also contributed to the rising divorce rate in later life.

Elders' remarriage is still regarded negatively. Remarriage is particularly difficult for female elders because of Neo-Confucianism tradition. Despite the long history of these traditions in Korea, however, people seem to be changing some of their attitudes. Increasingly, Koreans have begun to regard remarriage as a way to solve the problems of loneliness in older adults.

Korean families in later life are in a transition stage, and family relationship norms are in the process of reconstruction. In the midst of such dramatic and rapid changes, caring for elder parents has become a more serious problem. Society, in general, and the Korean government, more specifically, need to consider new ways to resolve the family care giving problems in order to ensure healthy and happy lives for the elderly. Policies should reflect the unique demands of elders in all social classes and provide appropriate support.

References

Bae, S. (1997). Haryu gyegeubui gobugwangye-e daehan saryeyeon-gu (A Case study on a Mother and Daughter-in—law's Relationship in the Low Class; in Korean). *Han-gukgajeonggwallihakhoeji (Journal of the Korean Home Management Association)* 15(4): 327-339.

Chang, K. (1994). Family and Political Life. In *Families and Korean Society*, ed. Korean Social Research Society for Women. Seoul: Kyungmunsa.

Cho, C. (1997). The Study of the Bilateralization of Korean Kin Relationship; In Korean. *(Journal of Korean Women's Studies)* 13(1): 87-114.

Cho, H. (2009). Nongchon-noin-gwa oeguginmyeo-neuriui gobugwangye manjokdo mit munhwajeokeung seuteureseu-e gwanhan yeon-gu (A Study on Satisfactions by Foreign Women and Their Mothers-in-law with Their Relationships and Their Acculturation Stresses; in Korean). Master's Thesis, University of Hanseo, Chungnam, Seosan.

Choi, J. (1994). Seonginjanyeoga jigakhaneun nobumowaui gyeolsokdo mit galdeung-e gwanhan yeon-gu (Research on Adult Childrens' Perception of Solidarity and Discord with Their Aged Parents; in Korean). *Han-guk-no-nyeonhak (Journal of the Korean Gerontological Society)* 14(2): 25-36.

Choi, J. (2009). Han-gukgwa miguk seonginjanyeoui nobumowaui gwangyeui jilgwa buyanghaengdong bigyoyeon-gu (Comparison of Adult Children's Quality of Relationship and Care Provision for Elderly Parents in the U.S. and Korea; in Korean). *Han-guknonyeonhak (Journal of the Korean Gerontological Society)* 29(2): 611-627.

Choi, J. & Kim, T. (1991). Nobumoga jigakhaneun seonginjanyeowaui gyeolsokdo mit galdeung-e gwanhan yeon-gu (Research on Aged Parent's Perception of Solidarity and Discord with Their Adult Children; in Korean). *Han-guknonyeonhak (Journal of the Korean Gerontological Society)* 11(2): 221-234.

Chung, H. & Ok, S. (2008). *Gajokgwan-gye (Family Relations;* in Korean). Seoul: Korea National Open University Press.

Chung, H. & Yoo, K. (2002). *Gajokgwan-gye (Family Relations;* in Koean). Seoul: Shinjung.

Daily Seoul. February 14th 2009. "Caregiving=Family Conflict."

Finch, J. (1989). *Family Obligation and Social Change*. Cambridge: Polity Press.

Han, K. & Yoon, S. (2004). Han-gukgajok chinjokgwangyeui yanggyehwa gyeonghyang: Sedaegwangyereul jungsimeuro (The Bilateralization of the Kinship Relation in Korean Families: Focused on the Intergenerational Exchange; in Korean). *Han-guk-in-guhak (Korean Journal of Population Studies)* 27(2): 177-203.

Hong, S., Yoo, E., & Jeon, K. (1996). Jung-nyeon-myeo-neurireul wihan gobugwangye hyangsang gyoyuk peurogeuraem (Development of an Education Program for Caregiving Middle-aged Daughter-in-law; in Korean). *Daehan-gajeonghakhoeji (Journal of the Korean Home Economics Association)* 34(5): 293-305.

Ilyosisa. May 6th 2009. The Voice of Family Court on "Divorce in Later Life." Retrieved from http://www.ilyosisa.co.kr/detail.php?number=3330&thread=22r05.

Jeon, G. & Lim, S. (1998). Nonyeongi bubugaldeunggwa u-ul-e gwanhan yeon-gu (A Study on the Marital Conflict and Depression in Old Age; in Korean). *Daehan-gajeonghakhoeji (Journal of the Korean Home Economics Association)* 36(6): 1-12.

Johnson, C. L. (1988). Interdependence, Reciprocity and Indebtedness: An Analysis of Japanese American Kinship Relations. *Journal of Gerontology* 43: 114-120.

Jeon, G. (1993). No-mowa seong-inttalganui sanghojakyonggwa buyang-gidaegam: Buyang-gidaeyoin-eul jungsimeuro (Interaction and Filial Duty Expectation between Elderly Mothers and Adult Daughters : Focusing on the Factor of Support Expectation; in Korean). Ph. D. Dissertation, Sungshin Women's University, Seoul.

Jung, O., Jung, S. & Hong, K. (2006). *Gyeolhongwa gajogui ihae (The Introduction of Marriage and Families*; in Korean). Seoul: Sigmapress.

Jung, T. (2008). Han-gukno-nyeonhak-eseo darun noinui simnijeok teukseong: Yeoksajeok gochalgwa miraeui gwaje (Psychological Characteristics of the Aged dealt with in the Journal of the Korean Gerontological Society: Historical Review and Future Task; in Korean). *Han-guknonyeonhak (Journal of the Korean Gerontological Society)* 28(4): 815-829.

Kang, H. (2008). Yangbanyeoseong jongbuui yugyo dodeok silcheonui uiui (A

Meaning of Confucian Moral Practice in Jongbu as Yangban: The Cases of the Ten Jongbu at Yongnam Region in Modern Korean Society; in Korean). *Sahoewa yeoksa (Society and History)* 78: 169-222.

Kerr, M. & Bowen, M. (1988). *Family Evaluation*. NY: Norton.

Kim, H. (2008). Gajok gan galdeungdaehwaui gujowa chaengnyak yeon-gu: Gobu, bubu gan galdeungdaehwareul jungsimeuro (A Study on Structure and Strategies for Confrontational Conversation among Family: Focus on Confrontational Conversation between Spouses and between Mother-in-law and Daughter-in-law; in Korean). Ph. D. Dissertation, Inje University, Busan.

Kim, H., Park H., & Hong, H. (2005). *Han-gukgajeongsaenghwalsa (Korean Life History*; in Korean). Seoul: Korea National Open University Press.

Kim, H., Park, H., & Ok, S. (2003). *Gajokgwangyehak (Family Relations*; in Korean). Seoul: Korea National Open University Press.

Kim, K. & Lee, S. (2001). Nonyeongi bubugaldeung mit gwallyeon-e gwanhan yeon-gu (Marital Conflict and Related Variables in Old Aged Couples; in Korean). *Han-guknonyeonhakyeon-gu (Korean Journal of Research in Gerontology)* 10: 31-54.

Kim, K. & Lee, S. (2003). Nonyeongi bubuui galdeunggwa saenghwal manjokdo (Marital Conflict and Life Satisfaction in Aged Couples; in Korean). *Daehan-gajeonghakhoeji (Journal of the Korean Home Economics Association)* 41(1): 1-15.

Kim, M. (2008). Noinui buyanguimugidae, bumoyeokhalmanjok mit janyeogyeolsongnyeogi uul mit salmui manjokdoe michineun yeonghyang (The Effect of Parental Expectation of Filial Responsibility, Parental Role Expectation and Intergenerational Solidity on Depressive Symptoms and Life Satisfaction; in Korean). *Han-gukgajokbokjihak (Korean Journal of Family Social Work)* 24(12): 161-188.

Kim, M., Shin, K., Kang, M., & Kang, I. (2006). Goryeonghwa han-guksahoeui buyangchegye guchug-eul wihan yeon-gu: Seong-gongjeok nohu salmui yuhyeongbyeol buyang chegye bunseogeul tong-hayeo (A Study on Development of Care System in Aged Korea: Analysis on the Care System among The Types of Successful Aging Life). *Han-guknonyeonhak (Journal of the Korean Gerontological Society)* 26(3): 617-639.

Kim, T. (1975). Work for Elderly in Chosun Dynasty. Master's Thesis, Korea University, Seoul.

Kim, T. (1999). Noinui gajokgyeolsokdowa hyouisik mit u-ule gwanhan bigyomunhwajeok yeon-gu (Cross-Cultural Study On Family Solidarity, Filial Piety and Depression among the elderly; in Korean). *Han-guk-nonyeonhak (Journal of the Korean Gerontological Society)* 19(2): 79-96.

Kim, T. (2007). *Nonyeonhak (Gerontology*; in Korean). Paju: Kyomunsa.

Kim, T. & Han, H. (1996). Sabyeol-noinui jaehon-e gwanhan yeon-gu (Study on the Remarriage of the Bereaved Old People; in Korean). *Han-guknon-yeonhak (Journal of the Korean Gerontological Society)* 16(1): 18-38.

Kim, T. & Jun, G. (1997). Nonyeon-gi bubuui sanghogan jijiwa yeokhalgong-yu mit gyeolhonjeokeung-e gwanhan yeon-gu (A study on the conjugal support, the share of household activities and marital adjustment in old age; in Korean). *Han-guknonyeonhak (Journal of the Korean Gerontological Society)* 17(2): 167-182.

Kim, T., Kim D., Kim A., Kim M., & Lee Y. (1998). Nonyeongi salmui jil hyangsang-e gwanhan yeon-gu (A Study on Improvement of the Quality of Life for the Aged; in Korean). *Han-guknonyeonhak (Journal of the Korean Gerontological Society)* 18(1): 150-169.

Kim, Y., Park, J., & Lee, K. (2008). Janyeowaui jiwon-gyo-hwangwa noinui buyangchaegim-e daehan insigi noinui jugwanjeok an-nyeong-gam-e michineun yeonghyang (Intergenerational exchange filial responsibility and subjective wellbeing among elderly in Seoul and Chuncheon; in Korean). *Han-guksahoebokjijosayeon-gu (Korean Social Work Research)* 18: 47-65.

Kim, Y. & Park, J. (2004). Han-guknoinui gajokgwangyemanggwa salmui manjokdo (The Family Network and Life Satisfaction of Elderly in South Korea; in Korean). *Han-guknonyeonhak (Journal of the Korean Gerontological Society)* 24(1): 169-185.

Koh, Y. (1983). *Jeontongsahoeui hyogae-nyeom-gwa hyeonsiljeok gwaje (Filial Piety and Future Task*; in Korean). Seoul: Asan Social Welfare Foundation.

Koo, J. (1999). Sieo-meo-niwa myeoneuriga jigakhaneun gobuganui galdeung (The Difference of Complication in Point of View of Mother-in-low and Daughter-in-law; in Korean). Ph. D. Dissertation, Ewha Womans

University, Seoul.

Korea Court (2005). Family Relation Registration. Retrieved from http://www. scourt.go.kr/minwon/min_8_6/min_8_6_1/index.html.

Korea JoongAng Daily. April 15th 2009. "90 % of Adult, No Expectation on Their Children's Care in the Later Life." Retrieved from http://article.joinsmsn. com/news/article/article.asp?ctg=12&total_id =3571003

Korea National Statistical Office (2002). *Social Survey Report*. Daejeon: KNSO.

Korea National Statistical Office. (2006). *Estimation of Future Population*. Daejeon: KNSO

Korea National Statistical Office. (2006). *Social Survey Report*. Daejeon: KNSO

Korea National Statistical Office. (2008). *Demographic Change Statistics*. Daejeon: KNSO

Korea National Statistical Office (2009), *Demographic Change Statistics*: KNSO.

Korea National Statistical Office. (2009). *Korea Society Index*. Daejeon: KNSO.

Korean History Research Society (1990). *Introduction of Korean History Research*. Seoul: Gisiksaneopsa.

Lee, E. (2008). Gajoktallyeokmodel-eul iyonghan chimaenoinui buyang-gajokwonui jeok-eung-e gwanhan yeon-gu (A Study on the Level of Family Adaptation to Family Caregivers with Senile Dementia Patients: An Application of the Family Resiliency Model; in Korean). *Noinbokjiyeon-gu (Journal of Korean Welfare for the Aged)* 39: 195-219.

Lee, H. (2003). Sibumo gobugaldeung yuhyeonghwawa gwallyeonbyeon-in yeon-gu (The Factorial Structure of the Conflict Source between Mother-in-law and Daughter-in-law and Related Variables; in Korean). *Noinbokjiyeon-gu (Journal of Korean Welfare for the Aged)* 19: 31-59.

Lee, H. (2009). Oeguk myeoneurireul dun nongchon sieo-meo-niui suyong-gyeon-heom-e gwanhan yeon-gu (A Study on the Experience of Accep-tance of Mother-in-law with Foreign Daughter-in-law in Rural Area; in Korean). Master's Thesis, Chungbuk National University, Cheongju.

Lee, H. & Kim, Y. (2004). Bubugwangyega no-nyeon-gi salmui jil-e michineun yeonghyang (The Effects of Marital Relationship (Love and Sexual Attitudes) in Later Life on Quality of Life; in Korean). *Han-guknonyeonhak (Journal of the Korean Gerontological Society)* 24(4): 197-214.

Lee, J. (2002). Gobugwan-gyegaeseoneul wihan geungjeongjeok sagohullyeon peurogeuraemui jeokyong (Application of Positive Thinking Training Program for the Improvement of Relationships between Mothers-in-law and Daughters-in-law; in Korean). *Han-gukgajokgwangyehakhoeji (Journal of the Korea Association of Family Relations)* 7(1): 117-136.

Lee J. & Choi, Y. (1997). Sabyeol mit ihonhan noinui jaehon-e gwanhan yeon-gu: Jeonju-si geoju jaehonhan noinui seong-gongsaryereul jungsimeuro (Study on Remarriage of Bereaved or Divorced Old People: Emphasis on Successful Remarriage in Jeonju Area; in Korean). *Daehan-gajeonghakhoeji (Journal of the Korean Home Economics Association)* 35(2): 255-272.

Lee, J., Jeong, H., & Chang, J. (1996). Jeolmeun myeo-neurireul wihan gobugwangye hyangsang gyoyuk peurogeuraemui gaebal mit pyeong-ga (Development and Evaluation of Enrichment program for the Relation-ship of Young Daughters-in-law with Their Mothers-in-law; in Korean). *Han-gukgajeonggwallihakhoeji (Journal of Korean Home Management Association)* 14(4): 13-26.

Lee, J. & Kim, M. (2001). Jung-no-nyeon-gi gihonnamnyeoui jaesansang-sokuisik-e gwanhan yeon-gu (A Study on the Consciousness of Inheritance among Married People of the Middle Aged and the Elderly; in Korean). *Han-gukgajeonggwallihakhoeji (Journal of the Korea Home Management Association)* 19(4): 151-165.

Lee, S. (2005). Nonyeongi bubuui oeroum-e gwanhan yeon-gu (Loneliness of Old Married Couples; in Korean). *Han-guknonyeonhak (Journal of the Korean Gerontological Society)* 25(1): 37-54.

Lee, S. & Kim, K. (2002). Nonyeongi bubuui saeng-hwalmanjokdowa u-ul mit gwallyeonbyeonin yeon-gu (Life Satisfaction, Depression and Related Variables in Old Married Couples; in Korean). *Han-guknonyeonhak (Journal of the Korean Gerontological Society)* 22(1): 139-157.

Lewis, R. A. & Spanier, G. B. (1979). Theorizing about the Quality and Stability of Marriage. In *Contemporary Theories about the Family*, Vol. 1, *Research-based Theories*, ed. W. R. Burr, R. Hill, F. I. Nye, & I. L. Reiss, 268-294. NY: The Free Press.

Lim, C. (1997). Jaehonhan namjanoinui jaehongajoksaenghwal jeogeung-e gwanhan yeon-gu (The elderly men's adaptation to remarried family life; in Korean). *Han-guknonyeonhak (Journal of the Korean Gerontological Society)*

17(2): 119-138.

Lim, J. & Jeon, G. (2004). Noinui jugwanjeok an-nyeong-gam-e yeong-hyang-eul michineun byeonin yeon-gu (A study of variables influencing subjective well-being in the elderly; in Korean). *Han-guknonyeonhak (Journal of the Korean Gerontological Society)* 24(1): 71-87.

Lim, S. & Kim, T. (2002). Nonyeon-gi bubu seuteureseuwa gyeolhonbul-anjeongseong (A study on marital stress and marital instability of elderly couples; in Korean). *Han-guknonyeonhak (Journal of the Korean Gerontological Society)* 21(3): 111-128.

Lim, S. & Lee, S. (2009). Noinui cheyukhwaldong chamyeo manjog-i buyang gidaegam mit gajokgineung-e michineun yeong-hyang (The influence of the satisfaction of the elderly with their participation in fitness on the expectation of support and family function; in Korean). *Han-guknonyeonhak (Journal of the Korean Gerontological Society)* 29(1): 89-99.

National Archives & Records Services (1991). The Second Revision of Family Law. Retrieved from http://contents.archives.go.kr/next/content/listSubjectDescription.do?id=002591

Ok, S., Kim, J., Park, H., Shin, H., Han, K., & Koh, S. (2000). Gajok/Chinjok gujoui haechewa jaeguseong: Nongchonjiyeok siltaejosareul jungsimeuro (Disintegration and reconstruction of the family/kinship structure among the families in the Seoul area; in Korean). *Daehan-gajeonghakhoeji (Journal of the Korean Home Economics Association)* 38(10): 157-180.

Park, C. & Bae, N. (2003). Nonyeongi jaehon-e gwanhan jiljeok yeon-gu (A study on the remarriage of old people; in Korean). *Sahoebokjiyeon-gu (Journal of Social Welfare Research)* 24: 91-122.

Park, G. & Lee, Y. (2003). Gobugwangyeeseo myeoneuriga jigakhaneun seuteureseu mit daecheo (Stress perceived by daughters-in-law and their coping; in Korean). *Noinbokjihak (Journal of Welfare for the Aged)* 22: 79-104.

Park, I., Choi, W., & Kim, A. (2008). Daehaksaeng-ui nakgwanseong-gwa gajoktongjegami noinbuyanguisige michineun yeong-hyang (The effects of undergraduate's optimism and family-control on their awareness of caregiving for the elderly; in Korean). *Han-guksaenghwalhakhoeji (Journal of Korean Association of Human Ecology)* 17(1): 13-26.

Park, I. & Um, K. (2007). Nobumoui uijonseong-i seonginjanyeowa nobumogan galdeung-e michinneun yeong-hyang (A study on the effects of parent's dependency on the parent-child confrontation-focused on the interaction effects of childhood abuse experience and filial obligation; in Korean). *Han-guknonyeonhak (Journal of the Korean Gerontological Society)* 27(1): 179-194.

Park, J. (1984). Nohubojang-gwa sajeokbuyang-gineung (Articles presented at a seminar held in 1984: A study on the support system for the aged and the function of private support system; in Korean). *Han-guknonyeonhak (Journal of the Korean Gerontological Society)* 4: 82-87.

Park, M. & Jung, J. (1999). Gagyeui sajeonsangsoge gwanhan tamsaekjeok yeon-gu (A pilot study of prearranged inheritance; in Korean). *Proceeding of Biennial Conference on Korean Society of Consumer Studies.* 430-455.

Park, Y. & Song, I. (2008). Noin buyanggajogui gajokgaldeung, buyangbudam mit sahoejeok jijigan-ui ingwagwangye yeon-gu (The analysis on the causal model of family conflict, family support and caregiving burden; in Korean). *Noinbokjiyeon-gu (Journal of Korean Welfare for the Aged)* 39: 53-78.

Shin, H. & Cho, B. (1999). Sahoegyohwan-nonjeok gwanjeomeseo bon nomoreul buyanghaneun seonginjanyeoga jigakhan daega, bogang mit gwangyeui jil (Rewards, costs and relationship quality perceived by caregiving adult children: A comparison between Koreans and Korean Americans; in Korean). *Han-gukgajokgwangyehakhoeji (Journal of Family Relations)* 9(1): 153-174.

Sung, M. (2006). Jiljeok yeon-gureul tong-han han-guk gajogui yang-gyehwa hyeonsang-e daehan jindanjeok jeopgeun (Bilateralization phenomena in Korean families: A qualitative approach; in Korean). *Han-gukgajeong-gwallihakhoeji (Journal of Korean Home Management Association)* 24(3): 59-72.

Sung, M. (2009). Han-guk gajok mit chinjok gaenyeom-e daehan yeon-gu: Gajokgwallyeon beobeul jungsimeuro (A study on families and kinship concepts in Korea: A focus on family related laws; in Korean). *Daehan-gajeonghakhoeji (Journal of the Korean Home Economics Association)* 47(4): 11-24.

Sung, M. & Ok, S. (1997). Han-gukgajeong-gwallihakhoeji (Historical review on filial piety norm-focus in reciprocity and fairness; in Korean). *Daehan-gajoenghakhoeji (Journal of the Korean Home Economics Association)* 35(3): 245-257.

Sung, M. & Ok, S. (2004). Yeoseong toejikjaui toejik hu saenghwal-e gwanhan jiljeok yeon-gu: Gyojik/Gongmuwonjik toejikjareul jungsimeuro (Qualitative research on women's post-retirement lives; in Korean). *Gajokgwa munwha (Family and Culture)* 16(2): 57-94.

The Dong-A ILBO. December 7th 2006. "The Portrait of 50's in Korea: The kangaroo children." Retrieved from www.donga.com/fbin/output?n= 200611210094.

Yang, O. (2004). Noin-gwa cheong/jangnyeon sedaeganui gyeolhongwajeong-e daehan uisik gochal (Research on marital process consciousness of elderly, young and middle age). *Proceeding of Biennial Conference on Korea Social Welfare* 3: 441-459.

Yang, Y. (2009). Noinbuyang byeonhwagwajeong-e daehan saeng-aesajeok jaeguseong (A biographical reconstruction of the process involving changes in elderly support: From the perspective of the rural elderly; in Korean). *Han-guknonyeonhak (Journal of the Korean Gerontological Society)* 29(1): 1-20.

Yoo, J. & Sung, H. (2009). Nonyeon-gi u-ul-e daehan gajokgwangye manjokdoui jungjae hyogwa (The moderating effect of family relationships on depression in the elderly; in Korean). *Han-guknonyeonhak (Journal of the Korean Gerontological Society)* 29(2): 717-728.

Wolf, M. (1972). *Women and the Family in Rural Taiwan*. Stanford: Stanford University Press.

Won, Y. (1995). Dong byeolgeo hyoengtaega han-guknoinui simnijoek hae-bokgame michineun yeong-hyang (Living arrangements and psychological well-being of the elderly in Korea; in Korean). *Han-guknonyeonhak (Journal of the Korean Gerontological Society)* 18(2): 64-79.

Index

Korean Family Studies Association

The Korean Family Studies Association, founded in 1977, is the academic organization for the multi-disciplinary understanding of Korean families, and published the first edition of its journal in 1979.

Authors

Chang, Kyung-Sup	Ph.D., Professor, Department of Sociology, Seoul National University
Chin, Meejung	Ph. D., Associate Professor, Department of Child Development & Family Studies, Seoul National University
Cho, Oakla	Ph.D., Professor, Department of Sociology, Sogang University
Chung, Hyunsook	Ph. D., Professor, Department of Family Welfare, Sangmyung University
Eun, Ki-Soo	Ph. D., Professor, Graduate School of International Studies, Seoul National University
Kim, Hye-Kyung	Ph. D., Professor, Department of Sociology, Jeonbuk National University
Kim, Myung-hye	Ph. D., Professor, Department of Anthropology, Chonnam National University
Lee, Jae Kyung	Ph.D., Professor, Department of Women's Studies, Ewha Womans University
Lee, SoonGu	Ph.D., Research Officer, National Institute of Korean History
Ok, Sun Wha	Ph. D., Professor, Department of Child Development & Family Studies, Seoul National University
Park, Boo Jin	Ph. D., Professor, Department of Child Development & Education, Myongji University
Sohn, Seong Young	Ph. D., Professor, Department of Gender Studies, Graduate School, Dongduk Women's University
Sung, Miai	Ph.D., Associate Professor, Department of Home Economics, Korea National Open University
Yi, Jong Seo	Ph. D., Associate Professor, Department of History and Culture, Ulsan University